Impressions of Russia

THE CROWELL HISTORICAL CLASSICS SERIES

UNDER THE EDITORSHIP OF *Herman Ausubel*

Impressions of Russia by Georg Brandes
WITH AN INTRODUCTION BY RICHARD PIPES

Lord Beaconsfield by Georg Brandes
WITH AN INTRODUCTION BY SALO W. BARON

Queen Elizabeth by Mandell Creighton
WITH AN INTRODUCTION BY G. R. ELTON

William Stubbs on the English Constitution
EDITED BY NORMAN F. CANTOR

IN PREPARATION

Americans of 1776 by James Schouler
WITH AN INTRODUCTION BY RICHARD B. MORRIS

The First Two Stuarts and the Puritan Revolution
by Samuel R. Gardiner
WITH AN INTRODUCTION BY WILLSON COATES

Hume by Thomas Henry Huxley
WITH AN INTRODUCTION BY ALBERT HOFSTADTER

Life of Andrew Jackson by William Cobbett
WITH AN INTRODUCTION BY MARCUS CUNLIFFE

❧ ❧ ❧❀ ❧ ❧

Impressions

of Russia

BY Georg Brandes

❧ ❧ ❧❀ ❧ ❧

WITH AN INTRODUCTION
BY Richard Pipes

THOMAS Y. CROWELL COMPANY

Established 1834 New York

INTRODUCTION

◆§ In 1887, the celebrated Danish literary critic and historian, Georg Brandes, visited Russia to deliver a series of lectures. He stayed for three months, and after his return to Denmark published a volume of *Impressions* in which he combined an account of what he had observed with a general survey of Russian history and literature.

Brandes belongs to a type of literary middleman virtually extinct today. In the nineteenth century, literature became confined, to a greater extent than it had been either before or since, within national boundaries. The emergence of national cultures and the preoccupation of writers, romantic and naturalist alike, with the local and specific had the effect of loosening the bonds which had given Europe during the hegemony of classicism a single, homogeneous culture. The rhythm of intellectual life animating the continent became disrupted. In 1830, when romanticism was already past its peak in England and Germany, it still had to fight for its existence in France; and in 1860, when it fell from favor in France, it was at the height of its influence in Scandinavia. This cultural fragmentation of a continent traditionally disposed toward unity created a need for critics and publicists capable of linking the diverse national cultures. Madame de Staël with her *De l'Allemagne* (1810–13), which discovered Romantic Germany for the French, set a model that was widely emulated later in the century. Among these emulators, Brandes was one of the most gifted and successful.

He was born in Copenhagen in 1842 of prosperous and cosmopolitan Jewish parents. Although formally affiliated with the synagogue, the Brandeses had little to do with it, preferring to espouse a brand of rationalism and humanism common among

assimilated Jews. Georg received an excellent secondary education, and upon his entry in 1859 at the University of Copenhagen
immediately attracted attention by his erudition and brilliance. At
this time he was a dedicated romantic and an admirer of Heine,
Musset, Kierkegaard, and Lermontov.

The great caesura in Brandes's intellectual development occurred as his university studies were drawing to a close. It en-
tailed a break with romanticism in favor of positivism, of which
he became the foremost exponent in Scandinavia. The initial
influence in this direction came from Feuerbach, whose atheistic
writings weaned Brandes away from Kierkegaard. Even more
important was his discovery of Hippolyte Taine and the whole
French positivist school of literary criticism. Taine's method, best
exemplified in his *History of English Literature*, was to treat
works of literature not as things in themselves, children of pure,
unfettered inspiration, but as a consequence of specific historical
circumstances. To him and other positivists the writer was not
so much the creator of a culture as its product. If the idea seems
commonplace to us, it is not because it is self-evident, but because it has become an intrinsic ingredient of the modern outlook. In its own time it was considered bold and new, and had to
face much opposition from the entrenched school of romantic
criticism.

Brandes became thoroughly captivated by the positivist
method, and when in 1871 his native university invited him to
deliver a course on modern literature, he took advantage of the
opportunity to present a full-scale positivist critique of romanticism. His lectures, which continued until 1875, were an enormous success by virtue of the freshness of their approach and the
excellence of their exposition. Published later in six volumes
under the title *Main Currents in Nineteenth-Century Literature*,
they established Brandes's reputation. Nevertheless, they failed in
their immediate purpose, which was to obtain for Brandes the
chair of literature at the University of Copenhagen. His attacks
on romantic patriotism and idealism ("he accounted for romanticism," writes one historian, "as the chairman of a committee *de
lunatico inquirendo* might account for a case of religious

mania")[1] shocked the rather provincial Danish public. Word spread that Brandes was a radical and an atheist (which was in part true). Since the academic authorities were none too impressed by the scholarly side of his treatment, the vacant professorship was given to someone else.

Although he failed in his academic ambitions, Brandes continued to gain prestige with the European public. His *Main Currents* was translated into many languages, as were his subsequent literary and historical studies, many of them devoted to great figures (e.g., Lassalle, Disraeli, and Kierkegaard). He introduced the Western public to the whole range of modern Scandinavian literature, being in large measure responsible for the international reputation of such writers as Holberg, Kierkegaard, and Ibsen. A man of catholic tastes and contagious enthusiasm, he could both select some of the best writing of his time and persuade the public to accept his choice. Of course, a critic of such influence was much in demand. In the 1880's, when he stood at the pinnacle of his fame, he was dined and wined from one end of the continent to the other. His sympathy for radical causes, especially for anarchism, won him much popularity in oppositional circles everywhere.

Brandes's reputation did not take long to penetrate Russia, which, as he tells us in his *Impressions*, was at the time most receptive to all modern Western influences. The Russians translated a part of the *Main Currents* and several of his other books shortly after their appearance, and were naturally eager to see and hear their author in person. Brandes himself had a keen interest in Russian literature, which at that time was still very imperfectly known in the West. He welcomed, therefore, the invitation extended to him by the Society of Writers to lecture in St. Petersburg.

The 1880's were a difficult time for Russia. The country had just gone through a decade of revolutionary upheaval, which pitted a small but determined band of anarchists against the whole apparatus of the imperial bureaucracy. The great majority of

[1] H. H. Boyesen, *Essays on Scandinavian Literature* (New York, 1895), p. 203.

Russians observed this conflict from the sidelines, until the sense-
less and brutal assassination of Alexander II produced among them
a feeling of revulsion against extremism. The government, headed
by the authoritarian Alexander III (1881–94), became persuaded
that liberal reforms of the kind initiated by the murdered tsar
led only to civil disorder, and resorted increasingly to a policy of repression. The time of Brandes's visit coincided with a
low point between two peaks of intense public activity: the so-
called "Populism" of the 1870's, and the Marxism and Liberalism
of the 1890's. The intelligentsia was discouraged by the failures
of anarchism, the country at large shied away from politics, while
the government exercised its authority in a manner calculated to
make no concessions to public wishes. It was a particularly gloomy
and lethargic period, and this atmosphere the account of Brandes
reflects accurately.

Impressions of Russia consists of two distinct and somewhat
perfunctorily related parts: one devoted to the country, the other
to its literature. Brandes used a similar plan in his book of Polish
impressions, brought out three years earlier—a fact which sug-
gests that he was not merely padding a rather succinct travel account. In preceding the literary narrative with a description of
Russia, he was being faithful to the positivist method, which demanded that literary works be explained by the environment that
gave rise to them. The first part, therefore, constitutes an introduction to the subject which really interests him, namely,
literature.

Brandes's knowledge of Russian history, whether old or new,
is not profound. He commits many mistakes, some of an elementary kind. It is not true, for example, that around 1840 the
imperial government would not allow any foreign books or newspapers to come into Russia (page 80), nor that the organs of
local self-rule known as *zemstva* traced their history back to the
Middle Ages (page 87), nor that the gentry received no compensation for the land taken from them at the time of the emancipation of the serfs in 1861 (page 95). But then no one today
would turn to Brandes for this kind of information. Where he is
reliable and of lasting value is in his descriptions of the quality
of Russian life in the late nineteenth century. What he has to say

of the "broad and proud frankness" of Russians in social intercourse, of their horror of hypocrisy, will strike anyone privileged
to have known Russians reared in that atmosphere as most per-
ceptively put. His remarks about Russian provincial life, about
the Panslavists, about the utter isolation of the intelligentsia from
the establishment are equally true and valuable. In the brief
sketches of the things he had personally observed, Brandes reveals
the sensitivity that has made him so influential a critic.

Although Brandes made his reputation as a leading proponent
of literary positivism, his commitment to this school was neither
wholehearted nor consistent. He was too subtle to be satisfied
with a theory that treated a writer as a mere product of objective
environmental forces. Brandes had great admiration for individual
genius, and in the 1890's went so far in his hero worship as to
accept Nietzsche's notion of the "Superman." He also firmly believed in the freedom of artistic creativity. These were legacies of
romanticism which Brandes ostensibly had left behind in the mid-
1860's, but to which he was temperamentally too much predis-
posed ever to abandon. He seems to have been aware of this para-
dox, for in his old age he once remarked that he was a romantic
who had spent his life fighting romanticism.[2] In dealing with individual writers, Russian or other, he actually made greater use
of the techniques of Sainte-Beuve than of Taine. What he sought
was the specific dominant quality of a writer's work, that which
made him "tick," and this he found not so much in the environment as in the writer's psychology and experience. Hence it is
that the second part of the book stands on its own merit, with
only a tenuous relationship to the survey of Russia provided in
the first.

Brandes reveals at once his independence in his relative cool-
ness toward the recognized giants of Russian letters, Pushkin,
Dostoevsky, and Tolstoy. In the case of Pushkin his inability to
read him in the original undoubtedly influenced Brandes's judgment. But the decisive consideration was ideological. Brandes dis-
liked the conservatism of the late Pushkin, the religiosity of
Tolstoy, and the combination of both qualities in Dostoevsky. His
literary sensitivity was too great not to respond to the sheer

[2] Henning Fenger, *Georg Brandes et la France* (Paris, 1963), p. 193.

genius of these three writers, and he praised them duly; but his praise was not unstinted. It is significant for his own outlook that in Dostoevsky's novels he was most attracted by Raskolnikov's musings over the rights of the extraordinary individual. Much else that he has to say about Dostoevsky is downright silly; and it certainly does Brandes no credit that having read *The Brothers Karamazov* he had nothing of interest to say about it.

Brandes reserved his most enthusiastic praise for Lermontov and Turgenev, two uncompromising individualists and liberals. His admiration for Lermontov goes back to his school days when he discovered *The Hero of Our Time*. This novel, which he describes so glowingly below, made a lasting impression on him; it was, as he later wrote, the first book that he "understood after reaching adulthood." In Turgenev he loved the purity of style, the restraint and understatement, the eschewal of all illusion. The chapter on Turgenev is the most memorable in the present book.

The kind of criticism which Brandes practiced is not in fashion today. We are not inclined to rate writers on the ground of their wisdom and behavior; nor are we content to take their words at face value. We prefer our critics to bare the technical underpinnings of literary works and to make explicit all that is implicit in them. What writers say is less important to us than how and why they say it. By comparison with the modern critic and his formidable analytic apparatus, Brandes may seem naive and unprofessional. But at least he is never guilty of assuming toward a writer the attitude of superiority so widespread in much modern criticism, whether formalist, Freudian, or Marxist. Literature is to him an intrinsic part of life and writers are men who know how to live better and deeper. He admires them with an enthusiasm bred of perceptivity and wide reading; and when he communicates this enthusiasm to us we feel not only instructed but enlivened.

RICHARD PIPES

Harvard University
January, 1966

Author's Introduction

෴ The cause of my trip to Russia in 1887 was an invitation by the Russian Authors' Association in St. Petersburg to deliver a course of lectures in French. They proposed to make all the arrangements, if I would give one-fourth of the receipts to their poor-fund.

While I was in St. Petersburg, I received a similar invitation from Count Kapnist, the curator of the university in Moscow, who also asked for the same portion of the receipts for the benefit of the poor students. On my way to St. Petersburg I also visited Helsingfors. After my lectures in Moscow, I spent some time in a villa in Central Russia, twenty hours' journey by rail south of Moscow. From there I went to Smolensk, and from Smolensk to Warsaw.

Thus in three months I became acquainted with widely separated parts of the country, and some of the most important of this great empire. I had the opportunity of observing both city and country life. I saw Russia both in winter and summer garb. The peculiar conditions under which I travelled brought me in connection with several hundred people of different races and of different classes in society; I met residents of Great and Little Russia, Finns and Swedes, Armenians and Poles, of both sexes, and was brought into close relations with fashionable and common people, conservatives and liberals, lawyers and doctors, authors and artists, princes and professors, journalists and peasants, officials and menials.

Although I am giving my impressions, I do not for a moment forget how imperfect must be my description of the Russian Empire in its entirety. I am not unmindful of how little of what I did see I was able to understand fully, nor of how inconsiderable a portion of a country like Russia and of its inhabitants was placed before me. But naturally I believe in my capacity for observation and in the soundness of my judgments.

G. B.

CONTENTS

LITERATURE

IMPRESSIONS OF RUSSIA

I

৶§ Alexander von Humboldt, in order to give a forcible illustration of the immense extent of the Russian Empire, once compared it to the moon. If you look at the moon when it is full, you see in the hemisphere of the satellite which is before you a smaller territory than that of Russia. About fifty thousand square miles are still wanting.

No other country has so large an extent of territory in one division. It is one-sixth part of the area of the land of our globe, and, although sparsely inhabited, has a population of about ninety-seven million souls, of whom sixty-seven millions are of Russian lineage.

So far as inanimate nature is concerned, the situation of the Russian Empire corresponds to its immense size. Boundless plains extend from the German frontier far into Central Asia, and from the extreme north to the Black Sea. In one of its remote quarters are the mountains of Caucasus, which rise, from a level lower than that of the ocean, to a height far above the highest of the European Alps. In the northwest, it has the largest lakes of Europe, the Ládoga and the Onega, and in the south, the Caspian Sea, the largest in the world. Finally, its rivers are as vast as its plains, its mountains, and its lakes. The largest of them, the Volga, is the longest and widest river in Europe. Although it does not discharge so large a volume of water as might be expected, and as the Danube does, for example, yet that is on account of the flatness of the country and the scantiness of the rainfall. Just as whole streams in Southern Russia are swallowed up by the earth and evaporated as they flow, so the immense flood of the Volga, pouring into the basin of the Caspian Sea, has not sufficed in a hundred years to raise the water level.

The great steppes, which have been compared to the ocean, have none of the ever varying aspects of the sea. Unchanging uniformity is their characteristic. The greatest river, which is as broad as a sound, and in comparison with which the Rhine is short, lacks the impetuosity and turmoil of less imposing rivers. A certain mighty sluggishness is peculiar to its flow. This sluggishness as well as this uniformity is Russian.

In this empire, where everything is immense, there is nothing in the natural conditions which is mild or temperate. This great tract of land is like a body without limbs. It has no indentations of any consequence; is not cut up into half-island formations or divided into islands, like the whole of Northern, Western, and Southern Europe. It has a continental climate: that is, long, severe winters and burning summers. The ocean, which always tempers the cold and heat, is remote; and the influence of the Gulf Stream, always softening, is not felt here.

Just as this immense continent has no indentations, so is its uniformity unbroken by either mountains or valleys. This land of forests, black mould, and steppes is one great plain. This is the reason why the cold blasts from the Arctic Ocean sweep down over the whole empire without meeting any obstruction, and why the moisture is wanting which the Atlantic Ocean and the Baltic and Mediterranean Seas give to Europe. With the exception of the Crimea and Caucasus, no part of this broad land has a southern climate. As some one has expressed it, Russia has a summer but no south.

It is quite true that there are very great extremes in this homogeneous climate. The average summer temperature on the northern coasts of Russia (37° Fahr.) is lower than the winter temperature in Sevastopol. But January in Odessa has the same temperature as January in Christiania; and although Moscow is on the same degree of latitude as Copenhagen and Edinburgh, the average winter temperature is 10° Fahr. in the Russian city, 33° in the Danish, and 38° in the Scotch.

Yet there is hardly any real difference between the natural conditions of European Russia and Siberia except the greater severity.

From that region, in the north, where only the reindeer can exist, to that country, in the south, which produces the grape and

Indian corn, there is in European Russia a gradual transition; yet to the Western-European neither the vegetable nor the animal life presents anything unfamiliar or extraordinary. Both the plants and animals that are common with us are found in the larger part of the empire. Of wild beasts there are found some bears in all the forests, while both in the forests and on the grassy plains and some of the steppes there are wolves in great numbers. The number of wolves in European Russia is estimated to be about 175,000. These wolves destroy annually 180,000 head of cattle, 560,000 sheep, 100,000 dogs, besides 150 human beings. Each wolf is estimated to consume annually the value of about 80 rubles.

Except this one wild beast, however, there is no dangerous or uncommon animal. While the inorganic world in this land is on a grand scale, the vegetable and animal products are the reverse. The trees, even in the forests, are not tall, and the whole animal world has no striking feature.

The decidedly essential feature which characterizes Russia is uniformity notwithstanding the immensity of everything. Although the country is enormously large, it is monotonous. Russia is a land not only of far-reaching plains, long and broad rivers, uniform climate, but also of regular geological formation. This immense country also constitutes one organic unit, since the woodland cannot do without the grain-land, the grain-land without the steppes, nor the steppes without the woodland. The steppes need the trees, and the woodland needs the cattle. And so also the country near the coast feels the want of the interior, and the interior of the coast. As Count Moltke has said, in his "Letters from Russia," "No part can do without the other: the forests of the north cannot dispense with the grain-producing south, nor can the industrious interior spare either of the other parts." The vision that this great empire will be broken up into a number of small kingdoms will therefore hardly be realized. What nature has united geographically, man cannot separate; and what it has separated, man cannot unite. The geography of the country, which has prevented the union of the three Scandinavian nations into one, keeps this sixth part of the earth together.[1]

[1] A. Leroy-Beaulieu: "The Empire of the Tsars and the Russians," vol. 1, bk. 1. Elisée Réclus: "New Universal Geography," vol. 5.

II

⚜ Russia is an agricultural country. There are comparatively few cities. The provincial towns all resemble one another.
When you have seen one or two, you know them all. Such a
provincial town has a public park, a cathedral, a governor's palace,
and a hospital. So much is essential; the remainder depends on the
better or worse condition of the inhabitants. Still, there is one
and a very important thing you are sure to find—a prison,—and
in a country town like Lomja, which has a population of twenty-
five thousand, there is one with six hundred inmates.

Life in such a Russian country town, on a clear summer day,
however little it may be praised by native authors, sometimes appears very attractive. The gay costumes, the red shirts of the men
and the embroidered jackets of the women, shine brightly in the
sun. Of those which I have seen, Briansk, a manufacturing town
on the river Diesna, was a type of the Russian monotony. On the
other hand, Smolensk [1] is delightfully situated on both banks of
the Dnieper. The larger part of the town is on the left bank,
which has a steep descent to the river, so that the numerous
domes and spires of the churches, seen from the opposite side,
appear towering over the landscape in strong relief. The general
situation, however, on account of the flatness of the land, is not
attractive, and the town, therefore, is only interesting to the
traveller as a commercial and manufacturing town or for the historical associations, like all the towns which Napoleon's winter
campaign has made renowned. The intellectual life in these provincial towns presents a sad picture: it is cards and brandy,
brandy and cards.

With the exception of Finland, Poland, and the provinces on

[1] Pronounced Smahlyensk, with the accent on the last syllable.

the Baltic, each of which has its own character, all the intellectual life in Russia is concentrated in the two capitals, St. Petersburg and Moscow.

At the very moment when the traveller at the frontier takes the Russian railway train, there are three things which meet him like messages from a strange world: the language, which, with its rich and soft melody, has not the least resemblance to any of the Western-European tongues; the alphabet, of which some of the characters are new to us and others have a different meaning than in ours (as, for instance, H is used for N); and finally a computation of time, which tears you away from your customary almanac by rolling the time back for twelve days, and thereby burns the bridge to the civilization of Western and Southern Europe. Would that it were only in these twelve days that Russia was behind the rest of Europe!

St. Petersburg is generally the first place visited by the traveller. St. Petersburg is, as said by Peter the Great in his old comparison, the window which the creator of modern Russia built towards the west. It must be conceded that for by far the largest part of the year the view through the window is obscured by frost flowers. What Russia most needed in that time was an open port. Archangel, in the north, was almost continuously closed by ice. Kronstadt was added, but that also is shut up for half the year. Since then the empire has gained new harbors, such as Vladivostok, in the far east, but not one of them is free from ice. Only from the ports on the Black Sea and the Sea of Azof is navigation almost always free, but these do not afford Russia free approach to the outside world, since vessels can always be stopped at the Dardanelles, so long as Constantinople is in the possession of the Turk. This accounts for the constant and ever increasing desire of Russia to possess Constantinople.

By the founding of St. Petersburg the Tsar desired to bring his country nearer to the west. The city, as has been said, was at once a symbol of his determination and the means for its execution. Although at the same time he allowed a canal to be constructed between the Neva and the Volga, he strove to force the wealth of the land from the east and south up against the current, and to open an outlet for it to the west.

St. Petersburg is a city intersected by an enormous number of canals and streams; it is built in a swamp and surrounded by a desert. It is an artificial city, without any country naturally tributary, and it derives the most of its support from officials and soldiers, although its trade and manufactures are of late more important. It is an unhealthy city, in which, as in the old capital of the empire also, the number of deaths is so much larger than the number of births that the population, suffering a loss of one or two thousand a year, would die out, were it not for a constant immigration. It is a half-educated city, in which, at the present time, three hundred thousand of the nine hundred thousand inhabitants cannot read or write. Finally, it is a beautiful city, in grand style, with half European and half barbarian splendor.

For the foundation of this city in the five years from 1712 to 1716, Peter the Great caused more than one hundred and fifty thousand workmen to be brought into the Neva swamp, where the most of them died of fever, contagious diseases, or hunger. To compel the masons to seek employment in this place only, he prohibited the erection of stone houses in the whole empire, under a penalty of confiscation of property and banishment to Siberia, and also commanded every nobleman who owned more than thirty peasant families to build a house in this new capital, the situation and size of which were exactly determined as the conditions of the individuals brought them under one or another class of householders. Perhaps in remembrance of what he owed to Holland, he gave to the city, when it was built, his name in its Dutch form, *Piterburg*.

It has developed into a city of luxury, where the number of servants in proportion to the number of the inhabitants exceeds that of any other city in Europe. In 1870 the number of families in Berlin which had three domestics was two per cent of the whole number, in St. Petersburg it was twelve per cent; and for that year the percentage of families in Berlin having eleven domestics was not given, but the number of such families in St. Petersburg was one per cent.

Driving from the railway station into St. Petersburg, you constantly expect to see the Neva before you—St. Petersburg and the Neva being so closely connected in our minds. But no! this is only a canal, and that only the river Fontanka, which empties into the Neva. Finally, the mighty stream lies before you, broad as an arm of the sea, ice-bound and covered with snow, between the tall quays and the islands, on one of which towers the fortress of Petro-Pavlovsk, with its gilded spire glistening in the sun. Then a world of reddish yellow palaces is disclosed, which, like all the Russian government buildings, awaken surprise by their wonderful color, being partly suggestive of a prison hue and partly of a flesh tint.

Before the Winter Palace the stranger is startled by the sight of a strange, ugly iron shed, which disfigures the beautiful square. This shed, however, gives a correct impression of the climate of the country. It is as necessary as the palace, even more necessary. In the middle of it there is a huge caldron, which in winter nights is filled with glowing coals so that the coachmen and servants, while waiting for their masters in the palace, may not freeze to death.

Here on the left bank of the Neva are also the huge, gay-colored buildings of the Admiralty, and St. Isaac's Church, built wholly of granite and marble. And here also the stranger first comes in contact with the propensity of the Russian to work out his results by the aid of the strength and the richness of the material, rather than by the beauty of the design. In the interior, the floor and walls are covered with polished marble of different kinds: there are columns of lapis-lazuli, sixteen or seventeen feet high, and of malachite, thirty feet high, with gilded bases and capitals; but there are no forms that impress themselves on your memory. Great art first meets the eye when it dwells on Falconet's bold memorial Peter the Great, where the Tsar is seen galloping up a block of Finnish granite on a rearing horse—perhaps the best equestrian statue of modern times. There are also along the Neva a large number of fine buildings in the Italian and French style, transplanted here. There are also very numerous chapels and shrines, before which every passer-by crosses himself again and again, in case he does not stop and say his prayers. On the Neva and on the quays there is a constant succession of sleighs. These sleighs, public or private, have only a single seat, for two persons, generally a gentleman and a lady, and the man and woman sit in such a manner that he always has his arm about her waist,—probably to prevent her being thrown out.

Everybody drives, even the servants who are sent about the city. The distances are so great that, as a rule, it is necessary, and there are twenty-five thousand public coachmen at command. People bargain about the price of every trip; and in the outset, when the stranger imperfectly understands Russian, nothing is more common than this conversation: "What do you ask?"— "Fifteen kopecks."—"Not at all! I will not give more than twenty-five."

We drive from here to the Nevski Prospekt, on a day in early spring, with pure, clear air and sun. The driver is a Russian peasant. During the summer he cultivates his land, but in the winter he earns his bread as *izvoshchik*. He sits there, with his face covered with beard, under a low-crowned hat, in a long and loose coat, which from the waist down is shaped like a wide, puckered shirt or a loose dressing-gown, and extends quite down to the feet. He wears an embroidered scarf about the waist. Strange to say, in the museum at the Hermitage, among the antiquities found in the earth at Kertsh, in the Crimea, on the ornaments like bracelets, are to be found figures of bearded Scythians, who in physiognomy, as well as in dress, remind one of these peasant coachmen. The type seems to have prevailed ever since.

It is a genuine scene of a great city, this Nevski Prospekt in the sparkling sunlight, with three and four rows of carriages side by side, in an endless procession. Elegant men and women are in the carriages. On the sidewalks are the less wealthy people, the women wrapped up like mummies for fear of the cold,—although the worst of it is over,—and apparently wholly unable to dress becomingly. The impression made by most of them is trivial and insignificant, but the appearance of some who have striven to be noticed for their dress arrests the attention. I recall such a one in a glaring costume of light green velvet, shining like a scarabæus, and another in a bright yellow velvet dress with embroidery down the back. Some of the coachmen look like genuine barbarians, being dressed in red and gold; those of the foreign ministers have a triangle in gold embroidery on the back and the colors of the country on the front of the hat. Our coachman and all coachmen cross themselves on the forehead, the mouth, and the breast before every shrine and before every one of the numerous chapels from whose burning lamp a light is thrown into the street. Most of this comes from habit. There is far less piety than there would seem to be from all the crossing and bowing, in the open streets, to which the stranger is a witness. While they are making the sign of the cross with the right hand, they are scratching themselves on the back with the left.

Some of the men have extremely expressive countenances. Almost all the women have chlorosis. The climate compels them to sit too much indoors. The water is undrinkable and the food bad. The poorer people live on barley bread, cabbage soup, and porridge in this land whose temperature demands more nutritious food than in England. And the national drinks—tea, kvas, and vodka (brandy)—have not the nutriment of Germany's lighter or England's stronger ales. In St. Petersburg anæmia is met everywhere.

Life in the principal streets is quite modern. But in the middle of the Nevski, near the Kazán Church, behind the memorial of Catherine the Second, you look into the Gostinny Dvor, bazaars with arcades, stall against stall, a spectacle which is anything but modern. You catch a glimpse of old Russia in the bearded peasant (*muzhik*) with his bast shoes, and his patched caftan or sheepskin, and then you see the priests in brown robes, reaching to their feet, a black cap over their long hair, and with an embroidered belt to which the beard almost reaches. They trade with the merchant, who stands there in antique Russian fur cap, while his wife, with real pearls about her neck, stands by and listens.

Nevertheless, if you really wish to see old Russia you must go to Moscow. It is easily done; for, though St. Petersburg and Moscow are two separate worlds, it is arranged by the modern means of conveyance that by leaving the first in the afternoon the other is reached the next morning. The two capitals are united by the only really express train in Russia.

On the more elevated land in the interior, surrounded by a wall which here and there rises into the towers with green roofs, lies a city which, in its different quarters, alternately possesses the characteristics of a great capital, a provincial city, and a country town. Here there are fine streets, with tall houses and passages, as in Paris, and there interminable ranges of low houses with spacious gardens. You can drive from this fine quarter into one which is almost wholly without pavements. In some places, it is like the country in this city of eight hundred thousand inhabitants and four hundred churches. There is open ground enough, but hardly any place where people can walk,—no promenades except in the outskirts. Yet everything is laid out on a broad scale; everything has the stamp of repose, just as in St. Petersburg everything seems to be planned for keen and immediate enjoyment.

Here the traveller would think he was on the highway into Asia. Strange sights are to be seen: a Tatar wedding-party in modern carriages; dark countenances, under turbans, in elegant European landaus. That was the sight which first met me in Moscow. Everything is to be seen here which we are accustomed to imagine as gay in the streets of a city: Persians with their tall sheepskin caps, Turks with their fezzes, and pagan Kalmucks; it is perhaps as unusual a variety as the sight of Turks and Persians in the streets of Venice.

The stranger's first visit is to the Kremlin. Here he stands on the navel of Russia. This is a holy place for Russian patriotism. Here is the central point of the empire; here the Tsar is crowned. Ascending the highest tower, Iván Veliky, you can see an immense city on every side, with gilded and green cupolas and roofs. Here stood Napoleon with his marshals in 1812 and saw the commencement of the conflagration of the city. Here stood Madame de Staël and uttered the well-known words, "Rome of the Tatars!" which depicts in a masterly manner the impression made by the fountain-head of the church of a barbaric race. But the old French proverb, "Scratch a Russian and you will find a Tatar," contains a truth, though with so many limitations that it will be wrong nine times in ten. The harsh rule of the Mongolian for two hundred and sixty years (1220–1480) in fact put Russia far back and had its baneful influence on the Russian character; but it did not succeed in changing the race, even if it made the blood less pure. The Russian flesh and blood is concealed under many Tatarean princely titles; under many customs originating with the Mongolians, the Slavic temperament has held its own uncorrupted. That appeared when Peter the Great undertook to scratch the Asiatic and found a European under the foreign crust. Even if Kief is more entitled to honor from the Russians than Moscow, on account of its greater antiquity, and even if it is, like Jerusalem, the holy city, —still, Moscow is always, for the inhabitants of Greater Russia, the mother city, *Moskva mátushka.*

The vivid colors of these roofs, the bright gilding of the cupolas of the churches, all this, which in a milder climate would be in bad taste, has its foundation in the climatic and historical relations, and most of all in the length and kind of the winters. If you conceive a winter where the snow for two hundred days together covers everything, woods and fields, roads and streets and roofs of the houses, with its monotonous sheet, you can understand that some splendor is needed in the air to enliven the world when the sun does shine for a day.

Winter is the characteristic season in Russia. Even if the wind is cold, still it is not by far so strong as in Denmark, so that a greater degree of cold can be endured than here. Winter stamps the whole life and character of the people.

The peasant is obliged to live immured in his hut, with the walls and windows carefully closed to the cold. He lives in bad air, by the light of a blazing pine knot, close to the great stove, on the top of which the whole family sleep at night. He sleeps with his clothes on, including his sheepskin. He does not undress the whole week through, except when, on Saturday, he takes his Russian bath. But with his sheepskin he puts on his vermin again.

With the higher classes the long winter has this result, that night is turned into day. Social life in St. Petersburg is even in a higher degree than in Warsaw a night life. Even the most of the sleighing parties take place in the night. In the silent quiet, the three horses abreast with the light sleighs whistle over the snow and ice fields. It is the combination of the silence of death and the furious speed which amuses and satisfies the Russian disposition.

In a southerly land like Italy vegetation is somewhat uniform during the whole year. The laurels and the olive trees are always green. In Russia, summer and winter present two entirely different countries and aspects of life. For a typical impression of winter the life in Siberia in that season may be taken as described by Korolenko, the poet of Little Russia, who returned from an involuntary residence of several years in the department of Yakutsk. He lived in a little house thatched with deerskin. In such a dwelling, at the approach of winter, blocks of ice are substituted for the windows, which are replaced by panes of glass only when melted in the spring. There is never a single day of thaw in winter. It begins by barely freezing and gradually falling to fifty to sixty degrees below zero. In order to breathe, they wrap themselves up in a sort of boa or respirator of fur, made of squirrel's tails. The sun breaks through the icy panes in strange and beautiful rainbow hues.

But the approach of spring awakes a new existence. The fluid element, which had vanished, returns. The real spring is detestable. But this disagreeable spring thaw lasts only a short time, and is hardly considered in Russia as one of the seasons. Still nothing can give the Western-European a conception of the effect on the mind and senses of this sudden plunge into summer.

It had been necessary to wear furs in Moscow; the days were raw and the nights cold; it snowed and froze until the streets, during the last of my stay (until the middle of May), changed to a chaos of mud. Then one day I was taken by an acquaintance to the Kursk Railway station, and we journeyed for a day and night towards the south. When we arose the next morning at five o'clock summer was upon us. There was the country-house surrounded with trees newly clad with foliage. There was a fragrance from these poplars and birches as intoxicatingly strong as the perfume of the plants in a conservatory, and far more fresh. There was no grass, only moss, but over the moss a never ending carpet of extremely fragrant lilies of the valley. The dense, fresh, primeval forest extended along the two rivers Diesna and Bolva; and the nightingales sang in rich chorus, as I had never before heard them. This was no accident, for this is the country of nightingales above all others. It is said that in the vicinity of Kursk and Orel (pronounced Aryól) the nightingale is to be found in the greatest numbers and sings the best of all places on the earth.

To sum up the characteristics, this is a land where everything is extravagant and nothing temperate. In the next place, just as the conditions are extraordinary, immense, so the uniformity is great, and as the natural uniformity is great, so is the variety produced by the seasons great. All is laid out on a large scale, cities and provincial towns. There is room to spare everywhere, as in the United States.

the conditions are very different, has that, on the contrary, is very, and so on almost unanimously … so is the reason inspired by the genius of Russia … would not on a large scale enter into … confidence in this, and it make excessive to in the fullest sense.

III

⁊ If the stranger has now looked about at all in this land, he will necessarily be inclined to reflect on the condition of the people who inhabit it, and will strive to reach clear conclusions as to the fundamental elements of their character.

The truth has been expressed in many different ways, especially in earlier times, that the Russians have invented very little, have contributed nothing, so to speak, to the development of civilization, but have only appropriated the culture of others. They are, it is said, a people of imitation, a people without originality.

It cannot be denied that of all the larger European nations this is the one which has borrowed the most of foreign culture, and whose native culture strikes one least. It shows itself in something external, as in this, that, while a travelling Englishman may be detected at the distance of a hundred paces, you must look well to recognize a Russian on his travels. It is, moreover, scarcely any extravagant exaggeration to say, as in the first part of the "Main Currents," that a square yard of the Roman Forum has more history than the whole Russian Empire.

And yet the observation is very superficial which characterizes the Russian people with the word exotic. The traveller in Russia who asks himself the question, What is there here original? will not fail to find an answer when he directs his mind from the trivial and unimportant to the most fundamental qualities which he can trace.

He is, very likely, first struck by the way in which the horses are harnessed to the carriages. In no other place is this done as here; in no other country are three horses used with one carriage in so stylish a manner. It is no slight or common sense of beauty which prompted this. In the next place, there is a very striking originality in all kinds of manual labor. This is seen in the patterns of embroidery (also well known here from the Russian embroidered handkerchiefs), in the harmony of bright colors which characterize all Russian ornamentation and decoration, from the ancient manuscripts down to the beautiful enamel in gold and silver of this present day, and, finally, in the style of architecture, which, although it is a composite of Byzantine and Mongolian, Hindoo and Persian, Gothic and Renaissance, still has obtained a marked national character as the embodiment of the Russian-Greek Church.

In the next place, this people have an original conception in their civil relations, the so-called *mir*, a municipality whose bond of union is home rule and common ownership of the soil.

Russia is primarily and in its very essence a patriarchal state, a state where the father has the authority and the children are in a condition of equality with one another. As a result of a development ordained by fate, Russia has become a bureaucratic state, where official power has destroyed all spontaneous and natural growth in the relations of public life. Nevertheless, the family, the municipality, and the state in Russia are three organisms, constructed on entirely homogeneous principles, but moving in different spheres. The great Russian family is not restricted to parents and children; it includes several generations and many families. Married sons, brothers of the father or of the mother, have down to a very recent period constantly worked in the same house or on the same farm, yielding obedience to the authority of the eldest, and with property in common. This family relation is now being broken up, because in it (as in the state) the paternal authority has been inflated till it has become unnatural and oppressive.

In the mean time, the municipality is only the larger family, as the state is only the union of all the municipalities into one great family, whose father is the Tsar. The Russian family has two decided characteristics: the unlimited authority of the father, and the undivided possession by the children. The Russian state, absolute monarchy, has developed the first; the Russian municipality, *mir*, the second. In fact, these two characteristics—the power of the Tsar and the ownership of land in common—are the two fundamental principles which distinguish the Russian people from all others. It is very true that many other countries, Denmark among the rest, have long known a similiar common ownership of property; but elsewhere it has been abolished with the abolition of serfdom, or with the emancipation from villanage; here, on the contrary, it still survives. While the common family (or the organization which may be termed a family partnership) is undergoing dissolution since the emanipation of the serfs, the municipal joint property has not only held its own since then, but it has even increased at the expense of private property. In the department of Moscow, since 1861, of 74,480 farms only nineteen have abandoned the joint proprietorship; and at the present time, in the whole of Greater Russia, of all the peasant farm lands 90–98 per cent are owned in common. Even in White and Little Russia common ownership has made inroads.

It is natural that the Russians, underneath the socialistic agitations of our time, should see in their *mir* the healthy germ of better social relations. They generally regard themselves in this particular as the pioneer or prototype for Europe.

Intellectual originality among the Russians is, naturally, much less easily grasped, but it is not on that account the less indisputable. Intellectually, the Russians impress the stranger by their realism, their practical, positive taste for the real, which has made them a great people and has won so many victories in the battle of life. It seems to be this quality which has given the inhabitant of Great Russia superiority over all the other races of the empire. While the Little-Russian possibly surpasses the Great-Russian in continued action, through his vivacity and delicacy, his sensibility and disposition, he lacks the sound common sense of the other. This taste for realism has shown itself to be the strong point of the Great-Russian. It is this among other things which explains how it is that, where a realistic tendency in modern times has prevailed in French literature, and books of this intellectual character have been brought to Russia, they have been received there as the representatives of something old and well known. A long time before, the Russian authors had solved the problem of the novel in a like manner. At the time when France was becoming the most infatuated with Romanticism, the whole Russian novel literature had already begun to produce the description of actual life, and Art had begun to follow on the track of Poetry.

The result of this realism is that the Great-Russian despises the Little-Russian as sentimental and effeminate, and looks down upon the Pole as on a being weak and unreliable, or, on a higher plane, romantic and fantastic. There is also the strongly developed realistic tendency which has deprived the Russian of all metaphysical qualities, and led him, as a rule, to take interest in only two groups of sciences—the physical and social.

The form of government in Russia is not now of the kind to give free scope for any sort of originality. And while independent thought in political affairs is not allowed any outlet, and is almost equally debarred from full and free expression in literature on account of the censor, there is no obstacle to singularity, individual peculiarity, and absurdity, which not infrequently becomes merged into mysticism, a Slavic peculiarity, but one which with the Russians is wonderfully united to realism. Gogol comes to us a representative of the past, and Tolstoï of the present time. It is this mysticism which is outwardly shown in the numerous sects which are found in Russia. The membership of the sects amounts to fourteen or fifteen millions, divided among some fifty or sixty different moral and religious systems.

The trait, however, which struck me personally more strongly than any other, and one which I met with in the most developed and also, so far as I could judge, the most typical individuals, was what they themselves called *une large franchise*, a broad and proud frankness. Nowhere else are men and women occupying the most advanced places in culture heard expressing themselves so openly and without reserve. They not only give utterance to their ideas and thoughts without hesitation, but they not infrequently expose traits of their own lives, traits which they must see may be judged differently, without any fear of losing anything in the opinion of others. Behind this transparency, which especially surprises us in the women, there lies: "Such am I; I appear as I am—too broadly and largely constituted to be reserved and prudent, and too sure of my position in life not to be dependent on my own judgment." The meaning of this in social intercourse is: "This is what I am. Tell me what you are. What is the profit of this reserve! Life is short, time is scantily measured out; if we are to get anything out of our intercourse, we must explain what we are to each other." And behind this frankness lies the emotion which works most strangely of all on one who comes from the north, a horror and hatred of hypocrisy, and a pride which shows itself in carelessness—so unlike English stiffness, French prudence, German class pride, Danish nonsense.

The basis of this is the broadly constituted nature, without frivolity, without narrowness, without bitterness—the true basis of originality in Russia.

And this, which is thus opened to inspection when this natural disposition is examined, this is a peculiarity which is unique among the national peculiarities of Europe.

The fundamental inclination, which numerous experiences disclose to the stranger, is: the inclination to have their swing. It is not simply the inclination to extremes. But it is this: when a Russian has got hold of a thought, a fundamental idea, a principle, a purpose, without regard to its origin, whether it originated with himself or was borrowed from European culture, he does not rest until he has followed it out to the last results. Therefore the Russians are the most arbitrary oppressors in the world and the most reckless liberators, blindly orthodox, following sectarian religions to self-destruction, free-thinking to Nihilism, sedition to attempts at murder and dynamite assaults. If they believe in the idea of authority, they bow down till the forehead touches the earth before it (*chelobitie*); if they hate the idea of authority, that hate forces percussion bombs into their hands. They are radicals in everything, in faith and infidelity, in love and hate, in submission and rebellion.

Finally, there is one more fundamental trait of the Russians, one which seems most vigorously to combat the idea of originality: the inclination to imitation, the power of echoing, of reflecting after the Russian spirit, the capacity to accommodate themselves to the strange and to adapt the strange to themselves. It is first and foremost a capacity to understand and then a disposition to appropriate.

It has been claimed that the Germans possess a similar quality of seizing upon everything foreign, and by translation or penetrating comprehension making it their own. They have this quality in the highest degree. But it is of a different kind with them. Herder's highly endowed, but ponderous and slow people understand ponderously and slowly national intellects: they grasped Greece, Calderon, and Shakespeare before any of the other European nations; but they are not able, on that account, to become so thoroughly imbued with the genius of the foreign race as to reproduce it and act in its spirit. The French, who did not appreciate the Greeks, came far nearer to them in their works than the Germans, who did comprehend them. The Russians, above all others, have the talent of grasping the manner of thought and range of ideas of other races, of imitating them and of dealing with them as their own intellectual property. The cultivated Russian understands and always has understood the living, the new, the newest in foreign countries, and does not wait till it becomes cheap because it is old, or has gained currency by the approbation of the stranger's countrymen. The Russian catches the new thought on the wing. Their culture makes a modern race, with the keenest scent for everything modern. It has been often the case in our own time that authors who have met with obstacles or aversion in their own country have found their first sanctuary in the Russian newspapers or from the Russian public. Who knows if in this respect Russia will not in the future play a rôle similar to that of Holland during the Renaissance, when it furnished a place of refuge to those authors who were persecuted at home? An omen of this is the hero-worship which exists in full bloom in Russia after having been almost wholly lost in the rest of Europe.

This remarkable capacity for assimilation is also met with, in matters of artistic handicraft, among the peasants. The peasant readily takes to any kind of work. He can imitate anything he sees. He knows ten trades. If a traveller somewhere in the country loses a cap with a peculiar kind of embroidery, ten years later the whole region is reproducing it. Another traveller forgets in a corner a piece of chased copper or enamelled silver, and this waif gives rise to a new industry. Some of the most celebrated producers of industrial art are self-made men from the peasant class, men who have groped their way to the position they now occupy. Mas-

lianikof, who as master potter has reached the post of superinten-
dent of the imperial porcelain-factory, was formerly a peasant,
and he has worked his way up, without any training in the works,
by his own individual exertions and conjectures; and Ovtchinnikof,
the celebrated goldsmith of Moscow, whose transparent enamel
was so much admired at the exhibition in Copenhagen, was also
born a peasant, and is indebted to nothing but his natural talents.
He has succeeded, among the other things, in reproducing the old
Byzantine art of using cloisonné-enamel to represent the human
countenance, and in getting on the track of one of the secrets of
the Japanese in the use of a fine red enamel with inlaid foliage of
silver, where the shadows of the leaves are brought out by a device in the process of firing.

In this popular intelligence, exactly the opposite of the English, the capacity for fructification, intellectual suppleness, is the
predominating talent.

It can easily be understood how a national character of this
kind should be developed in this land above all others. We see
before us an enormously large but scantily populated country, very
backward in education, and which it is necessary at once to re-
claim by new settlements and to elevate by European culture,—a
land with broad, unoccupied territory, as in the United States, and
at the same time governed in much the same manner as Turkey.

It is a great winter-land, and the first effect of the cold is to
produce inertia. That is possibly the cause of the national inclination to indolence, which has obtained its typical expression in Gon-
charóf's novel "Oblómof," famous both in and out of Russia, and
a monumental picture of Russian sluggishness. Oblómof is a
character so slack, so tired, so indolent, so disinclined to activity,
that he loses his dignity, his self-respect, his sweetheart and his
fortune, from pure, insurmountable indifference.

The want of sufficiently nutritious food makes the blood thin,
the requirements for protection against the cold make the temperament nervous. Passivity becomes a fundamental trait, which
is sharply and clearly manifested in the popular amusements.
While the Spaniard takes his pleasures in bull-fights, either as
participant or spectator; while the Englishman boxes and rows, the
Frenchman fights, the Pole dances,—the Russian finds no happi-

ness in any kind of sport. His delight is to hear a hand-organ or harmonica play, to swing and to ride on the gravitating railway of which he is the inventor.

In every Russian *traktir*, where the common or better class of people assemble to enjoy the national food and to drink tea, there is found a great automatic organ, sometimes reaching to the ceiling; and the coming guest orders the waltz to suit his taste, never tired of hearing a favorite melody. The swing, with its rocking ease, is an indispensable accompaniment of every Russian festivity. But the gravitating railway, with its passive voyage into the unknown, is the most characteristic amusement for the Russian temperament. Without any exertion, without moving a limb, the participant has the complete sensation of having his full swing.

Passivity shows itself, in public and private life, in the submission to the powers that be. But, at the same time, sluggishness has its strength in passive resistance. Absolutism not only cows, but it hardens. This stolidity becomes the popular ideal. It is not the one who takes the lead,—the daring, the defiant,—who is admired; but the one who, without complaint, knows how to endure, to suffer, and to die. This characteristic may be seen more at large in Dostoyevski's "Recollections of a Dead House in Siberia," in which, according to the popular view, he who endures the lash and the knout without asking for mercy is the object of veneration,—such as, among other nations, is bestowed on the hero or conqueror for dealing blows.

This explains the fact that, although the Russians are a brave people, and a remarkably steadfast people in war, they are the most peaceful and unwarlike nation in the world. The Russian officers have little class feeling. They never, like the Prussians, form a military caste, distinct from the people. They have no *morgue*, no cruel haughtiness. While the German officer, even when his education is the best, feels himself to be a sort of priest, —a military *sacerdos*,—the Russian officer, even when he is rude, is, according to his own conception, a mortal like others.

In the next place, it seems as if the hard contest with the harsh climate, which at the same time has made the people hardy and inactive, has given them the apparently contradictory qualities,—good nature and gruffness.

The popular temper seems to be at once unfeeling and kindly. There is a Russian indifference to their own sufferings, and a Russian sympathy for the sufferings of others, to which this indifference contributes.

The Russian peasant often shows himself indifferent to death. He generally has no special fear of death, and he is indifferent as to inflicting death on others, especially if it is a question of children or old people. Horrible murders are thus sometimes perpetrated among the peasants, without passion or malice. Compare, for example, the child-murder in Tolstoï's instructive drama, "The Power of Darkness."

Still more striking is the trait, which is here stated from a verbal account, given by a Russian general.

The following incident took place in the time of the Crimean War: A severely wounded soldier was dragging himself along with difficulty, and in great pain, after his battalion. His wound was so severe that there seemed to be no hope of his recovery. His comrades then said to him, with the deepest sympathy: "You are suffering too much, you will soon die. Do you want us to end your pain? Shall we bury you?"—"I wish you would," answered the unhappy soldier. So they set to work and dug a grave. He laid himself down in it, and the others buried him alive—out of pity.

When the general, who did not hear of it till it was all over, afterwards said to the soldiers: "He must have suffered terribly," they answered: "Oh no! (*Nitchevo!*) we stamped the earth down hard with our feet."

This mingling of gentleness and ferocity is remarkable. It is typical of the Russian common people. What is otherwise inexplicable becomes clear when we see the utter darkness of the ignorance in which the soul of the poor Russian peasant vegetates.

In all probability, also, the strife with the natural conditions has developed the practical qualities with the Great-Russian,—the taste for that which is available and useful in handiwork. In this aspect, it is suggestive that the most celebrated and most typical Russian, Peter the Great, when he wanted to reform his country, felt himself drawn to the mechanical inventions above everything else. Anatole Leroy-Beaulieu, in his characteristics of that monarch, has pertinently made prominent that, on his journeys, he

did not visit the universities, but the workshops and the dock-
yards; that he brought back to Russia anatomy, surgery, the art
of the apothecary, mechanics, ship-building, engineering, as well
as a whole army of workmen and master mechanics,—but that
there were no learned men or thinkers in his train. With his own
hands he essayed the whole range of manual labor: entered the
army as a drummer, served in the navy as a pilot, knew how to
build boats, forge iron, and engrave. In the armory in the palace
of the Kremlin, in Moscow, there is shown a horseshoe which he
hammered out on the anvil, and a bowl which he modelled. The
genial muzhik shines out through this ruler as through so many a
gifted Russian nobleman.

As the severity of the climate is the cause of certain national
qualities, already spoken of, so it seems to be the connecting link
between the extraordinary uniformity of nature and the melancholy which is so characteristic of the Russian disposition. The
Russian is melancholy,—yet not splenetic in solitude, like the
Englishman. It is a melancholy pervading the community. It is
this which easily glides into sectarian mysticism.

The union of the natural and historical conditions has produced the Russian *mir*. Call to mind one or another small country
town, settled by Russian immigrants, in the vicinity of one of the
remote cities in the north, on the Volga, only a century or two
ago. Before it extend the boundless steppes, from which hordes
of wild Tatars, the so-called Nogaï, are constantly threatening;
the forests round about are full of wild beasts and of subjugated
Tatar tribes, the so-called Cheremissians, who are constantly rising in rebellion. An impassable swamp separates the country town
from the castle of the Tsar, which in time of danger is the only
place of refuge of the inhabitants. In winter, the swamp is frozen
over; the cold reaches the neighborhood of —60° Fahr., and the
blasts from Siberia pile up mountains of snow, which almost bury
the whole town. Is it not evident that in such circumstances there
is no use for the saying, "My house is my castle"? Such an idea
would be madness. Here, it is not only unsuited to the surroundings,
but impossible, to live alone, each family and each farm by itself.
Each one daily needs the help of his neighbors for protection
against the Tatars, for defence against the wild beasts, for the

clearing of the woodland, and for breaking up the soil. The first and most important thing is to take care not to starve to death, and to preserve their own lives and the lives of those dearest to them. Bread can nowhere be bought, and to keep the road open to the castle requires the united aid of all.[1]

When every country town was composed, as a rule, of only a few farms, it was of the greatest importance to have as strong a league as possible between these towns. And thus it came about that all the thoughts of the peasant were concentrated on giving to this league,—the *mir*,—his world, his true fatherland, as perfect an internal structure as possible. Necessity taught him to unite with his equals, and to manage his own affairs in union with them.

Russia, as is well known, has been a constantly growing empire since the time of Peter the Great. Since then, it has annexed annually, on an average, a territory as large as Denmark. While its western boundaries in our time cannot be extended or are even insecure,—for in a great war neither the Baltic provinces nor Poland could be depended on,—its Asiatic boundary is elastic, and is constantly moving towards the east and south. The significant condition of things is here manifested, that such an immense empire is continually growing larger, and, impossible as it may seem, all the new races are immediately assimilated: the Russian race still maintains its supremacy and moves on everywhere, however far the boundaries are extended.

It seems as if the natural conditions of empire had been a controlling force in this direction. The broad endless plains have from an early time awakened a migratory passion among the peasants. They never emigrate to North America, like the peasants of other countries; they go to new places in the Russian Empire. The Russian peasant has always been given to roving. He has been accustomed to make a day's journey to fairs, and to pass weeks and months in a pilgrimage to Kief; nay, even to this day the Russian peasants in crowds make pilgrimages to Jerusalem. For this reason they are exceedingly well fitted for colonizing a new country. Although they are bound to Russia, they do not feel at all bound to their homesteads. Nature is, so to speak, uni-

[1] Tikhomirof: *La Russie politique et sociale,* p. 100.

form, wherever they go. They can wander for weeks together over the steppes without seeing any special change. They can build new houses (*izbás*) for themselves in a few days anywhere. For, from a fear of fire, which in Russia, on account of the droughts and the construction of the houses, is more frequent than in other countries, the peasant never ornaments his *izbá*. The new house contains everything which was contained in the old. He misses nothing in it. The new soil which he is cultivating brings forth just as good a harvest as the old. And by his emigration he has satisfied his desire for adventure, for new experiences, and for seeing new faces.

There is this peculiarity about the steppes, that they continually invite one to go on and on. Level as the sea never is, it evokes limitless reveries, passion for wandering about, thirst for novelty, and the inclination to let every idea be pursued to its never-reached end.

The uniformity of the country gives to the Russian the roaming propensity, the contrasts of the climate make a certain pliability necessary in the face of the great and sudden changes, which may be the basis of the Russian flexibility in intellectual matters, and is perhaps connected with the spasmodic in Russian manners and mode of life.

It is the suppleness in the Russian's nature which makes him so susceptible to foreign impressions. The intellectual transition to the Russian talent for imitation, and the ability to appropriate everything which is foreign, flows from this flexibility. Looking at it in this connection (that is, from the standpoint of its cause) this quality of comprehension and assimilation, it seems to me, has its character of originality. Looking at it abstractly, the lack of originality becomes the foundation of a new originality in the culture of Europe.

It is quite certain that this Russia has always been the pupil of the whole world. It is quite certain that this Russian people is indebted to each and all the nations of Europe. The foundations of its empire were laid by Scandinavian chiefs; almost all the names of the Varings are Norse, and so are the "Russian" names of the Dnieper Falls preserved by Constantine Porphyrogenetes;

even the name *Rus* is in all probability a Norse word, even if
other explanations are not absolutely excluded.[1] Modern Russian
civilization exhibits strong proofs of the Byzantine and Tatar
influences. The Russians as a nation have been to school to the
Poles, then to the Germans and Dutch, and then to the French.
Finally, they have received impulses from the whole of West-
Europe, and their *belles-lettres* have been influenced by the whole
of civilized Europe. All this cannot be denied, and it is equally
true that when we stand in St. Petersburg and look at this Winter
Palace, built from designs by the Italian Rastrelli, and the beautiful equestrian statue, the work of the Frenchman Falconet, or
when, in Moscow, you gaze upon the walls and towers of the
Kremlin, built by Lombardian and Venetian architects, or when,
finally, in front even of Vasíli Blazhémnoï, the model of all time-
honored Byzantine Muscovite churches, we learn that it also, with
its domes, which are like bulbs and pine-apples, dentated and
peeled fruits and buds, with its towers in all forms and hues, was
built by Italian artists of the Renaissance,— then we unquestionably wonder what the Russians themselves have done. But it will
also be noted that the Russians have compelled the foreigner to
work in their spirit or adopt and develop the peculiar Russian
style.

At the present time, the unlimited capacity of receiving that
which is foreign means scarcely anything else than the intensified
ability to fructify. It is this which, among other things, becomes
ardor, enthusiasm, deification of genius, hero-worship.

All springs from the *broadly constituted nature (shirókaya
natura)*. The Russians have an expression, *Chernozióm*—the black
earth, mould. They mean by it the broad and deep belt of fertile
soil, *humus*, which extends from Podolia to Kazán and even across
Urál into Siberia. The wonderful fertility of this soil is ascribed
to the slow decay of the grass of the steppes, which has been
going on for centuries.

The richest and broadest Russian natures remind us of this
belt of rich soil. Even the circumstance that the Russian nature

[1] See William Thomsen: "The Relations between Ancient Russia and
Scandinavia, and the Origin of the Russian State." Compare Elisée Réclus,
cited before, tome v. 301.

has been lying fallow for hundreds of years increases its wealth.

You occasionally meet a man or woman who exactly embodies this Russian soil—a nature which is open, rich, luxurious, receptive, warm without glow or heat, but which gives the impression of inexhaustible exuberance.

A foreigner who had delivered a course of lectures in the Polytechnic Museum in Moscow, where the university for women founded by Professor Guerrier and his colleagues was situated until it was recently closed, related the following little trait of Muscovite enthusiasm: "At the time when the university for women was in existence, I went, one forenoon, into the hall where I had lectured the evening before. I was going to have some changes made in the arrangement of the chairs. I was sitting alone in the hall, and waiting, when a door was half opened and a young girl looked in and withdrew smiling. A few moments later a hundred young girls came quickly in through the door, all in black woollen dresses, formed a circle around me, and began to clap their hands. Then one of them, the daughter of a celebrated deceased poet, said a few words to me, and they clapped again. I believe it is the pleasantest impression of my journey."

Every one who knows how to see will discover similar little traits of surprising warmth and simplicity, during a trip in Russia. It is, possibly, this receptiveness, this prodigality of nature, this inexhaustible richness of the material life, which makes the greatest attraction of Russia, and which betokens its future and more decided originality.

Black land, fertile land, new land, grain-land,—that is its constitution. The broadly constituted, open, rich, warm nature,—that is Russia's. And when you are turning over these qualities: the unlimited extended, that which fills the mind with melancholy and hope, the impenetrable, darkly mysterious, the womb of new realities and new mysticism, all these which are Russia's,—then it strikes one that they suit the future almost as well, and the question presses itself upon us whether, when we are striving to penetrate the secrets of this land, we are not gazing into the very future of Europe.

IV

꧁ As may be imagined, the foreigner has little chance to see the real Russian people in motion in the open air. All public life, meetings, conferences, unions, are forbidden—nay, impossible.

Still the traveller who is in Russia at the right season can get a distinct impression of the character of the masses.

In St. Petersburg, Easter is the gayest season for the common people. In the largest open place, the Field of Mars, where the soldiers are drilled at Easter, four or five large theatres of unpainted wood are erected, side by side, and in these theatres plays are acted, with short intervals between, from morning till night. In the vicinity of the buildings there was a large, permanent market, and, especially on holidays, a great crush of spectators and purchasers. The whole goes under the name *balagani*.

The principal amusement of the poorer people, who have not the means of paying the cheap admission fee to the theatres, is this: On the open balcony which encircles the theatre walks from side to side a youth, dressed like an old man, with an enormous wig of long white hair and a long white beard,—who, sitting down, with his legs hanging from the scaffolding, collects a crowd. He is called *Stárik* (the old man). What he says is the most childish and harmless nonsense,—"If I had plenty of money I would eat this and that for breakfast, so and so much for dinner," etc. [absurd quantities],—and they laugh. Or, "You, down there, don't forget to take off your boots when you go to bed at night,"—and more nonsense of equal value. He speaks just as we do to children of six or seven years, when we want to make them laugh.

We go inside and see a real play. At the best theatre, *Suvórof* is given, a national play in three acts. It is now two o'clock in the afternoon, and the piece has already been played four times since nine o'clock in the morning. It takes about an hour. The auditorium is as simple as possible—a shed; the seats are unplaned, wooden benches, like those used at the Passion play in the Tyrol. The audience is made up of very simple people: servants, peasant men and women from the vicinity; petty tradesmen and their wives, from the suburbs. They wait in silence, Russian silence, till the curtain rises.

Suvórof is the popular national hero of Russia. A short distance from the theatre stands a bad academical statue of him, in ancient Roman costume, with bare legs, which resembles almost anything, only not at all, externally, a careless Russian general. Thus the actor, hoarse as he is, has more of the real Suvórof than the statue. This great man was, in reality, a genuine Russian eccentricity, undoubtedly the only genius among the generals of Russia. While Kutúzof, the loiterer, whom Tolstoï, from philosophic-religious reasons, has glorified and idealized in "War and Peace," was a nullity, who appropriated Barclay de Tolly's plan of the campaign, and for whom circumstances conquered, Suvórof was a real military genius, irresistible even at the head of only a mere handful of men. His crossing the Alps from Italy to Switzerland was undertaken under greater difficulties than either that of Hannibal or of Bonaparte.

Very significantly he is represented in the play exclusively from national patriarchal aspects. He is glorified in the Russian spirit on account of his fatherly disposition, and not for his courage or his victories. And—suggestive enough in regard to the Russian taste—in this piece about a war hero there is no burning of powder, no shooting. No, the common man here sees with surprise and pride Suvórof clad in an old, worn-out uniform, like a common soldier, even carrying his baggage in a bag on his back, —living with the soldier, and eating as he does the same food, a father to all.

There is a well known anecdote of Suvórof, that when he awoke in the morning—and he was generally the first—he used to crow like a cock to awaken his associates. As *General Cock-a-doodle-do* he has been famous throughout the whole of Russia.

In the play this characteristic is abused to such a degree that the hero shouts his Cock-a-doodle-do thirty times, or speaks of its use on earlier occasions. And the screech is every time followed by the exultation of the audience. So also are the scenes in which he declares to the common soldier that he is as good as a general when he does his duty, and offers him his hand,—a scene where he sends away the decorated bearer of a flag of truce, who is astonished at the sight of his simple barracks,—scenes where he comforts and assists his subordinates, jokes with them, and exacts the same things from himself as from them. When a play like this is compared with the national plays of other countries, about the military heroes of general reputation, it strikes one that invariably, in the latter, dash is the quality which is illuminated with Bengal lights, while in the former it is patriarchal simplicity, the paternal relation of the leader of the army to the soldier, that is emphasized.

The same patriarchal trait appeared in another sight of the Easter festival, in the open streets. Young girls of the upper classes of the Imperial Girls' School were driven in a long procession through the streets in the imperial carriages. The pleasure for them was only that of being allowed to take a drive in a stylish court carriage, with coachman and footman in the imperial livery; for there was nothing special to be seen.

The theory of this is that the Tsar stands in a sort of higher paternal relation to all these children. When he once a year visits one of these schools,—to which only the children of the nobility are admitted,—it is a custom that, as a sign of his favor, he drops his pocket-handkerchief, and the girls all scramble for it, and it is torn in pieces, so that each one can get a fragment. He takes the most brilliant girl to the table, and tastes of the food of the institution. It is valued as the highest distinction when he gives one of the girls his plate with what is left upon it. It is the custom and usage for her to swallow it with delight shown in all her features. Great was the stupefaction of Alexander the Second when a young girl, a Pole,—from whose own mouth I had the story,—whom the Tsar had taken to the table, as the most distinguished scholar of the institute, and to whom he shoved what was left of roast meat and potatoes,—nodded to a servant, and calmly gave him the Tsar's plate to take away.

The Tsar has always stood in the position of their common father to the people of the lower ranks, although the foundations of this feeling have of late been somewhat shaken. At the same time, as the present government in Russia has placed itself upon a war footing towards the advanced classes of the people by the very act of putting the greatest impediments in the way of the passion for learning and travel, so it has foolishly decided to forbid the holding the celebration of the twenty-fifth anniversary of the abolition of serfdom. The now emancipated serfs consequently think it proper to infer that those who are in the highest places repent of what was done.

In the cities, the Russian common people are found in the genuine Russian tea-houses, where they have the melodies ground out for them in the organs, and enjoy the pleasure of having music at tea. There also the workman or the peasant is generally to be seen on his Friday, or when he has got a little too much in his head, with his harmonica in his hand, that instrument which demands so little skill and has superseded the balalaïka of earlier times. I shall never forget a slightly intoxicated young workman in Smolénsk, who was reeling along happy in the middle of the street, working away on his accordion while the inhabitants from all the street doors accompanied his wanderings with looks and smiles. Seeing him suggested the rôle the accordion plays in Tolstoï's "Power of Darkness." We cannot help comparing mentally the gay tramp of young men through the streets of Rome, keeping step to the melody of the guitar, or the artistic four-part songs of the Germans. Here is delight in music which is elementary and only half developed. Gentleness and naïveté in this popular pleasure are united with rudeness and stupid melancholy.

In the vicinity of Moscow, on the first of May (Russian style) there was an opportunity of seeing a celebrated national festival, which annually takes place in Sakolniki Park. It is a wood of tall spruces, traversed by many broad carriage-roads. From the grand avenue radiate seven principal roads, which are mutually united by cross-roads. There are also smaller roads and paths, which lead to numerous villas in the Russian Swiss style.

Even the promenade on the first of May, which was meant as a sort of Corso, and for which it was necessary to engage your carriage days before if you would have a suitable conveyance, by a genuine Russian arrangement lost its whole Corso character. All of these numerous roads, for the whole distance from the city, were guarded by Cossacks and gendarmes on horseback, who were stationed by the side of the road, about twenty yards apart, so that there should be no riot, and for the sake of good order it was decided at the last moment that the lines of carriages should not cross each other in the park, notwithstanding the fact that there was room enough. Thus, instead of being able to enjoy the usually varied scenes of a Corso, there was nothing to be seen except the back of the driver, the tails of the horses,—and your lady's face, if you were fortunate enough to have one with you.

In the park, on the great lawns, the common people were collected in great swarms. But neither song nor music was to be heard, nor a single shout or noise of any kind. The people amused themselves in perfect silence. Here were gravitating railways, which afford a pleasure very much like that of the toboggan slide at night: the combination of silence and furious speed which answers for the enthusiastic phase of the national character, and to the Russian favorite word, which is the peculiar characteristic device of the passionate Russian woman,—*Avós*, "Fire away," the French *vogue la galère*. In the next place, the second, also characteristic popular amusement, which corresponds with the lymphatic temperament of the nation, was supplied to the common people in constantly used swings of all kinds. At the same time the humor with which we in Denmark amuse ourselves in the parks on a spring day, was wanting. The lines between the different classes of society, also, are nowhere with us, outside of the metropolis, so sharply drawn as here.

While in cities like London, Paris, and Berlin the museums and other places of education are constantly filled by the common people, seeking instruction suited to their capacity, and for whom, even when they possess only the most moderate abilities, the use of such places has been made easy, nothing whatever corresponding to it is to be found in Russia. The Hermitage in St. Petersburg, with its large and valuable collection of objects of art, is commonly inaccessible and little visited. The museums in Moscow are also rarely open, and have even less of an instructive character. Not even the memorials in the large cities have any educational qualities. They glorify the Tsar and the generals or national heroes, and are designed only to aid in the deification of the Tsar and national self-esteem. In this respect they are behind Berlin, where, since the establishment of the kingdom, no small number of statues have been erected which represent neither kings nor warriors. The re-action in Russia even at the present moment is so great that even the possession of a statuette of Falconet's Peter the Great is taken as a sign of disloyalty rather than the opposite: Peter was a man of the West, a European.

Besides the emperors and generals in bronze, only one single statue is to be found in St. Petersburg. It is a very unpretending and modest memorial of the fabulist Krylof, in the imperial summer park, the playground for children. It is placed just as that of Hans Christian Andersen is in the Rosenburg Park, only the Russian statue is better, and the various reliefs on the base, which represent the whole animal world crowded together, are more amusing, though on the other hand, less artistic than the Danish. In Moscow there is a large group of the two liberators from the yoke of the Poles, the butcher Minin and Prince Pozharsky, whose celebrity dates from 1612, and to whom also a memorial is erected in Novgorod. There is besides this a modern statue of Pushkin, which is not remarkably good. Smolénsk is the birthplace of the musical composer Glinka, and there is found a statue of him, a square-built little man, not particularly suitable for the plastic art. Nevertheless, they had the original idea of putting slender cross-lines in the iron railing which is around the memorial, to represent the musical staff, and thus encircle the composer with his best known melodies.

While other European states do something, even if not all they might, for the instruction of the people, the government here dislikes popular education, and puts innumerable obstacles in the way,—nay, even does what it can to oppose it. As has already been said, the cities do not afford nearly as many opportunities for the instruction and cultivation of the common people as the cities of other countries. As in the country the fight against knowledge can be carried on with much greater emphasis, a still more appalling ignorance is the result, in spite of the excellent natural capacities of the people.

It may be said without exaggeration that there is now, as in the time of the Tsar Nicholas, a constant exertion on the part of the rulers to make real knowledge impossible and to destroy all individual and independent will.

Three kinds of books are published in Russia:—First, the forbidden, that is, nearly all valuable literature, except when with ineffable art and resignation it is shaped so as exactly to suit the demands of the Russian censor; second, the allowed innocent *belles-lettres* and purely technical works, yet with this limitation that in the German Conversations-lexicons of Myers and Brockhaus all the articles about Russia and all the biographies of Russians are blackened over on account of the spirit in which they are written, though they necessarily contain almost nothing but known facts. The anxiety even extends to foreign lands. In a French book which was sent to me from Russia last year, the censor had cut out a leaf, on which, as the context showed, was something not unfavorable, but not absolutely favorable, to the deceased Tsaritsa. Third, the last category of books consists of those recommended for use in educational establishments and schools for the common people. An idea can easily be formed as to what these are.

The solicitude lest the popular standard of knowledge should be raised is so great that obstacles are put in the way of elementary instruction of the youngest children. When, a few years since, a lady of high rank, of whom nothing whatever of a revolutionary character was known, the daughter of a well-known minister, who under Alexander II. had carried through a legal reform, a princess of great wealth, who could not possibly be mistaken as having any wish to excite the peasants to unlawful trespasses on foreign soil, wished to found an orphan asylum in the country where she lived, she sought permission for two years in vain and then received a refusal. Leave must be asked in such cases, and this kind of petition is not granted as a rule.

Thus it is no wonder that the condition of the peasants in most respects makes an impression of profound ignorance and of an Asiatic spirit of submission.

The lady of rank, on her estate, is greeted by every peasant or workman, by every young or old woman of the lower classes, who would ask assistance of any kind, by falling flat on the face at her feet. Not only every one who would beg, but every man or woman who would ask a favor, falls on the knee before her and touches the forehead to the dirt of the road. No remonstrances can make them give up this custom. Significantly enough, the striking of the forehead (to the earth) is even at the present time the name of petitions to the Tsar (*chelobitnaya*).

The superstition is as great as the ignorance.

In turbulent times it not infrequently assumes a formidable character. When, in the time of the Tsar Nicholas, the cholera broke out in St. Petersburg, the common people ascribed such a mysterious origin to the epidemic that they attacked in a frenzy some boys who had been seen *pouring the cholera* into the Neva, and in one of the market-squares they rose in a great revolt against the police, because they had not arrested two persons who had *brought cholera powder into a house* to spread the contagion. It was on this occasion that Nicholas, who was just driving past in his sleigh, and witnessed the tumult, quelled it at once by raising his arm in anger, and calling in a loud tone: "*On your knees.*" This is the scene which is portrayed in relief on the base of the memorial to him.

The supersition of the people still continues. In a manufacturing region in middle Russia, where I was staying, the lightning struck several times, or some other misfortune happened, on Trinity Sunday. To avert the wrath of Heaven, this year, the workmen asked the monks in a cloister some miles away to lend them the miracle-working image of "the Blessed Virgin with three hands," which in that district is regarded as endowed with holy, supernatural power, and this picture was brought to the country town, with great pomp, in a special railway car, accompanied by the singing of the priests and the swinging of censers. The people collected at the station in such numbers that those who were on the front part of the platform were compelled to take refuge in the railway carriage, to escape being crushed. The picture was brought into the church, where a Te Deum was sung. The day passed without either storm or accident, and there was not a workman who had a doubt as to the supernatural cause thereof.

Another illustration of the spiritual point of view of the peasants and priests is the following from the same time. Not far from the little town Biezhitsa the huge head of a mammoth was found. A young princess, whose country-seat was in the vicinity, bought this head of the peasants. Some one or other who wanted to play a trick on the public or the clergy wrote to the local newspaper of the department that the peasants, after the head was dug up, had brought a priest, who had read the prayers for the dead over it and then buried it again.—Could one believe it! On this account the whole clergy of that region were excited, and just because what had been stated in the article was untrue and nothing had happened. What if it had been a human head, and they had neglected to read the prayers for the dead! The consistory in St. Petersburg sent a mandate to the most distinguished prelate, required an examination into what had happened, and commanded that the clergy of the district should take the measure of the head that had been found (literally—"inasmuch as it is of *anthropological* interest"). The day after a whole procession of priests arrived at the country place and held a great council as to how they ought to act to show that this was a mammoth and not an *antediluvian man*, as they expressed it, until the private tutor, a Panslavist naturalist, who was able to inspire confidence, fortified by his diploma, measured the head and gave the formal declaration that this head had never rested on the body of a prehistoric Christian, but on a mammoth. The subject is well fitted for a Russian farce, only it would never be printed or acted.

The workmen in this district lived in barracks. One hundred and fifty workmen slept in a narrow room. Bunks were built up on the walls, so that they lay and slept as in berths on board a ship, except that these bunks or benches were so wide that the workmen lay with their heads against the walls and their feet towards the middle of the floor. There was no other furniture in the room, nothing whatever,—no pillows, no carpet, no chair, no table. The furnishing was exactly like a dog-kennel. This unfortunate condition depends on the fact that there are everywhere found contractors who keep hundreds of workmen in the vicinity of the large manufactories, to let them out as soon as there is need of them. The food they get is a porridge which is scarcely cooked. The rest is uneatable bread and undrinkable kvas with a few pieces of cucumber in it.

A female physician gave the following account of a visit to one of these barracks: A woman was expecting her confinement in a little room where eight persons were lying about her. When I was called, I was obliged to shove them aside in order to deliver the woman. They saw what was coming, shrugged their shoulders a little, and went to sleep.

The poorest workmen in this manufactory, where mandrels are made, earn 17 cents a day, the more skillful 27 cents, and the best workmen 43 cents.

This is the human material which the young men and women, who strive to make the great populace share in the advanced ideas of the age, must educate and rely upon. It is plain that the education will take time, and the aid they are now able to find is of no account.

Two short dialogues of Turgenief are given below, which, on account of the censor, were omitted from the "Poems in Prose," —entitled "The workman and the man with the white hands."

In the first, the workmen wonder at the stranger, and reject his claim of being one of them, while they point to their own working hands, which smell of filth and tar, and to his delicate white hands: "What do they smell of?"—"Smell, yourselves."— "It is strange! We should say they smell of iron."—"Yes, of iron. For six whole years I have worn handcuffs on them."—"Why?" —"Because I thought of your happiness. I wanted to make you poor fellows free, I rebelled against your oppressors; on that account I was put in prison."—"Prison!"—"Yes."—"Why were you rebellious?"

In the second dialogue, which occurred two years later, the same workman speaks to another about the young gentleman who once talked with them: "He is to be hanged to-day; the order has come."—"Has he been rebelling again?"—"Yes—again."— "Well Dmitri, don't you believe we could get a piece of the rope he is hanged by? They say it brings good luck to the house."— "Yes. Piotr, let us try."

This, then, is the human material which the young men and

women who "go out among the people" try to educate and elevate. They do it with an untiring, heroic zeal, which is beyond all praise and without parallel in any land. They leave relatives and friends, expose themselves to cold and hunger, hatred and derision, scorn and insult, they brave imprisonment, sickness and death, with no other reward than that their own conscience gives them. No honor of any kind awaits them; their work is hidden, their offering is unrecognized. Their outer life is a series of struggles and sufferings.

They constitute the outwardly active element of the Russian *intelligentia*,—a world by itself, with its own moral qualities, precarious at times, but always of more value than the mercantile compound, which in other parts of Europe goes under the name of moral,—a pure young world, with the fiery faith of youth, and the passive character of Russian heroism, constant even in torture. The faith in their historic mission, and the consciousness of their spiritual power, sustains them.

Tikhomirof, who has been one of the leading spirits in revolutionary agitations, and who now lives an exile in Paris, greatly deploring the attempts at assassination which alone have made possible the re-action now prevailing in Russia, is always fully trustworthy when he portrays single traits, though not always when he generalizes. He speaks of a young prisoner who was constantly refractory and asking for unheard-of favors, such as permission for the prisoners confined in the cells to talk and walk together. "It is necessary to protest," he continually repeated.—"But what can you accomplish?" said his comrade. "You forget that you are under lock and key. How are you going to find the power of compelling the authorities?"—"The power! How? In myself, in you. . . . *I am myself the power!*"—"My dear friend, that power the others can crush in a minute!"—"Crush it! let us see first! let them try!" [1]

Without doubt, in a classical sense the fundamental trait of invincibility is the strength of the party of agitation in Russia.

A conception of the stoicism of Russian prisoners can be gained by reading, in Dostoyevski's "Recollections of a Dead House," the number of lashes they endure without a complaint

[1] Tikhomirof: *La Russie politique et sociale*, p. 280.

or a groan. In later times, there have been repeated instances of
the resolution with which political prisoners have sought death
to avoid disclosing their accomplices. One has killed himself by
the aid of petroleum, and another has cut his throat with a
fragment of glass, all access to weapons having been denied them.

Out of Russia, an already extended list of revolutionary spirits
in this land has attracted the attention and kept curiosity on the
alert. We call them Nihilists,—of which the Russian pronuncia-
tion is *neegilist*, which, however, is now obsolete. Confined to
the terroristic group in Europe the number of these persons is
certainly very small. Perhaps, as is thought in Russia, there are
five hundred in all, who busy themselves, even if reluctantly, with
thoughts of resorting to bombs and murderous weapons to inspire terror. But it is not exactly this group that is meant when we
speak of that nihilistic force in society which extends everywhere,
into all circles, and finds support and strongholds at widely spread
points. It is indeed not very different from what elsewhere in
Europe is regarded as culture, advanced culture: the profound
scepticism in regard to our existing institutions in their present
form, what we call royal prerogative, church, marriage, property.

The *nigilists* even do not call themselves by this old name,
to which currency was given by Turgenief, in "Fathers and
Sons." It dates from the time when Russia by the death of the
Tsar Nicholas had been liberated from the system of compulsion
intensified to the highest degree under an absolute monarchy, and
when not only the liberation of the serfs was in the air, but
thought, which for a generation had been paralyzed, at once felt
itself free, unhampered, and unrestrained, and speech, which so
long had been the serf of the government, was made free, or by
a sort of inward necessity assumed freedom. At that time, everything which had the ring of a human voice was pure criticism,
negation, revolt against all ancient authority. With the wrath and
enthusiam of youth, their inexperience ran away with them. The
young men showed their democratic proclivities by not combing
their long locks, not washing their hands, and going about fan-
tastically dressed; the young women asserted their independence
by wearing their hair short, a plain dress, and using the blunt
speech of the peasant. Hatred of the old traditions of society, its

hypocrisy and its old customs, went so far that everything which had hitherto been held sacred was despised on account of the respect it enjoyed.

Yet this period was of short duration. Niekrásof (in the "Cabinet of Reading") makes a son answer his father's complaints in the following manner: "Nihilist is a stupid word. But if you understand by it a man of liberal ideas, who does not intend to live at the expense of others, but works, seeks for the truth, is striving not to live a useless life, looks every scoundrel straight in the eye,—nay, sometimes gives him a thrashing,—in that sense I do not see anything bad in it, and in that sense am I a nihilist."

At the present time, the discontented youth, in their own language, call themselves *Nyelegalni,*—that is, outlaws. To obtain a correct idea of them, you must, at the outset, forget the old Bazárof (in "Fathers and Sons"), who was at one time a true conception, but is so no longer, as well as the young people in "Virgin Soil," who are foreign creations, and were never a true representation, but particularly Dostoyevski's "The Possessed," an ultra-reactionary caricature of a tendency in which he participated in his youth, but to which by the lapse of time he had taken an aversion. And it must be remembered that no other sketches of this youth can be found, in books which are published in Russia, than such as are intended to pass the censor. And it would be easier for a camel to go through the eye of a needle than for a sympathetic sketch of the outlaw elements of society to go through the Russian censorship.

A plainly clad, very intelligent young girl came to a country town in the department of Orel, who supported herself by the modest and unartistic employment of painting portraits of the dead from photographs. While very young, with some other young girls she had gone among the people in the country to teach the peasants to read and their wives to sew; she wished for once and all to live with them. The authorities arrested these young girls, separated them, and sent them all by the administrative process to different remote towns, despatching this one to a very small town in the department of Vólogda. There she made the acquaintance of Viera Sassúlitch, who was also exiled, and they lived there together for several years. In this way she became infected with revolutionary ideas. She was especially on her guard with the families of rank and wealth in the vicinity. But she met a lady to whom, after further acquaintance had inspired her with confidence, she said: "I see you are human; I class you as one of us."

The most of these young girls are plain, rather unattractive, hardly ever sensual. They are wholly entranced by their ideas. Several ladies who were present as spectators at the celebrated political trial which goes by the name of the Trial of 193 report that all the women who were implicated in it looked like pale nuns, thin, very serious, care-worn; only one of them was at all pretty.

The construction which obtains in the Russian *intelligentia* of the freedom which can be found in the intercourse between men and women is directly the opposite of the French and Polish. Nowhere is the relation between the two sexes judged with more liberality, and in the cases where nature has broken over the boundaries of law with greater toleration. No one in the more cultivated circles of Russia finds it strange if a man and a woman seek one another's company by themselves. No one on that account immediately believes that there is any bond of love between them; least of all, are the sexes regarded here (as in France) as on every opportunity attracted to each other from brutish impulses. The Russian mother is generally not afraid to leave her daughter alone with a young man. Perhaps the indifference for *qu'en dira-t-on* is nowhere greater than in good society here.

When Bourbaki's army, in 1870, was forced to cross the boundaries into Switzerland, and the soldiers were obliged, after forced marches, to pass the night in the open streets, in a pouring rain, no house, where there were only women, would open its doors to them. Only two young Russian women, who were studying in Switzerland, gave up to some soldiers the only room they had, and passed the whole night in their company rather than let them sleep in the street, entirely unconcerned what stupid and cruel popular judgment would be given to this step. Also nothing is more common than the bond of friendship between young students of both sexes, where common interests, common ideals and plans for the future, form that connecting link which in other countries is due only to the attraction of love. Here the latter, naturally, may be an element, but just as often it is wanting. The intellectual curiosity and the youthful zeal for reform are greater than elsewhere.

It must, however, be understood that these young women would like to live a full human life. Anatole Leroy-Beaulieu, who, plainly, has obtained the far larger part of the material for his valuable book about Russia from a small circle composed of those who were formerly liberal but are now strongly conservative, has described the nihilist women as living in a distinct kingdom of disorganization, where "the free-love" principle has introduced a "manner of life customary among monkeys," and he speaks with a surprised recognition of the fact that in these brutish circles there are, nevertheless, now and then found vestals, who actually abstain from using the freedom which they support in principle.

Tikhomirof (1886) cites against him that free love, only not interpreted as it is understood by the European populace, has long ago been the recognized principle of the whole Russian *intelligentia*—a principle which is not even discussed any more, just as we no longer discuss religious freedom or the freedom of the press. It can be said that since Tchernuishevski wrote his principal work, "What is to be done?" (1863),—nay, substantially, since Alexander Herzen wrote his romance, "Who is to blame?" (1847),—this problem is regarded as substantially (so far as morals are concerned) solved. Love is not understood in Russia, as in other countries, as mere sensualism. And there is found within the Russian *intelligentia* a true worship of love,—as of a holy thing, lawful in itself.

The respect for the formal legal bond between man and woman is comparatively weak; the view of the marriage relation as a means of support is unpopular; sympathy in the case where repentance at leisure has followed the marriage in haste often has a humorous coloring here. It not infrequently happens that, when, for one cause or another, a greater incongruity of temper than usual has been found to exist, the husband and wife give each other complete liberty and continue their common life as good friends. The young girl has here, perhaps even more frequently than elsewhere, her ideal of life; she does not wish to live a useless life. It would not be possible for her to surrender herself coldly and brutally like the very unreal nihilist in the play, by a Danish author, "The Lodger" which is otherwise very admirable. She would also be ashamed of entering into a matrimonial contract simply for profit. But she would not be ashamed of forming a connection with a man without the consent of her parents, and without legal formalities, if she were seriously in love with him. She is more indifferent to the judgment of the world than are the women of the other countries.

This mental and moral attitude has no connection with frivolity or thoughtlessness. It is a fact shown by statistics that two thousand women annually, of their own accord, accompany the exiles to Siberia, frequently to hard labor. In this way, a lady of high rank, Baroness Rehbinder, some years ago went with the celebrated physician Dr. Weimar, who was implicated in the trials for the attempts at assassination.

It can generally be said of those who "go out among the people" that, when the home life is oppressive or obstructive, they seek emancipation from it at any cost. It was in this view that what at the time was called *sham marriage* was invented, though it has nearly gone out of use. The young girl found a comrade of the same views of life as herself, who consented to marry her *pro forma*, but who neither had nor claimed any control over her, and by whose aid she escaped from the surveillance of her family. Sometimes it happens that the two (as in Mrs. Gyllembourg's "Light Nights"), after having become better acquainted, actually marry; in other cases the man is said to have abused the rights formally conferred upon him and a separation is the result. Generally the newly married couple have separated from each other immediately after the wedding, each being free and independent. As is well known in "Virgin Soil," Turgenief has described a kindred case, the relation of brother and sister in the case of Nezhdanof and Marianne, after he carried away the young girl.

However much these young women feel themselves drawn towards the common people, it very seldom happens that they fall in love or marry out of their own rank; and, if it does happen, it usually brings its own punishment. The following is an instance from my own circle of acquaintance: A young girl loved a man of her own, the higher classes. They were both exiled by the administrative process, but were sent to the opposite ends of Siberia and could never learn the least thing about each other. In the country town where the young girl was, after the lapse of a few years, she became acquainted with a young workman exiled for the same political reasons she was. She met him daily. He fell passionately in love with her; they had a child. Other exiles, on the way home, came to the town. Among them was a young man of the same class in society as the young girl, who knew something about her lover. She was never wearied of asking him questions, and sat and talked with him through the whole night. At daybreak, as she was sitting with the child at her breast, the workman killed her in a fit of jealous frenzy. He thought that in her face he read regret for having stooped down to him. Two years after, the child was brought to St. Petersburg, to her parents.

Very significant and instructive is an unprinted and prohibited novel of Korolenko, the title of which is "Strange," and the plot as follows:—

A woman has been sent in exile to a distant province. One of the gendarmes who has accompanied the young lady is the narrator. She has not been able in advance to find out where she is to be sent to, and is thus, by two gendarmes, taken almost through the whole of Siberia. One of the gendarmes, an uncultivated but fine fellow, feels so deeply affected by her youth and charms that he actually falls in love with her, and cannot obey his orders. He tells her the name of the town which is selected for her abode. "Good!" she says; "there are several of *ours* there." Immediately on her arrival, she goes to a young man, whose name she knows, but whom she has never seen, and takes lodgings in his house. She falls ill, of a lung disease.

A month later the gendarme comes again through the town, seeks her out, and finds the young man by her bedside, and with astonishment hears them still using the formal "you" to each other. It is impossible for him to understand what kind of bond it is which unites them; it is clear that it is not love; but the companionship of ideas is foreign to his scope of comprehension. He makes known to the young girl his attachment for her, but she drives him away with the greatest abhorrence. She does not dislike him personally; but solely because he is a gendarme, from principle, from love for the cause to which she has devoted her life; he is for her not a human being, only an instrument in the hand of an evil power. The poor gendarme cannot possibly understand this any more than what has been stated above.

An author, who has a European reputation, gave me the following account of his connection with this circle: "About ten years ago, while I was living in Berlin, I frequently received letters from discontented Russians, of both sexes, some of them asking me to write for them some pamphlets, which they could translate and distribute among the peasants; and others, in relation to a monograph I had written about a celebrated revolutionary individual,—a book to which I am chiefly indebted for my popularity in certain social circles in Russia. A juvenile naïveté shone through the style of some of the letters; but the tone of warm juvenile enthusiasm, united to an energy of style,—which is uncommon even in men of ability,—in one letter, where the Christian name of the writer was only indicated by an initial, awakened great surprise in me. As I remarked, in my answer, that it was not new to me to find enthusiasm and energy among the young men in Russia, I received, to my amazement, the following reply: 'It is very possible that you have been accustomed to find these qualities among our young men; but it does not apply to my case, for I have for some years already been a grandmother.' An extended correspondence was the result of this letter. But, after the lapse of some time, this, and other correspondence of a similar nature, had to be suspended, on account of the innumerable precautions my correspondents were obliged to take. As several of my books had at that time just been forbidden in Russia, they did not dare to write my name on the envelopes. They changed the name, so that I was obliged to inform the letter-carriers of it. At the time of the attempts at assassination, all correspondence of this kind was suspended."

Not infrequently they are very young children who embark upon the peculiarly Russian plans for the improvement of the world. For, even if the old sometimes possess a youthful enthusiasm, yet in Russia, as elsewhere, it is the rule that years and

experience bring both men and women to regard the existing
state of things as stronger than it is, and the prospect of being
able to overthrow it, as much less promising than it appeared to
them in their youth. The observation has also long since been
made that, in the numerous political trials of the last twenty years,
hardly any one has been convicted who was over thirty years
old; even those who were twenty-five years old were uncommon,
the ages of the majority varying from seventeen to twenty-three.

In the spring of 1887, a young girl of sixteen was arrested in
St. Petersburg, whose parents were well known everywhere in
good society. Out of regard to the high standing of her father,
she was set at liberty; but yet with such conditions that she now
remains under the surveillance of the police. A group of young
students had a weekly meeting in her mother's house,—to read
Shakespeare aloud in Russian, as it was said. The fact of these six
or seven students meeting together so regularly aroused suspicion;
and the police sent a warning, received an explanation, and answered: "It would be better to abandon these readings."

They apparently complied. Then the young students were
arrested. A manuscript translation of a little socialistic tract, written by a man by the name of Thun, was found in the rooms of
one of them; and a card of invitation was found, in the same handwriting, signed with the young girl's name. It was of no avail that
she denied all knowledge of the tract contained in the manuscript.

She was very peculiar: homely, with beautiful eyes; difficult
to become acquainted with, for a little thing would silence her.
In the presence of a dashing woman of the world or a beautiful
coquette, she opened not her mouth. She contended that it was
impossible to say a word in the presence of that kind of woman.
She had the whole severity of youth; forbearance was a virtue she
knew only by name. And she had youth's naïve faith in the effi-
cacy of every kind of propaganda. Her mother, a lady of thirty-
five years of age, was high-spirited and passionate, with all the
luxurious vital powers of the Russian blood. The whole emotional life of the daughter had been absorbed by the intellectual;
she managed her mother as if the latter had been her own grown-
up child.

Still more rare than this type, there is among these women

the patient, light-hearted, on whom no opposition makes any impression. A letter from a young married woman, who had been exiled to a town in Siberia, but without being confined in prison, was somewhat to this effect: "Dear Friends,—I can imagine that you are somewhat uneasy about me. But never in my life have I been happier. It is quite pleasant to be separated for a while from my beloved husband, who was beginning to tire me. But that is truly one of the most unimportant things. I have been received here not as a criminal, but as a queen. The whole town is made up of exiles, descendants of exiles, friends of exiles. They actually vie with each other in showing me kindness—nay, homage. Every other evening, I am at a ball, and never off the floor. This place is a true ball-paradise," etc.

More frequent than this arrogance is a humility, a profound, boundless modesty, which is genuinely Slavic. In a small house with a garden, in a remote quarter of Moscow, lived an extremely finely endowed young girl, who for many years had been severely ill; and, as a result, from time to time, especially when excited, lost the power of speech. She lived a purely intellectual life, wholly absorbed in intellectual pursuits; and, on account of her poor health and weakness, was hardly a woman. But a purer and stronger intellectual enthusiasm, and more arduous exertions in that direction, are not often seen. She translated a great deal from foreign languages, and also wrote, herself. There was a combination of energy and the most profound humility, which struck the stranger who conversed with her. Her father had been a well known professor of mathematics. She and her two sisters, bright and healthy girls, supported themselves respectably, orphans as they were, without aid. The worship of the gifted invalid by the two sisters, especially by the younger, was very touching.

One evening, in company, a distinguished foreigner, who had spent some time in St. Petersburg, described another young girl of the same turn of mind and of the same plane of culture, only seventeen years old, and of far bolder temperament. "I have," he continued, "met her for a short time in society, but we were almost immediately separated. I merely noticed that she had beautiful, clear eyes, and cordial, but very decided manners. The day before my departure, I received a long letter from her, which

seemed to me to be very interesting, because it gave me the impression of being characteristic of a whole family. She wrote,—

" 'Permit me to express to you in writing what I had not any
opportunity to say otherwise. I do not speak in my own name
alone, but in behalf of a large part of the young people of Russia,
with whom you have not had time to become adequately acquainted. I should have said it to you, day before yesterday, at the
D—s'; but could not in the few moments we talked together. You
regretted having known, comparatively, so few of the young people. That is partly because the time of your visit was very unfortunately chosen, so far as the Russian youth are concerned. It
is just the time of examination in all of the public institutions of
education. But, entirely apart from that, the Russian youth could
not make themselves known to you. Life deprives us of its highest
good,—freedom, and all the happiness which is inseparable from
it; but do not believe us insensible to that which alone gives meaning and value to human life. Quite the contrary. If fate has sent us
so few blessings, we love those we do receive all the more dearly,
and prize them the more highly. We prize above everything the
science which emancipates. It is not allowed to the Russian youth
to express in writing what they feel; but it would pain me, as a
patriot, if you should get an unjust impression of them. You once
called Rudin the typical representative of the Russian weakness of
character. "Weakness!" I exclaimed to myself when I heard it.
Oh, no! Do not forget that Russian literature is only an in-
complete reflex of the life and character of the Russian people.
Do not forget that they would make us deaf and dumb, and that
we are still too few in number not to be compelled to be so. But
we are really not like Rudin. Rudin is intelligent, and has a certain
quality of intellectual perception, but has no depth of soul; he
loves no one and no thing. He is allured by the beauty of ideas;
he is not drawn on by true and earnest love for the human race.
It is on this account that he is a failure in his relation to Nathalie,
and especially in life, even if he does not succeed as a hero. But,
great God!—do not believe about us that we are a failure in the
wearisome battle of life, which we are in, day in and day out.
How unjust! my strong and living faith is that Russia will some
day come forth cured of its political disease, and disclose itself

liberally and manfully. I believe not only in the Russian people, but I believe in our intelligent youth, in their receptiveness of everything which is true and therefore beautiful. It betrays itself in the profound respect for the men who understand how to find out and unveil the meaning of things, and to open for us wider horizons.' "

There is, perhaps, nothing in this letter indicative of uncommon abilities, and the seventeen-year-old child is visible behind it; nevertheless, there is a personality in it which may be typically Russian, and which it would be impossible to find in a Scandinavian girl of that age,—and a will gleams out through the words, flashing like a steel blade, a will which is full of promise.

One can form a vivid conception of this progressive youth of both sexes, as they enter upon life, face to face with the common people, whose elevation is the object of their aspirations.

These young people represent the highest culture of the age; among the peasants there is an ignorance which renders it almost impossible to begin the communication of information. An exiled mathematician, who had returned from Siberia, a very practical young man, told me that in the country town he was regarded as a man with a supernatural insight, simply on account of his large library; and after he had taught some peasants there, in the spring, how to graft fruit-trees, they came to him the next day from the whole neighborhood with sick children and sick cattle, and besought him to undertake a general cure: "Make them well, little father! make them well!" When he assured them that he had not the power to do it, there was not one of them who would believe him. They begged, cried, asked him what they had done to him that he would not help them: "You know very well you can, if you will!"

In Benjamin Constant's old work on "Religion," it is related that at the beginning of this century, when a Russian general in full uniform rode out into a country town in a part of Siberia but little frequented, he was regarded by the natives as God himself, and that the memory of his appearance got such a firm hold among the people that when ten years later a Russian colonel came to the same place he was greeted as the "Son of God."

That would hardly be possible now. Still, the following hap-

pened last year. A cultured Russian passed through a town inhabited by Cossacks of Little Russia. He was asked the question:
"Will you be so good as to tell us if you have been in the other
world?" He was offended, since he supposed that the inhabitants
meant to indicate to him that they did not believe what he had
said. But the fact was that one of the inhabitants of the town had
returned from a pilgrimage and had told them that he came from
the other world, and those recently deceased in the town had
requested him to bring greetings to their relatives. He had gone
away again, loaded with rustic presents, to the departed relatives
of the credulous Cossacks. Now they wanted to find out from the
Russian gentleman whether these gifts had reached their proper
destination.

In the presence of such ignorance and naïveté mutual understanding is difficult,—most difficult, perhaps, because the peasant
does not like to be treated as children are by their teachers. As a
matter of course, he does not like to have morals preached to
him. When an attempt was lately made on an estate to give a new
drama of Tolstoï, aimed against intoxicating liquors, and in which
the devil personally appears as the maker and distributer of spirits,
the peasants expressed their disgust at it. It was, they said, a tale
for children.

But the same peasants would readily believe that, if the harvest
was poor this year, it was because the priests were now on a
fixed salary. Heretofore the latter said the mass earnestly, to get a
good harvest and rich tithe: this year it was all the same to them;
therefore they prayed negligently and without real heartiness.
Drought followed. And the same peasants explained the last Rus-
sian-Turkish war by saying that in the country of the Turks there
lies in the ground a huge beast, of great age, and under the claw
of his left hind-leg an immense treasure of gold is buried, which
the Tsar wanted to wrest from the Turk.

It must not be forgotten that by the last returns seventy-six
out of one hundred of the soldiers could neither read nor write.

On the other hand, let us examine the moral idea which underlies the whole struggle of the intelligent people of Russia: The
wish to be useful, to see those about them happy in freedom. This

idea crops out in many different guises, now in the costume of the utilitarianism of Bentham and Mill, now in the garb of Tchernuishevski's phalanstery, now in Dostoyevski's strait-jacket, but it is the basis of the philosophy of the enlightened reformers of the fatherland and their friends of reform.

In speaking of the relations of the two sexes, attention has been called to the equality between the man and woman, and to the greatest possible sum of human freedom as the right of both. On this point we can compare the manner of thought and action prevailing among the peasants. External considerations are almost wholly excluded from the marriage question in this class. Nowhere else in Europe does the heart play so small a rôle in affairs of this kind. That early marriages do not indeed of themselves bestow the happiness of love is shown here; for as a rule the age at which they marry is eighteen for the men and sixteen for the women. A result of the extreme youth of these marriages is that the "old man," the head of the family, is often a man less than forty years old and who uses to the full extent his power and the respect which must be shown to him. For a long time past he has sent his sons into the fields and been at home alone with the sons' wives. For centuries he has gone about among all the young women in the house, like a Turkish sultan, and none of them has dared to defy him. A whole range of Russian national songs treat of the cane of the father-in-law. The result is that the Russian peasant never has treated woman as man's equal helpmate. The proverbs run: "Love your wife as your own soul and beat her like your fur!"—"If you cannot thrash your wife, whom can you thrash?"—"It is my wife—my thing."—Even in the seventeenth century the father, on giving his daughter in marriage, bought a new whip to give her the last domestic discipline coming from him, and then gave it solemnly to the son-in-law, with the direction to use it early and unsparingly. On entering the bridal chamber, the ceremonial custom was for the bridegroom to give his bride one or two lashes over the shoulders, with the words: "Now forget your father's will and suit yourself to mine." The national song, nevertheless, directs him to take a "silken whip."

What a stride it is from this to the conceptions of the youngest generation about the right of women freely to give themselves away and freely recede, and their ideas of the common work of the sexes for the freedom and happiness of the masses!

And yet, if the distance is enormous between these alert and sprightly young people and those for whom and among whom they would labor, the contrast between an *intelligentia* with its system of morals and the official world of Russia, which holds in its hands the whole administration and all the material means of the country, is not less immense.

Here is an intelligent *élite*, for whom the rule of ethics is not the official patent morality,—nay, even not the legal—for the motto, "Nothing unlawful," is, for many who belong to it, the stamp of the Philistine,—but for whom above all ethics stands that which they call *the divine spark*,—this spark which Dostoyevski traces out and finds even in criminals and the partially insane, and for whom morality is what they call "the unconscious condition," —that is, that in which the individual does what is right without exertion, without self-conquest, because it agrees with his nature.

Imagine an *intelligentia* with these rules of ethics, as a spiritual guiding power in a state which is ruled and governed as Russia,— where the most ignorant bigotry, in the darkest of the Christian creeds, is the law and fashion, which from the court is diffused downwards, and where a single man's will, even if he has none, is the supreme controlling law.

These two underlying powers are drawing away from each other on every side. What does it lead to? Can any mortal draught the parallelogram of these forces, the resulting tendency and its course?

We are reminded, in considering it, of the passage in Gogol's "Dead Souls," where Tchitchikof's *kibitka* is lost in the distance, driven with mad haste,—

"And dost not thou, Russia, drive away like a *troïka*, not to be overtaken! The road smokes behind thee, the bridges creak. Thou leavest all behind thee. The beholders, amazed, stop and say,—'Was it a flash of lightning? what means this blood-curdling course? what is the secret power in these horses? What kind of horses are you? have you whirlwinds in your withers? have you recognized tones from above, and do you now force your iron limbs, without touching the earth with your hoofs, to fly hence through the air, as if inspired by a God? Russia, answer whither thou art driving?' There comes no answer. We can hear the little bells on the horses tinkling strangely; there is a groaning in the air, increasing like a storm; and the Russian land continues its wild flight, and the other nations and kingdoms of the earth step timorously aside, without checking its career."

V

⌐§ In the spring of 1887, the fiftieth anniversary of the poetic *début* of the old poet Polonski was celebrated in St. Petersburg. This festival offered an opportunity of obtaining a glimpse of the official world, and of becoming acquainted, at the same time, with many of the literary and artistic celebrities of Russia.

Yakof Petrovitch Polonski (born 1820) is very highly esteemed, and is exceedingly popular as a lyric poet. He, Maikof, and Plestcheyef are the leading living lyric poets of Russia of the older generation. The last (born 1825), like Dostoyevski, belonged to the "Petrashevskians," who were sentenced to death in 1849; but, by commutation of his sentence, he was sent to the Urál and put into the Orenburg battalion of the line. It was not till 1857 that he was restored to his rights of inheritance and rank, and given permission to reside at the capital of the country. Plestcheyef to this day belongs to the liberal group in St. Petersburg. Polonski and Maikof, on the contrary, have a close connection with the government. This does not imply that they have at any time participated in politics or cherished principles hostile to freedom; but, since they are both men of moderate means, and it is just as impossible in Russia as in smaller countries to live as a lyric poet, even by the aid of an occasional novel, the government endeavored to improve their condition by giving each of them an office in the censorship. This combination of lyric poet and literary censor, which is so tragi-comic in itself, is decidedly a peculiarity of Russia. In any other country it would be taken for granted that if any one needed absolute freedom, it would be a lyric poet, and that if any one was not adapted to curtail the liberty of others, it would be he.

More or less weakness of character and poverty have united to bring these poets to the point of receiving gratefully the bounty of the government.

Since Polonski was censor as well as government officer, it could be anticipated that the whole official world would be present to assist at his jubilee. Since he was to be honored as the representative of *belles-lettres*, it was not less certain that the larger number of the authors in St. Petersburg would be present. In fact, it was only the extreme liberal party, of which the reviews *Vyestnik Yevropui* and *Sevyerni Vyestnik* are the rallying-points, that did not participate in the festival. The only really liberal authors who were present sat, humorously enough, as guests—one even as an honored guest—between those who had forbidden the publication of their books and prevented the delivery of their lectures.

On one side of Polonski sat Vyshnegradski, then *ad interim*, but since fully constituted, minister of finance,—a fine-looking, elderly man, with broad shoulders, but with a countenance that did not inspire confidence; and who, prior to his assuming the office, had been somewhat criticised. The unthinking mob, which in Russia, as elsewhere, likes to throw mud at anything which shines, had set the following absurd report in circulation, and it obtained general currency, though, naturally, no credit: It is said that, on his appointment as minister, he was taken to the Kazán Church, before a celebrated image of a saint, adorned with jewels, and there was obliged to take a solemn oath that the treasury of the state should be sacred to him. He took the oath readily; but by a strange accident, it is added, after the ceremony, some diamonds and rubies were missing from the vestments of the saint. This story is of about the same kind as the accounts which are found in the Russian national songs,—of how the Cossack chief Platof pays a visit to the Emperor Napoleon, in Paris, disguised as a merchant, gives the *Frenchman* a description of himself, then leaps upon his horse and rides away before the emperor's nose. But the story is, nevertheless, indicative of the suspicion which the continual robbery of the public funds by officials has created among the people, even towards men in the highest places. A foreign author, who had described the Russian situation in Poland as that, when eighty thousand rubles were appropriated for a road, forty thousand must go into the pockets of the officials, repeatedly heard in St. Petersburg the answer: "Lucky fellows, those Poles, if it is really the case there! Since here, when eighty thousand rubles are appropriated for a road, eighty thousand goes into the pockets of the officials."

Since the Zemstvos have been deprived of jurisdiction throughout the land, it would seem that stealing goes on, regardless of consequences, in the most barefaced manner. It appears to the common people as if every disorder on the part of the officials escaped punishment now more than ever before.

By the side of Vyshnegradski sat a patron of literature,—a general in uniform, with a face as red as a lobster, and faience eyes, and expressed his good wishes for lyric and novelistic literature of the right kind in and out of Russia.

Polonski, who was placed at the middle of the left side of the table arranged in the form of a horse-shoe, is a tall and dignified old gentleman, with a mild, intellectual countenance, and a long, white beard. His hair, smoothly combed back, has still preserved its dark color. He came in with a cane in his hand, for he is slightly lame; in his face there was a somewhat uneasy expression of satisfaction at receiving homage. Later, the expression of pleasure at the consideration which was shown him broke through all his embarrassment. There was something childlike in this character,—stamped by the circumstances under which it had been developed, and which plainly had many excellent qualities. The friendship with which Turgenief continually honored him, and which does honor to his life, could not otherwise be explained. (The Vesná collection, published by the Danish author, Thor Lange, contains a series of genial letters from Turgenief to Polonski.)

Opposite to him at the table sat his brother in Apollo and in the censorship, Apollon Nikolayevitch Maikof, with his speech under his arm, with his long, white hair falling down as German professors sometimes wear it, a sharply cut countenance with a pure, strong profile. He rose first and moved a little away from the table and began to read from his paper,—not, as elsewhere is the custom, with his face towards the company, but, as was the case with the later speakers, turned towards the honored guest, so that those who would hear what was said must gather in a throng about him. When he came to the statement of the fact that the Tsar, in honor of the day, had doubled Polonski's salary as censor, there was loud applause from all directions, and with surprising servility came shouts of "The hymn! the hymn!" meaning the national song. They all rose to their feet and sang it. Then the telegrams were read. When Katkóf's came, it was received with demonstrations of shouts and applause,—and a silence, not less significant, on the part of some. When these shouts of joy for a man whose name is the symbol for every suppression and reaction in the interests of their fatherland were heard, it could be seen that in this hall there was assembled an extract of everything in Russia that gags, paralyzes, and brags, although on that account the presence of many distinguished and finely cultured men is not to be denied.

Among those who shook their heads and looked inquiringly at their neighbors, when the mention of Katkóf's name awaked such a storm of applause, was the celebrated Slavophile, Orestes Miller, the historian, a small, grizzled man, with a round head, animated features, and an expression of sense and enthusiasm, united with the conservatism of a professor. He has long sought to occupy a middle standpoint between the fanatical slavophiles of the Aksakovian school, who see an original production in all Russian works, and the scholars who investigate in the European methods, like Stasof, who, as, for instance, in the question about the subjects of the Russian epic poems, has supported the view that all this is the echo of tradition which a long time previous had been spread among the most distant nations of antiquity. Miller has written a valuable essay on the greatest national hero of the Kief-cycle, Ilia of Murom. In the more modern literature, Dostoyevski is his ideal, and he was just expounding to his neighbor at the table the excellence of that author's "Karamazof Brothers," when he was interrupted by the shouts for Katkóf. He little suspected that not a year after he should receive his dismissal from his professorship at the University at St. Petersburg because in two introductory lectures in succession he had stamped the character and effect of the Katkofskian re-action as injurious to Russia,—oblivious of the fact that the Tsar himself, in a letter to Katkóf's widow just after his death, had called him *Russia's greatest patriot.*

Not far from him sat a younger man, whom love of literature alone had brought into this circle, a wild and free bird in defiance of anybody, Vsevolod Garshin. He was strongly built, dark-haired, with the stamp of a self-educated man. He rolled his eyes about in a strangely watchful and wild manner: he had had repeated attacks of insane melancholy, and fears were entertained for his future condition. On no one did the reception given to Katkóf make so profound an impression as on him. But who could then imagine that, not many months later, the almost universal servile attitude of the Russian press at the death of Katkóf should be the occasion which caused him permanently to lose control over his faculties. The panegyrics over a man whose influence he regarded as the root of all evil in the new era of the Russian Empire gave a shock to his brain. At first he continually groaned,—"No, I should never have believed that our press was despicable to that extent, to that extent low-minded:—What shall we do? what shall we then do?" And again and again he broke out in sobs. After that he sat for half a year in his black melancholy, and wept continually. When he was asked the reason, he answered, "I weep for Russia."—In the hope of causing his recovery, the directors of the railroads, by which he was employed, gave him a leave of absence and the means to travel south; but, the day before he was to set out, the sick man put an end to his life by throwing himself over the stairs from the upper story of the house in which he lived with his young wife.

After Maïkof, a stranger to Polonski, who happened to be present, spoke, by invitation, and, although there was nothing in the speech, received hearty applause. It was not difficult to make an impression of eloquence here; for it seems that, with the exception of the advocates, no man in Russia has the talent of speaking, nor the courage to try. Not a single Russian arose who did not have his speech on paper in his hands, and who did not read it. Even among the advocates, there are not many who have a reputation for eloquence; perhaps the best known are Alexander Passauvert, "the great advocate," Prince Urussof, Koni, and Utin.

Yet it is significant that he who is most popular and makes the most money is the Pole Spasovitch, author of the volume which treats of Poland in Pypin's great work about Slavic literature. It is certain, in any case, that even if in Russian Poland, as here, all public and political life, which are indeed the natural school of eloquence, are wholly prohibited, yet the Poles have access to three parliaments out of Russia; and their natural gifts, from ancient times, lead them in the direction of weighing and selecting their words. One will seldom hear a more eloquent man than the Pole Joseph Koscielski: he is a member of the Prussian House of Lords and of the German parliament.

Among the persons present at the festival for Polonski, whose acquaintance a foreigner would be interested to make, the old lyric poet Pleshcheyef must also be mentioned,—a man of large frame, with white hair and beard, one of the few old men in Russia who have been true to the convictions of their youth; and Dostoyevski's widow, a lady between forty and fifty years old, with delicate, regular features, who must have appeared to great advantage by the side of the irregular, plebeian, good-natured physiognomy of her husband. An uncomfortable husband he must have been, even less fitted for matrimony than poets in general, and fully as irregular as any one to whom it has never occurred to make his books a series of arguments for mystical religion and pious asceticism.

A short time after, there was a similar festival in jubilee-delighting Russia, with speeches and telegrams, for the old marine painter Aïvasovski, whom they would thank for "having raised Russian art to the height it now occupies." Aïvasovski is chiefly indebted for his fame to the fact that there are very few Russians who have thoroughly known the ocean, and many who have never even seen it. None of them was qualified to criticise or sit in judgment on his marine views. When he was young, he may have painted some fine pictures; later, he has only repeated himself, and manufactured his sea-views as waffles are served,—hot and fresh on the spot. Always the same story; always the same waves, seen from right or left, in sun or moonlight. The exhibition of his painting, some time ago, in Copenhagen, was a *fiasco* not without good cause.

A day or two after the jubilee, he responded with a dinner
to one hundred and fifty persons, consisting of those who had
been present at the festival in his honor, the whole Academy, the
Minister of Education, the President of the Synod, the Tsar's tutor,
Pobyedonostsef, and others. Each guest received Aïvasovski's portrait, a large photograph, representing him sitting before a canvas,
and this canvas, one-fourth the size of an octavo page, pasted to
the photograph, was a painting by his own hand. In this manner
he distributed to his guests one hundred and fifty small paintings:
waves, shipwrecks, moonlight effects on the water. The rector of
the university delivered a long, ineffably silly speech. He said that
the Black Sea might vanish (be dried up?), but the memory of it
would never disappear; for it was immortalized by Aïvasovski's
paintings. The press, on this occasion, was represented only by
Suvórin, the editor of *Novoye Vremya*, as the other newspapers
had been unable to see in Aïvasovski an artist of any rank.

Taken as a whole, the official world in Russia is doubtless no
worse than elsewhere. The spirit of deference, timid snobbery,
and arrogant leaders of society are its characteristics everywhere.
At the same time, perhaps the lack of culture and the natural
simplicity is even greater, which is the more unfortunate because
the higher officials in Russia have a far greater uncontrolled range
of power than in any other European country.

Russia, as is well known, is divided into departments: Russia
proper, into fifty; Poland, into ten;—and on the frontier three,
four, and five of them are placed under one governor-general. In
addition, the largest cities, like St. Petersburg, Moscow, Kharkof,
Odessa, have governors-general, who possess a military dictator-
ship. Until the abolition of serfdom, in 1861, the governor was the
absolute ruler in his department,—a lesser Tsar, over about a million and a half inhabitants. Since then, the situation is changed
only to the extent that he is surrounded by a group of heterogeneous committees of control. But the whole of this apparatus is
of extremely slight practical importance, since nearly all of these
committees consist of officials under the governor, or of other
officials of low rank, the watchword of whose life is and must
be official servility. Instead of sharing in the governor's respon-

sibility, these committees diminish it, without limiting the full extent of his power to any perceptible extent. It is only necessary to read Saltykov's gory description of Russian provincial governors, in the work, "Our Pompadours," to get an idea of the plane of intellectual development which these men occupy, and of what can happen any day.

To this must be added that, even since the legal reforms of 1864, the governor has retained the privilege of reporting to the Minister of the Interior the persons whom, "in the interest of the public welfare," he desires to send to the distant provinces of the empire by the administrative process,—a privilege not limited to him, since "the third section of his Majesty's private Department of Justice," the secret police, who have the superintendence both of the officials and their subordinates, have the right, without judgment or evidence, to send to prison or to exile every one who is suspected by them. How is it possible that such institutions should not bring to the surface all that is evil and cowardly, hidden away in human nature, in those who, at the same time, represent the machinery of state and are in a situation to place others under its wheels, and must themselves continually take precautions not to share the same fate?

It is quite true that there are Russian officers of high rank who, from their judgment and humanity or from their strong sense of justice and plain manner of proceeding, understand how to make themselves respected in the most difficult circumstances, like the distinguished Governor of Warsaw. On the other hand, there can scarcely be any doubt that the Governor-General of Poland, General Gurko, possesses very few qualifications for his high office, or that old Prince Dolgorukof, Governor-General of Moscow, discharges his duties badly. He is an extremely obliging and polite old gentleman to foreigners, and yet he has a stamp of shallowness and vanity, which makes a painful impression, when we remember that the weal and woe of so many people depend on the state of his emotions and judgment. That he has many friends among the rich, conservative merchants of the city was shown by the exhibition, in his ante-chamber, of complimentary presents,—a collection of costly gifts sent to him on his jubilee,—

which filled one great case after another. But when tact and magnanimous forbearance are demanded, official zeal would evidently run away with him.

An incident which happened in the autumn of 1887 plainly showed this. A concert was given at the university, in which an orchestra of the students took part. In the midst of a solemn pianissimo passage, the sound of two blows on the ear were heard. It was a student who gave them to Inspector Brysgalof,— "an impertinent camel," as one of the professors called him, a creature of Katkóf, who had done all he could to deserve and excite the hatred of the students. The blows were accompanied by the words: "From all the students."—There was a general commotion; the police, Cossacks, all were called up to prevent the young men from escaping from the university. It came to a general fight: many students were struck and wounded in the courtyard, when they resisted arrest.

The whole affair was taken as a good excuse for the authorities still further tightening the reins by which the young men at the university are driven. No less than eighty-six students were exiled on this account by Prince Dolgorukof. What remained after this kind of thorough purification were the extreme conservatives, who are more autocratic than the government itself, who lament from the bottom of their souls the liberation of the serfs, and who, according to circumstances, mix a dose of Slavophilism or of Panslavism in their way of looking at political life.

VI

❧ In Russia, as elsewhere, it is not the official world with which the foreigner has the greatest desire to become acquainted. He seeks in every large city, as soon as possible, to be introduced to those whom the inhabitants themselves regard as the *élite*. As I have elsewhere expressed it: There is always a great difference between the tea which the Chinese drink and that which is sold throughout the rest of the world. He who is fond of tea will in every China seek for the tea drunk by the natives.

The foreigner, who, after having become acquainted with one slavic race, comes to another, soon sees that, in order to understand the new race thoroughly, he must make use of the one already known as a standard of comparison. For only thus can he find the resemblance, without which all comparison is meaningless. By comparison with the qualities of the intellectual aristocracy in Warsaw could the peculiarities of the most advanced and interesting persons in St. Petersburg and Moscow be grasped in their delicacy. The Russians have very few qualities in common with the Scandinavians and the Germans; and even with the Finns, who live under the same rule, and generally use the same language, there is hardly any similarity. The attitude of Finland to Russia has been admirably compared to that of an honest, quiet tradesman, who has lived sensibly but monotonously and a little tediously, to that of a rollicking student, at one time dissolute and then famished, ready for all sorts of follies, but also for business, and who is always thinking more of the problem of human life than of the rent he has to pay. The capital of Finland, in spite of the differences and battle of the languages and what revolves about it, on a flying visit makes a predominating Scandinavian impression on a foreigner. It is certainly true that a large, free, cosmopolitan culture is found among the best educated Finns, partly owing to their close connection with a power of the world which it would be quite impossible to find in a place of the same size in a Scandinavian country. Nevertheless, frivolity, slander, and philistinism flourish here, as in other parts of the North. There is no real standpoint of comparison with Russia to be found here.

With Poland it is entirely different. Nay, the similarity at first sight is so striking that it overshadows the dissimilarities, and conceals the Russian peculiarities. But, in order to find it, we must begin by eliminating all the traits which the Poles and Russians have in common.

In this way we naturally approach the qualifications which have any precise character; but they are not so insignificant as they may seem. The common observer sees no difference between the cultured classes of the European nations. As he moves among these people, who are everywhere dressed in the same manner, and who everywhere observe the same rules of life and of politeness, they seem to him the same; and even if he thinks he discovers some differences, they seem in reality to be purely accidental. On the other hand, he who is inclined to critical comparison, and is, therefore, accustomed to discriminate between essential and unessential qualities, typical and accidental traits, and is skilled in tracing the individual propensities back to the national, and these again to the characteristics of the race, will always be on the alert to avoid hasty generalizations: he looks through the skin, hears through the word, and constantly corrects one impression by the aid of another. If, for instance, he would give his impressions of a great capital, like Berlin or Warsaw, then perhaps for months he would fasten his eyes on lists of hundreds and hundreds of men and women whom he has known, while he constantly points out their characteristics to himself, compares these with each other and with characteristics of a like number of individuals of other nations, to find out the most fundamental traits and the common characteristics. It is thus that the natural scientist finds by comparison the constituent qualities of the different kinds of animals.

At every single personality, every single trait, or every group of traits, which is observed, we must ask ourselves, "Could not this be found outside of Russia?" After that which is common to the human race has been determined, then that which is common to the Slavic races, then that which the aristocracy or peasants in all countries have in common, then comes the investigation into that which is peculiarly national.

In the first conversations, the foreigner will scarcely find the men who pass for the most clever in Russia cleverer than those who are regarded as the most gifted in Warsaw; and he is more likely to find them less gifted.

The essential trait, to which attention is called earliest, is, without doubt, that the chief interests of the Russians are modern. The chief interests in Warsaw are not of this kind, as there Poland—a historic thing, the dream about a past which shall be made into a future—absorbs the thoughts of the best people. In Russia hardly anything relating to the past is thought about. Within the Russian *intelligentia* the historic sense is even perceptibly weak. Peter the Great, even, had done his part to saw it off, or rather to pluck it up by the roots. That the men of revolutionary ideas of Russia lack it, is in part because the modern founders of the empire had shaped its tendency in the direction of the present,—the newest, as the only thing at hand. To this extent he is to be regarded as the father of the so-called nihilism; and the Slavophiles have thus one more reason for regarding him with ill will and horror.

The Russian intelligence, moreover, is less unhappily situated than the Polish, because it is not hemmed in by any foreign and hostile nationality. It has connections in the official circle—nay, quite up in the family of the Tsar; and it is by no means so denationalized as it was in the first ten years of the century.

For example, the young Duke George Alexander (of Mecklenburg), son of the Princess Imperial Katharina Mikhailovna, grandson of the celebrated Princess Imperial Helen, and permeated with traditions from the time of his grandmother, is not infrequently met in liberal circles. Although he is a prince of the imperial family, he does not hesitate to make the first call on a foreigner who does not belong to the nobility, if he thinks that the acquaintance would be of any advantage to him. He is a young man of large and sound culture, with many interests. A more unconventional officer than he would probably be sought for in vain in the Russian army. His mother's palace in St. Petersburg, by its size, reminds one of Christianborg in Copenhagen. She is also the owner of large estates in different parts of Russia, and the young prince impresses one as being well acquainted with Russia. He is polished, quiet, and intelligent; his manners present an attractive mingling of German solidity and Russian intellectual freedom. He is an interesting illustration of how the intellectual currents which are blended in the highest circles of Russia in our time result in a half cosmopolitan, half national culture.

His grandfather, the Prince Imperial Mikhail, and his elder brother, Nicholas, were taught by the well known Swiss, Cæsar La Harpe, the same person who had previously been the tutor of Alexander the First, and in their schoolboy days received a thorough course in the liberal culture of the eighteenth century. So completely were the young imperial princes to be educated without regard to the traditions of Christianity, that, as is shown by the memoirs (edited by Durof) prepared for the Tsaritsa Katharina describing the methods of instruction adopted by La Harpe, the following was taught to them as to the founder of the Christian religion: "Jesus, surnamed the Christ, a Jew, from whom the Christian sect takes its name." [1] The young imperial princes, however, were forced by the tediousness of their teacher to let the philosophy he taught them go in at one ear and out at the other, and to employ all their leisure hours in the drill yard, where the beating of drums and the parades were their chief delight. Mikhail, who had some mathematical talent, became a zealous artillery officer, and still was no more absorbed in the peculiarly military problems than in the arts and sciences of peace. He would have readily given utterance to his older brother's memorable sentence, "I detest war: it spoils the armies." [2] Reviews and parades, orders and epaulets, were everything to him in his youth. When Nicholas became Tsar, from enthusiastic zeal for his authority, he excluded his brother from every position whatever, that was in the slightest degree influential; and, from indignation

[1] *Jésus, surnommé le Christ, juif, dont la secte des Chrétiens tire le nom.*
[2] *Je déteste la guerre: elle gâte les armées.*

at this, the latter on all occasions expressed himself in bitter derision about his surroundings, sneering at everything and everybody, with the reckless irony of a discontented man.

It was to this man that in the last year of the life of Alexander I. (1824) the young Princess of Würtemberg, who on being received into the Greek Church took the name Helena Pávlovna, was married. During the twenty-five years of her married life, she was compelled to suppress all her interests, and to be apparently absorbed in court festivals, audiences, and tedious drives, and dared to occupy herself with reading and music and to enjoy the society of artists and scientists only during the time which etiquette dealt out as sparingly as possible. At the age of forty-five she was a widow, and seemingly lived some years only for her daughter Katharina Mikhailovna and the children whom the latter had from her marriage with the somewhat bigoted reactionist, Duke George of Mecklenburg-Strelitz. At the death of the Tsar Nicholas, a new epoch was begun in her life, and she opened her palace to everything intellectual to be found in the different parties in St. Petersburg. The leaders not only of the Slavophile, but of the liberal party frequented her house. Conversation there was spirited and without restraint. The mistress of the house was still handsome, and she liked to see fine-looking men about her. Her household contained only handsome men, among them Abaza, afterwards Minister of Finance. She also patronized the distinguished vocalist, who afterwards became the wife of the latter, and now as Julia Feodorovna Abaza is one of the ladies in waiting at her daughter's court. By the side of the politicians of the different shades, artists and scientists, Russian and foreign, had free access to her house. For a long time it was the custom that distinguished artists or scholars who came to St. Petersburg took up their residence, by her invitation, in the beautiful palace at Mikhailof Square. She had lost the power of continuous activity or work during that long period of her life when her whole existence had been absorbed by the etiquette of the old court. But interest in and love of knowledge was fresh in her to the last.

It is her inheritance which Katharina Mikhailovna's heir has entered upon with greater earnestness and penetration in spite of his youth and in spite of his oppressive situation under the existing Russian rule.[1]

A point like this makes one feel sharply the distance from Russian Poland, where no thread from the world of intelligence reaches completely within the court circles.

At the present time there is no central salon in St. Petersburg. Formerly, Countess Alekseï Tolstoi formed such a centre. The widow of the celebrated poet, one of the most cultivated women in Russia, is now an elderly woman and no longer an attraction to society. Among the advanced Russians it is the style nowadays to answer questions relating to that subject with: "A salon! a circle! an intellectual aristocracy! Really, what do you expect? There is nothing of the kind here. The house where you live is an oasis. All around it is a desert."—And if you ask for their great men, where they are to be found and seen, the answer readily slips out: "I don't know them; I have never heard of them. We are perhaps in advance of the Germans in this one thing, that we do not have great men like them. We lack a Felix Dahn, a Gustav Freytag, and Julius Wolff, and so on. We do not have the solid and learned, earnest men, who on the other side of the frontier write novels in four volumes, and historical works in fifteen. There is an utter want of that kind of genius among us. We have not even the Prussian *Feldwebel* with clinched fists, in whom our neighbors see the new Pericles. He is deeply indebted to us. The stupidity of our statesmen is his genius. To that extent you can find his genius here."

This trait of depreciating and speaking ironically about themselves is of very frequent occurrence among the progressive Russians, more frequently than among the Poles of the present time, and united with an irony pointed at foreign self-conceit, which it is difficult to find elsewhere.

Just as the Russians, as a rule, do not extol the geniality or the industry of their countrymen, so also the more refined and more sceptical among them glorify just as little their intellectual powers or their trustworthiness. "Look out for a Russian," you will hear in St. Petersburg: "he has more imagination than intel-

[1] Comp. (Julius Eckhardt): *Aus der Petersburger Gesellschaft*, 5th ed., p. 30 and following.

lect, and more intellect than moral sense." This is hardly true about the common people of Great Russia, whose quick apprehension, constancy in work, and perseverance in adversity, are crowned by the most meritorious virtue,—a great gentleness,— and who, however credulous they may be, and however easily on that account they may be frightened for the moment, still have an equipoise in their nature, a consistency in their method of thought, and a quiet courage, which makes them composed and steady in times of danger.

Among the cultivated Russians, on the contrary, the foreigner will often enough meet with instability and capriciousness, of which the young men of Turgenief afford so many examples. Little traits which illustrate it will be at his service by the scores:—

A young Russian sees a young Englishwoman on a public promenade in Heidelberg. He does not rest until he has won her, and she gives him her hand. They come to Russia. He has little property and does not care to work to any extent. He has hardly passed the honeymoon before he declares that there is no congeniality, no affinity to be found between him and his wife. They then live in different cities: he amuses himself as well as he can in St. Petersburg; she remains in Schüsselburg, educates her daughter, in the English style, to independence, lives constantly in recollection of her husband. He amuses himself, travels, as a choice lies in a boat on the Black Sea and dreams. He is now forty years old and has not yet found his career. He has for a long time been a farmer, but wishes to change his occupation and become an advocate.

Is not that Russian? asks the foreigner. It is human, and common to the Slavs. A Pole has certainly not very infrequently done about the same. A Frenchman might, I dare say, become tired of an Englishwoman, but would hardly enter upon a new career at forty. A German would apply for a divorce, remain at his trade, and immediately marry again. It is Slavic, it is true, but hardly peculiarly Russian.

"Tell me your family drama," says the foreigner to his Russian acquaintances. They tell a story like this: There were two brothers L., of the aristocracy, one married but childless. His wife becomes *enceinte,* and informs her husband that his brother is the father of the child. A duel between the two brothers follows, in which blood is spilt, but no one killed. The wife leaves her husband, who is living and has lived with a ballet-dancer, marries the brother, and by him has a large number of children. The fathers and mothers-in-law are delighted. They immediately received the newly married pair with open arms, and society approves of what has been done. Is this Russian, or not?

That which is specially Russian must be the contentment and tolerance of the fathers and mothers-in-law.

Professor T. of the University became infatuated with a lady who was married to one of his colleagues. He moved into the same apartments with Mrs. M. They had both their names on the door, each received in their rooms, and were invited everywhere together.

This is more characteristic. In the capitals of other countries marriage would have been essential.

Baroness L. was first married to a young, fine-looking man, who held a high official position, left him to marry his superior officer, who was thirty years older than herself. Since this marriage she for some years travelled about with a young Austrian count of a celebrated family, then came back to Russia, while her husband by his official situation is tied in Madrid. In St. Petersburg she has a young artist living in her house, sees a young poet every day, shows a lively sympathy for several other men, and is not the less, after some hesitation on the part of society, received everywhere, being still young and remarkably pretty. She drives to a ball at the house of the minister of Foreign Affairs, and sits there dressed as a gypsy queen, with a gold ring on her forehead, takes an active part in the social life of the highest circles, and makes eyes with the young gentlemen. The next day she sits clothed in a simple woollen dress, without ornaments, knitting a stocking in a garret with a poor gray-haired lady, who knows the addresses of all the exiled, and takes care of money sent to them. She writes a novel for a prominent French periodical, about interesting countesses from Russian *high life,* who fall and rise again, and she writes pamphlets at one kopek for the collection of popular writings in Moscow. She stands on almost confidential footing with several young men of the radical wing of the liberal party; but on still more confidential footing with the prefect of police of a great city, through whom she can and does obtain pardons in large numbers.

This combination ought not to exist outside of Russia.

Nicholas Y., a very well educated young man, had revolutionary tendencies in the sixties. A young girl, very handsome and enthusiastic, fled out of the country with him. She was then a Nihilist, had taken part in commotions of the students, accompanied him from place to place—"civilly married" to him, as she called it, which means in Russia not married at all. They went to London. When they returned, in 1878, both were changed. He, a capitalist, re-actionist, working to get exorbitant railroad grants in Bulgaria. She, exclusive, formal, an Anglomaniac, correct and strikingly dressed, with several diamond ornaments on a dress of black velvet. It would not have been believed that they had ever led a life of independent and rebellious ideas and emotions. On his death some years after, it is said that she found among his papers several which placed his character in a light of which she had never dreamed, and which was unfavorable to her. Then she had another transformation, sought the most extreme liberal circles, and has now wholly devoted herself to the literature and politics of the progressives, declares that she is living her youth over again, because she believes that in the present times she finds once more the vigorous impulses from the sixties.

This inconstancy, which emanates from the very receptive nature of the cultivated Russian, is less surprising than elsewhere, and is accepted by the customs of the country.

This class, moreover, in the higher stratum of society also not infrequently manifests a certain cynicism in the presence of brides by the "civil" rules to be found elsewhere only among Bohemians.

Critic F. reads aloud in company an article about M.'s poems. M., who enjoys a certain prestige as a lyric poet, is a small, robust, thick-set man, about thirty years old, with a dark Jewish-Mongolian countenance, a kindly, attractive smile, and rather embarrassed demeanor. His poems are ponderous, rich in sentences, and belong to a kind of lyric usually characterized as deep. The critic positively overwhelmed the absent poet with his praise. In bombastic, incoherent prose, he extolled the wonderful beauties, which were not to be found in reading the poems through the first time. The comic aspect of the situation was that Mrs. M., who was divorced the previous year, is present, listens to the panegyrics upon her ex-husband, and by the side of him she now prefers expressed to the author of the article her objections to his view of the subject.

One must go to the South German circles of actors and authors to find anything like this. That which bears the special Russian stamp on it is perhaps that no one in the company seems to find anything out of the way in it. It is a peculiarity of Russia that, when a marriage tie is dissolved, it is generally the wife who desires to enter upon a new union, and very often the husband, in order to make this possible for her, assumes the blame, so that a divorce may be decreed, although he thereby makes it impossible to be married again himself. The following is a case which happened last year: an estimable and finely educated advocate, who was married to a young princess, received the confession from her that she was in love with an officer of the guard. He declared himself to be the guilty party, and she, by reason of this accommodation, not very easy for him, married her lover without impediment.

These glimpses of fundamental traits from the St. Petersburg family dramas shape themselves into a typical picture. But the peculiarities are brought into the clearest light when we compare prominent Russian individuals of the higher circles with prominent Poles of the same class.

The typical Polish nobleman of our time is a grand gentleman whose practical interests are agricultural, whose diversions are amusements and the theatre, whose intellectual interests are concentrated in the advancement of the cause of the Catholic Church and thereby of the Polish aristocracy. To him the Church is the precious pledge of the nationality, and in his mind the aristocracy stands as the indispensable leader of the nation. He publishes, at his own expense, some old national work, he subsidizes the national theatre in Posen or the Polish press in Warsaw, enters into alliance with Rome and with the Jesuits,—that is, if he is a zealous Conservative and a zealous Pole. Otherwise, he only thinks of amusing himself, lives for the ballet, never misses a horse race, marries the daughter of some rich Jewish banker to gild his tarnished coat-of-arms, and then continues the life of his youth with greater dignity and fewer creditors. He never does any real work. The old aristocratic disdain and aversion for labor exist to this day unchanged in Poland. A young Polish nobleman who works is cited everywhere as a phœnix.

It is quite different in Russia. In the aristocracy here, for the most part, the broad-shouldered, persistent muzhik shines out.

Here is a type: He is of a princely family; that is to say, he belongs to one of the only half a hundred Russian families who are of real princely blood, because they are descended from the old rulers of the country. He has inherited hardly any property. Without any trace of the Ranudo-like [1] disinclination to work, which is the characteristic of the Polish nobleman, he studies engineering first in Russia, then in Germany; on his return goes to work with an axe in his hand, builds bridges, and lays out railroads, at first in the employment of others, and afterwards on his own account. Not that he loves work on its own account. As a practical Russian, he means to become rich, very rich. He becomes a manufacturer, gives up his manufactory to become a financier; as a speculator on the exchange develops a sagacity and prudence which are not surpassed by old bankers; has the keenest scent for money-making, and at forty years of age is a millionnaire. He has a practical and coarse-grained nature, a mathematical head, a calculator of probabilities, who has never known any kind of enthusiasm, and has never had a glimpse of artistic taste. If he travels to Italy, it is not to enjoy nature, or see works of art: he is to be found dallying with roulette at Monaco.

He is practical but not narrow-minded, and not depraved. He is not like the Polish landed proprietors, who in Galicia (until in more recent times it was prohibited) tortured their Little-Russian peasants, and prevented their going to church, by locking the doors of the Greek church to them, and giving the keys to the

[1] Don Ranudo (read backwards *O du Nar* "Oh, thou fool!") is the principal character in Holberg's comedy of that title.

Jews, so that the peasants must buy them back in order to worship
the Lord on their festivals;—he has himself no kind of religion,
and he is willing that all men should have theirs. Nor is he like the
Polish landed proprietor in Galicia of the present day, who lives
by the manufacture of spirits, and by forcing as much of it as
possible into his peasants. His heart is without any sensitiveness;
he is as harsh as he is obstinate; but he does no man any harm.
In his youth he has been a humanitarian—not from emotion, but
from force of a process of reasoning in which the right is the
logical justice; now he is so no longer to that extent, as he no
longer believes in the utility of the efforts of single individuals in
respect to the great sum of social misery, and as he is entirely
incapable of the enthusiasm which leads to action even if the
profit of the action is infinitesimally small. Very sharp-sighted as
he is, he feels an almost personal hostility to all metaphysics; he
has written a book, a sort of philosophy of mathematics, in which
he advocates the necessity of introducing object lessons into the
department of mathematics, and combats the use of the words
line, point, etc., as unreal abstractions.

Like so many persons with mathematical minds, he is skilled in
music, well informed in all musical technics, conversant with
modern music, and eager to hear a great deal of good music well
performed.

As coarse as a peasant, unrefined but not frivolous, narrow
but not shallow, reckless and loving money but upright and sometimes almost liberal, he is a decided materialist from conviction
in all matters as to which he has any knowledge. He cannot with
calmness hear even a lady submit to him for consideration personal immortality as ever so weak a possibility with which imagination might amuse itself. To the question why he has preferred
the ballet-dancer whom he keeps in preference to any of the
other actresses, he answers: "She is a bit more tidy than the
others," and it seems almost to be the moving cause, for in her
regard for him he neither believes nor can believe.

But, in spite of this candid materialism, openly exposed, this
man is far from being an out-and-out materialist. He would not
be a typical Russian if he wholly lacked an ideal element. And he
has it. Tchernuishevski's old book, "What Is to Be Done?" ("A

Vital Question" [1]) is his Bible. Its rebellious propositions and contents are to him the truth in regard to the traditions of the old society. He demands, not aloud but in his quiet thoughts, a reform in the relations of the sexes, would have that freedom introduced which is proper for a man of age, who has left the official religion and the official morals equally far, far in the rear, and there, at this point of his spiritual life, is a nook where the social Utopia sprouts and blossoms in shade and twilight.

Next, the following type is more characteristic: he is also a prince, but probably of Tatar descent; the name indicates this, but the physiognomy is entirely European. He is very fine-looking, very elegant, with eyes which, in spite of his being almost fifty, shine like those of a youth, or rather like those of a magnetizer. He is unusually gifted, possessing at once great artistic, linguistic, and oratorical powers.

Being without money, he chose a practical career while yet very young. But he met with a mishap at the outset. Somewhere in a foreign country, in a semi-private circle, he had made a speech of a political tendency which had caused displeasure. On his return home he was punished by exile to a little country town in Esthonia, where he was obliged to remain for ten or twelve years, exclusively limited as to society to men, of whom not one stood on the same plane of culture as himself, and shut out from all activity, all development, and all means of livelihood. At last, he lost all hope of ever being liberated from his place of exile, and in a sort of desperation married a young woman of the neighborhood, who, indeed, was both pretty and good-hearted, but separated from him by so deep an abyss in culture, that she, on her part, has never desired to enter her husband's circle in society at St. Petersburg as princess. She lives only for her home and her son.

He came back finer-looking and more elegant than ever, thoroughly cured of political enthusiasm. As if in scorn, freedom was given him in the guise of a government appointment in which he must work in its service directly against that system of thought for which he had suffered. Cold as ice, materialist in his manner

[1] Translated from the Russian by N. H. Dole and S. S. Skidelsky; published by T. Y. Crowell & Co.

of thought and in all the relations of life, he has allowed himself only one passion: the passion for collecting. He collects books, manuscripts, bronzes, women. In literature and art he gives his allegiance to the principle, *Art for the sake of art;* [1] in life, to the principles from the time of the court of Louis XV. Among French authors, he specially affects the line of Flaubert, Zola, Huysmans; among the Russian poets, Andreyevski, a lyric writer, whose poems are not on emotional subjects, have no emotional relations, and who has had the artistic, exceedingly odd idea of turning a whole novel of Turgenief into verse.

He has much passion, but hardly a flash of emotion. He is frank, entirely truthful,—perhaps, except when it is a question as to his age,—reserved towards men, open towards women, who worship him, and in whom he trusts after having educated them. More than one is bound to him as if by enchantment, although he has constantly taught them to root out every germ of emotion as a germ of misfortune, and although his conversation with them chiefly turns upon his relations to his other mistresses.

Now and then, this man shuts himself up in his room, and sits lost in silent adoration of a statuette of a favorite French author, with a long, thick mustache, more sincerely loved by him than perhaps any Parisian woman has ever been. He makes a journey to Paris simply to buy a particular edition or a single autograph.

He has no convictions outside of the literary and artistic. But within this circle he has his Russian enthusiasm as a passion, wholly absorbing him, irrational in the midst of all his intellectual coldness.

What is common to the Slavs is easily comprehended in him. On closer examination and comparison, that which is essentially Russian may also be comprehended. In Poland there is an eminent nobleman, K. J., who belongs to the same class of men. He is elegant, cold, prudent, and yet, in certain directions, enthusiastic. This Pole and this Russian, to every one who knows them both and is able to compare them, are equally brilliant; but the Pole is vainer, the Russian more directly fond of sensual pleasures. There is a remnant of chivalrous tradition in the Pole, which the Russian

[1] *L'art pour l'art.*

has shaken off. The Russian satiety goes deeper than the Polish, and at the same time leaves room for more force. The Pole presents a weak side from his Polish dilettante desire to distinguish himself in every department; the Russian is of harder metal. The Polish ideal is, and continues to be, grace; the Russian, force.

If we now place the two typical Russian characters sketched here side by side, we shall notice that, however different they are, they have this in common, that the anticipation and struggles of their youth have been made of no avail by circumstances, so that they have been forced by necessity to be smaller men than they were framed for, hardened, practical materialists, in no situation to do anything profitable for others than themselves, and entertaining their ideals as one cherishes a harmless eccentricity.

The two currents in Russian intellectual life, which at once strike every observer, the tendency towards Western Europe, the disposition to acclimatize and further develop the general European culture, and the tendency inward, the national self-absorption, with a hostile attitude towards "the Gentiles" in the west, are most plainly personified in those Tsars of great historic renown, Peter the Great and Nicholas, two fundamental Russian types.

If you go still farther back, you find both these characteristics united in the old Muscovite Tsars, Iván III. and Iván IV. the Terrible, the latter being especially important. He has well been characterized as a combination of Louis XI. of France and Henry VIII. of England: a mystical, bloody tyrant and prudent monarch like the former, and having about as many wives as the latter. It looks as if Peter the Great broke with all the traditions from the old Muscovite princes when he began his violent reforms. And their coarseness, stubbornness, power, cruelty, and mystical faith in the might of the Tsar rise up again in this century in Nicholas. But even then Iván III. turned to the different European courts in order to procure from them physicians, artisans, and artists. He invited into Russia foreign masons, metalfounders, and goldsmiths, and caused architects and engineers to be brought from Bologna and Venice. Iván IV. also caused handicraftsmen to be brought from various parts of Europe; he approached England and, in spite of the opposition of the clergy, brought the art of printing into his empire. In other words, in the more remote times the contrast between the condition of the learners to the culture of Western Europe and the originality in the strongly marked institutions of the Muscovite Tsar and the long-bearded Byzantine Russia (governed from a palace which was a compromise between a barrack and a Greek Catholic monastery) was far weaker, far less sharp, than since that time. It was only when Peter I. at a blow abolishes the dignity of the Patriarch, takes from the Greek Church its landed estates, interdicts the national dress (nay, the beard), even abandons the long Byzantine costume in order to dress in an ordinary uniform, and stations a herd of foreigners, more or less unscrupulous, but unacquainted with Russian peculiarities, at the head of all the affairs of the empire, that the tendency towards Western Europe comes to the front as exclusive. And it was only when Nicholas wrapped himself up in a decided hate towards the ideas and reforms which emanated from the liberal west, when he limited the number of the students at each of the universities to three hundred, discontinued instruction in the common constitutional law of Europe, intrusted the philosophical instruction to the clergy of the orthodox church, caused the manuscripts from which history and kindred branches were taught to pass under the supervision of the censor, and about 1840, speaking in general terms, would not allow any foreign newspapers or books to cross the frontier, that the tendency which closed Russia to Europe was developed not less exclusively. At that time, it went so far that all the instructors in geometry in the land were ordered, when they were teaching the properties of triangles, to remind their pupils of the holy Trinity, and that the performance of Lessing's "Emilia Galotti," Goethe's "Egmont," and Schiller's "Fiesco," were forbidden, while Rossini's "William Tell" was allowed only with the words and title of "Charles the Bold."

And if the heterogeneous old Russian types appear sharply in these Czars, Iván III. and Iván IV., Peter and Nicholas, the modern Russian type of civilization is shown not less clearly and peculiarly in the person of Alexander I., with its commingling of energy and feminine receptivity,—of comprehensive liberalism with care for all the oppressed and love for the title of liberator, on the one side, and inertia, the mysticism of Mme. de Krüdener, a propensity to diffuse conceits or Utopias like the Holy Alliance, on the other.

This nature in our time is found in many a young Russian of rank, who travels to Berlin to seek out and passionately attach himself to Eugene Dühring or Edward von Hartmann, calls himself positivist or pessimist and to that extent regards himself as standing on the heights of modern progress,—but, returned home, with tearing haste is developed into a Russian high conservative, enthusiastic for the mission of absolute power, for the omnipotence of the dominion of the Slav and the glory of the Greek-Orthodox Church. One of these younger men, Prince Z., a good man, but not a good poet, a philosopher, who is accustomed at least once a year to sit at the feet of Edward von Hartmann, immediately after Katkóf's death, sought to succeed him in charge of his newspaper in Moscow and carry it to greater lengths in his spirit. He failed in solving this problem, not from lack of good will but of power.

In the mean time, most significant for Russia, and yet entirely in analogy to the situation elsewhere, is the intellectual division into the Western European and Slavophile groups. It is noticeable and extremely Russian that the primitive national party of the Slavophiles, not less than the Western European, owes its origin to the study of foreign philosophy and poetry. It is just as true that the great revolutionary spirits of Russia are a product of the movements which at the beginning of the thirties took possession of the University of Moscow. Some of the professors, who had studied in France and Germany, at that time awakened the interest of the young students for French socialism and German philosophy. In all secrecy and from prohibited books, the young men in separate groups appropriated, some of them the ideas of Saint-Simon and Fourier, and others the views of life of Schelling and Hegel. They gradually divided themselves up in such a manner that one party, to which Herzen and Bakunin belonged, united that manner of thought which was nearly allied to that of Hegel's most advanced disciples (Ruge, Feuerbach) to the French Socialistic ideas, which were proclaimed by Louis Blanc, and in modern French light literature by George Sand and many others;

while, on the other hand, the natural philosophy of Schelling and the enthusiasm of the German romanticists for everything national and old German was kindled in the party of the Slavophiles, who, wholly in the spirit of these Germans, demanded a purely Slavic culture and posed as the representatives of the national principle in its full sharpness. They cast longing looks back to the time of Peter the Great. The Muscovite Russia was the home of their thoughts and dreams. The horrible rule of Iván the Terrible, in spite of everything, was dearer to them than the modern liberalism, so destitute of character, and parliamentarianism. Their most precious study was Slavic antiquities, and they thought that they were diving into the Russian national spirit when they had dived deep into the Byzantine theology.

To that extent they substantially gave a voice to the forces and efforts which had existed since the time of Peter the Great. In those days there was no other element of opposition than the Raskólnik, that is to say, the old orthodox party, which, since the time of the reformer Nikon, had seceded from the State Church and been split up into numerous sects. The Patriarch Nikon had wished to regulate the ceremonies of the church. From his time on, the church demands that its followers shall cross themselves with three fingers and say three hallelujahs in succession, and fearful consequences have overtaken those who resisted. But the Raskólnik have defied the knout, exile, and execution for their conviction that one ought to cross himself with two fingers and only say two hallelujahs in succession. They have allowed themselves to be burned alive for their conviction, for they believed that they would suffer everlasting damnation if they consented to the number three. It is even only a year or two since that these sects have been suffered to have their own chapels and pray as they pleased—excepting, however, such sects as are still declared to be dangerous and are persecuted. The most interesting group of them at the present time is the so-called *Dukhobortsi* (Warriors of the Spirit), who are in the largest numbers in the department Voronezh, and who were exiled to the Caucasus, to a region without water. They have shown such energy as to have converted this desert into one of the most fruitful and richest regions in the Caucasus. They work in common, old and young, women and children. They can all read, although they have no schools; they teach their children themselves. They do not recognize holy images. They hang up in their houses, in the corner where the images are usually placed, an embroidered towel. They do not carry the cross, but, regarding it as a symbol and memorial of Christ's sufferings, detest instead of honoring it.

In time of war they have rendered the greatest service to the country, when there was need of transporting supplies or the wounded over the sometimes impassable roads of the Caucasus; they freely rendered their service to the State, which had treated them so harshly, and gave their wagons and time without compensation. Yet it is characteristic in this connection that in all these sects the most profound hatred of the heathenish, heretical institutions of Western Europe has been nourished.

But the national consciousness and hatred of the foreign mounted from the lowest classes of society to the highest during the great national struggle against Napoleon, who in 1812 inundated the land with hosts of Frenchmen, Germans, Italians, and Spaniards. The great prosperity of the national literature followed the great contest with its victorious exit, which, both in Pushkin and in Griboyédof, however much the one is influenced by Molière and the other by Byron, is controversially turned against the foreign influence in the empire. To a certain extent the Slavophiles thus only continued the agitation, which had been planted and had reached maturity. This intellectual current must not be confounded with the Panslavist, to which there is a certain resemblance in name. The Panslavists themselves have been European radicals like Bakunin, in so far as they, in the service of the national cause, to the advantage of the dissemination of the peculiar Russian communism and association, wished the union of all the Slavic races and the foundation of a great Slavic empire, monarchical or republican. The Slavophiles, on the other hand, have directed the most vigorous assaults towards those sympathizing with the Poles in the west; they represent the narrower Russian national feeling, and like to look back to the old Byzantine basis of culture and faith for the Russian national life.[1]

[1] Comp. Julius Eckhardt: *Jungrussisch und Altlivländisch; die russische neue Aera.*

If we turn back now to our starting-point, the comparison between the Russian and Polish intelligence, we shall see that the Russian intelligence is obliged to make almost as painful a choice of forces as the Polish. The dilemma of the modern Polish patriot is this, that, if he decides to labor uncompromisingly for progress, he undermines the Catholic Church, and thereby, for the time being, the Polish nationality, and labors in reality for the oppressive government,—the force at hand most hostile to himself and to progress of every kind. If, on the other hand, he chooses intellectual stagnation, he plainly sees the danger that the nationality, which is protected thereby, and of which they were and are so proud, will fall behind in European culture, and become antiquated and outstripped.[1] The corresponding dilemma of the progressive Russian patriot is this: to the best of his ability he would shake off foreign influences. But at the same time that he considers that what this brings in its train is ruinous to national originality and growth, he sees that the Russians are less advanced than the inhabitants of any of the European countries except Turkey.[2] However strongly he may complain, like Tchatski, the celebrated typical Russian in Griboyédof's "The Misfortune of Having Intelligence," that Moscow imitates Paris in manners and customs, in language and modes of expression, in fashions and follies, nevertheless, like Tchatski, he winds up by turning abruptly on the Russians themselves, who feel that they are only fit to be imitators, and who, when a man has five or six ideas by means of which he rises above the people, and dares to express them freely, fall upon him like barbarians. All the attacks on the intellectual supremacy of the foreigners become at last an attack on that Russia which submits to and finds its profit in it. Tchatski, in his last soliloquy, utters the painful cry, "It is also my fatherland." And thousands have ended with this cry of distress.

In other words, the progressive Russian who desires the broadening and development of the nationality of his people, and that the foreign element should be kept at a distance, soon comes to the conviction that the fragments of Western European culture in his land are always worth more than the unquestionable

[1] Comp. Georg Brandes: *Indtryk fra Polen.*
[2] Eckhardt: *Jungrussisch und Altlivländisch,* p. 18.

national roughness and the equally national barbarity. He cannot indeed distinguish between the people and the government, for a great people have the government they deserve. He sees that for whatever finer culture, scientific insight, and artistic taste he himself possesses, he is indebted to the civilization of Western Europe, and that it is the Russian people's own fault if they have only used this civilization to varnish the brutality of their form of government and the barbarity of its administration. The more nobly and earnestly he wishes for his country the gifts of justice, humanity, and freedom, the plainer it becomes to him that they can be obtained by unremittingly and uncompromisingly opposing the ruling national tendencies of the century. He feels the impossibility of wishing for progress and freedom of thought at the same time with the strengthening of national feeling in Russia. Not only the sentiment of fatherland, but that national feeling which he feels in his heart to be justified here, become re-actionary from necessity. The freedom-loving patriot can long enough and enthusiastically enough demand the development of the people from within. He can only by virtue of the points of view supplied by the culture of Western Europe judge what there is in his own country which ought to be promoted or repressed; and, wherever he makes his exit, if he desires to see human and civil rights respected in his land, and to see strong emotions and productive ideas disseminated and rooted there, he comes out by returning to the deficient western culture, only too often caricatured in Russia, which the sects detest, and which the national party of the Slavophiles abhors and condemns. For on the plane of development Russia has at this time reached, he inevitably finds himself compelled to choose between the two forces,—either the national with the sacrifice of the ideal of progressive freedom and culture, or the decidedly liberal, but then also without any firm footing on Russian soil, and with only a weak connection with the national spirit.

All the most remarkable men of Russia have this dilemma to contend with. Minds like Pushkin, Gogol, and Dostoyevski chose definitely to pursue the former direction; those like Alexander Herzen and Iván Turgenief, the latter.

VII

๙§ In the year 1887, the hostility in Russia towards the German Empire reached its height. They had the feeling that the future conflict was not very distant, and the foreigner frequently heard expressions about the impending European war. As a rule, these expressions were desponding. There is nowhere such a lively perception of the very great weakness of Russia as in Russia itself. But what without qualification was significant for Russia was the almost universal wish for defeat. The foreigner heard this not only in Northern but in Southern Russia, and it made no difference whether the speakers were Russians from the east or the west, provided only they were able men who loved freedom. I have certainly heard the wish expressed, as if by common consent, by more than fifty Russians, of the most varied classes of society, and entirely unacquainted with each other, that there should be a decisive defeat in an ensuing war. We can scarcely imagine a more instructive symptom than what I have here stated of the deep despair which exists as to the present condition of the country. No other possibility of liberation from the predominant misery presents itself than that which is offered in the weakness which an unsuccessful war will entail on the ruling system.

It is not the first time that this sentiment has flourished in Russia, and that wishes apparently so unpatriotic have been cherished by men who have the greatest love for their country, and are the best educated. It was the case in the time of the Crimean War, and the wholesome results which accompanied the defeat are distinctly remembered.

The terrible oppression which exists at the present time is by no means of so old a date as is sometimes believed by those who think that Russia, as a matter of course, is and constantly has been behind Europe. This is a re-action toward the short but powerful and remarkable period of freedom and emancipation in the first ten years of the rule of Alexander II. On the whole, in Russia freedom is the old, and oppression the comparatively new. The oldest Russian law-book (*Pravda Russkaya*) does not recognize corporal punishment. Serfdom was first introduced in the sixteenth century, and Pskof, the last free city, like the old Novgorod, a republic governed by a popular assembly for centuries, by the cruel order of the Muscovite Tsar, Vasíli, was deprived of all its privileges, its inhabitants carried away to the interior of Russia, "in order to live happily by the grace of the Tsar," and replaced by a newly imported race of men. In the eighteenth century the deliberative assemblies of the provinces, the Zemstvos, which in the Middle Ages had spoken loudly and energetically, first lost all their importance, and the theory of absolute power, on which the authority of the rulers now rests in Russia, first took form in the nineteenth century. It is not even of domestic origin.

Alexander I., in the first period of his reign, manifested an almost modern spirit. He appeared to be a man sincerely fond of freedom. He loved his age, despised the proceedings of the revolutionary re-actionists, was for a long time an admirer of Napoleon, continued for a long time to wish well to France, and cherished plans for the elevation of Poland. It seemed as if under him the power of the Tsar, like everything else in Europe, was to be humanized, and as if the voice of the people would be heard. So, under the strong re-actionary counter-shock towards the French revolution and empire, it was two persons who were not Russians, the Piedmontese De Maistre and the Frenchman Bonald, who shaped the great theory of re-action which was victorious throughout Europe, which the *doctrinaires* of Russia passionately appropriated, and which, easily manipulated by them, became the new corner-stone of the Tsar's throne.

The present condition in Russia is, then, neither the result of a stagnation for a thousand years, nor of a uniform progress towards the better, which has been too slow and much delayed, nor of a retrograde movement in culture uninterruptedly continued for a long time. It is the product of a re-action now twenty-five years old, constantly fortified anew by insurrections and attempts at assassination.

It is not that there is a want of good will and earnestness on the part of the Tsar. Justice is done everywhere and in all circles to his character. It is known that he likes to see honorable, upright men about him, and also that he was angry at the corruption and deceit which during the last Russo-Turkish war extended even to the highest officers of the army, and had so large a share in the unfavorable progress of the campaign. In other words, it is admitted that he is a man of honor; but a great man, a great leader, is at this moment needed on the imperial throne of Russia. It is, perhaps, a misfortune for a people to need great rulers. A country like Holland or Switzerland certainly has no need of any. But it is a greater misfortune not to have a great ruler when one is needed.

The Tsar's virtues as a private man are readily recognized. For the first time for centuries, for the first time probably at all, he furnishes an example of an occupant of the throne of Russia, about whose relations to the other sex even evil tongues have not the slightest thing to report. The men, as well as the women, who have occupied it, have for all time been renowned for their erotic extravagances. The emperor seems to be a pattern as a husband and a father. About this exemplary imperial family, the Russian court nevertheless runs riot with its elegant frivolity and its numberless irregularities, without re-acting upon it, but also without being influenced by the spirit which emanates from it. All the world knows that the Prince Imperial Alexis lives openly with the beautiful Countess de Beauharnais, sister of General Skobelef, whose husband, a cousin of the Prince Imperial, the Prince of Leuchtenberg, has seen his profit in resigning his rights to a prince of the imperial family. The beautiful German Princess Maria Pávlovna, consort of Prince Imperial Vladimir, of whom the author of the book *La Société de St. Petersbourg*, instigated by his hatred to the Germans, relates all imaginable evil, is, as it were, an incarnation of the passion for court pleasures. It is not necessary to believe what is said of her by the pen inspired by hate; but this much is true, that there is a sort of recklessness which stamps the tendency she gives to the amusements of the court. She arranges parties in which they amuse themselves with all kinds of games, but chiefly with playing hide-and-seek (*cache-cache*). In such games now and then a lady of the highest rank will be found hidden away with an officer of the guards in an empty bath-tub. One of the amusements of the youth in these court circles, also, is to get up sleighing parties, in which the finest ladies are taken out in basket sleighs drawn by officers. The sport is that the officers at a certain time upset the sleighs, with all their contents, in the snow. They laugh at the result.

In certain higher circles of the court, where a different spirit rules, there is no other amusement than dancing. They dance continually, on all occasions, with a real mania. They make up for their detention for many months at Gátshina by whirling away in an endless round dance. Where they do not dance, the tediousness is overwhelming. Tea-parties in these upper circles are described as tiresome. The guests arrive; after a while the grand persons appear, and take their places in silence. Evidently no one dares to ask so exalted ladies about anything. Then from their side drops a question as to the state of the health of one of the ladies present. As a rule she answers briefly, and therewith the conversation dies away. If she is very ingenious or very good-natured in relation to the embarrassment of the grand company, she shapes her answer so that it makes a new question almost necessary; but when the little series of questions and answers having intimate connection with this subject is exhausted,—as trustworthy eye-witnesses assure me,—twenty or twenty-five minutes may elapse in a pause of complete and painful silence, during which the guests look smilingly on the exalted visitors, who, in turn, distribute their smiles upon those about them.

Even if there is a little more noise, the impression may sometimes be not less painful. Eye-witnesses have described the following scene: the old courtier, Count A., fell while waltzing, and remained sitting on the floor. This evoked a laugh from the Tsar. Stimulated by having been the occasion of such a burst of good humor on the part of one whom it had been the study of the count's life to please, the old man danced out, and let himself fall again, this time with comic gestures. Renewed laughter. From that the aged courtier devoted himself the whole evening to evoking smiles from the lips of the august being by playing the clown. While all this was going on, his daughter, the present Countess O., one of the ladies in waiting to the empress, sat straight and stiff, with contented mien and a smile in her eye, swallowing her anger at her father's abasement, and really satisfied with the obvious favor which fell to his lot. The scene reminds one of what is immortalized in the well-known painting of the court of the Tsaritsa Anna Ivanovna, which is widely known in Russia by the copper-plate engraving, and in which the members of the first families of Russia are represented playing leap-frog in the ball-room of the palace for the amusement of their sovereign lady.

Court life was far from being so spiritless as now in the time of Alexander II. The court bigotry, so closely connected with shallowness, was also unknown during his time. Now you find large circles among the aristocracy who belong to the Radstock-Pashkof sect, which was founded not many years ago by an impostor. In these circles they pass their time in reading "The Evangelists," damn all who don't think as they do, and, above all, pick their neighbors to pieces. Fanaticism and a malicious propensity to gossip generally go hand in hand here. A large part of the members of this stratum of society send their sick to the priest John in Cronstadt, whom they believe able to work miraculous cures by the laying-on of hands. Even Loris Melikof sent a daughter to him when she was ill.

The vigorous Greek-orthodox re-action in the highest circles is comparatively new, and is now in full bloom. It began under Alexander II. It was not that this monarch was favorable to it; far from that. But his consort, a German princess, at first from a desire for popularity, afterwards from a want of an object in life, when she felt that she had entirely glided out of the existence of her volatile husband, took up the cause of the Greek-orthodox Church with constantly increasing warmth. Thus it happened for the first time from time immemorial in this empire, where the clergy occupy an inferior position and have little influence, that a priest of the imperial household, the wise and fanatical Bashanof, became influential at court. It was to this man to whom it also happened to prepare the present Tsaritsa, by instruction in the Greek religion, for her change of confession. And among the court ladies who were smitten with zeal for spreading abroad the sound doctrine, and combating Roman Catholicism and Lutheran Protestantism, especially when found within the boundaries of the Russian Empire, Countess Antonie Dmitrievna Bludova, a slightly deformed, energetic, and intelligent girl, made herself very conspicuous. It was she who, under Alexander II., cemented the union between the Muscovite Slavophile party and Aksákof and Katkóf, and was the first to master the Polish Marquis Wielopolski's plan for a reconciliation between Russia and Poland, with a hostile attitude towards Germany. Through her father, the well-known powerful minister, she accomplished the appointment of Wielopolski as governor in Poland; but then, after the revolt in 1863, she was converted to the doctrine of the necessity of the eradication of Roman Catholicism, and actually initiated the horrible religious persecutions in Lithuania and White Russia. It was she who stood at the head of the idolizing of Vilna's executioner, Muravief, in St. Petersburg, after the attempts at revolt were drowned in the blood of the Poles; and it was she who, on an appeal to the liberal Prince Suvórof for a subscription for the memorial present which was being procured for the hero, at a public dinner received the courageous answer, which deprived the prince of all popularity, "If you will make the general a present of a gold axe, my purse is at your service, countess." She took care that Katkóf's most fanatical and bloodthirsty articles were laid before the Tsar just at the moment when he was in a receptive mood for that kind of reading; and when, after Karakósof's attempts at assassination in 1866, a decisive re-action took place, she contributed perhaps more than any one else to bringing about the result of placing the whole educational system in bigoted hands, hostile to culture. From that time to the present, this religious re-action has continued uninterrupted, partly from fashion and partly as a prudential precaution. The political re-action took it up in its current, and carried it farther on.

This political re-action can be dated from 1863. An orgy of ideas had preceded it, in which the whole nation revelled in hopes of progress, and became intoxicated with plans of emancipation.

The result of the Crimean War had put an end to the system of the Tsar Nicholas. The time was passed when fanatical nar-

rowness and cruel harshness alone ruled over everything in the
Russian Empire. Not only had the books and newspapers of
Europe been excluded, but the greatest obstacles had been put in
the way of travellers across the frontiers, whether going or coming; nay, the hatred to the age had gone so far in the first man of
the empire, that he detested railways and prohibited their construction, so that Russia, at his death, had only the single line
between St. Petersburg and Moscow, and this one was managed
in such a manner that the merchants preferred to send their goods
by the old teamsters, in common wagons, as the safer and cheaper
way.

The defeats in the Crimea brought the deliverance. In however great respect for his father Alexander II. had been educated,
he was compelled at once on his accession to the throne to repeal
some of the most absurd of these laws. This was received by the
people who had been so long gagged and fettered as if from this
time any kind of criticism of Nicholas's system of government
would be allowed, and as if it was the Tsar's own intention now
to change everything. During the Crimean War, Herzen had already established his Russian printing-office in London; and his
weekly newspaper, *Kólokol* (The Bell), gave the signal for the
free and reckless inquiry into all the blunders and follies of the
old *régime*. Never had such language been heard in Russia, never
had any one wielded such a pen. The boldness carried away the
readers and conquered all minds. Herzen was soon the most influential man in Russia, the idolized dictator of the intelligent
youth. He seemed to be omniscient; nothing which happened in
the land, from which he had been banished, escaped his attention,
so thoroughly was he informed. He published secret state papers,
like the memoirs of Catherine II.; he threw light upon embezzle-
ments, frauds, infamous and cruel deeds, committed in various
parts of the empire. He had so many connections, and in such
high places, that on a day when *Kólokol* contained serious charges
against one of the imperial adjutants-general, and a number
printed in St. Petersburg, without the compromising passage, was
laid before Alexander, who was a constant reader of the paper,
a week or two later the Tsar received the original number in an
envelope, with a few lines which gave the reason why it was

sent in this manner. So widely spread was his newspaper, that in Nizhni alone, in 1859, one hundred thousand copies, which had been introduced from Asia, were seized by the police. There was at once formed a group of parties with different shades of opposition or progress. There was the opposition to the Germans flourishing at the court, on the part of the higher nobility who had been set aside by Nicholas in the interest of absolute power. There was the opposition of the Slavophile, who, as unaristocratic as possible, idolized the people. Finally, there was Herzen's, Ogaref's, and, in a short time, the sceptical, radical, and gradually socialistic opposition of Bakunin, who had escaped from Siberia. And all these groups of opposition, under these conditions, for the first time in Russia created a press.

Until the forties there had not existed in the great empire any other press than the official. Under Nicholas the newspaper, "The Russian Bee," an academical organ, which was conducted in the spirit of the old classical poets, Lomonósof and Derzhavin, carried on the same war against the romantic tendency inaugurated by Pushkin as Oginski's organ in Warsaw had carried on against Mickiewicz and his friends. It was the great Russian critic Byelinski who gained a hearing for the national poetry of the nineteenth century. It was under the control of the literary impressario, Krayevski, who is still living, that the newspaper "The Annals of our Fatherland" was published, and it was sustained by the genial articles of Byelinski. When he died, in 1847, worn out by his literary strife, by poverty and disease, the Annals were continued in *Sovremennik* (The Contemporary), to which journal the poet Nyekrásof contributed, and which in 1858–62 was in the main inspired by Tchernuishevski, who, as an author of novels and works on political economy, had made a deep impression on his time.

But the importance of the press in Russia must be dated from the end of the Crimean War, and from the *début* of Herzen as a journalist. For before this time the influence of the writers was extremely small, chiefly because the more intelligent circles spoke and read only French, with persistent contempt for the journalistic productions in their mother tongue; besides, they were compelled to limit their attention to purely literary questions, especially such as this, whether Russian literature ought to be purely national or not.

Now, at the close of the sixth decade, hundreds and hundreds of newspapers and periodicals were at once established. How numerous they were is best shown by a fact stated by Eckhardt, that in 1858–60 not less than seventy-seven large newspapers were compelled to suspend publication, without being perceptibly missed. Then, as it still happens down to the present day, the large monthly periodicals, each number as thick as a good-sized book, began to give abstracts of books in the natural sciences, literary history, or economy, to furnish political comments, and to publish long society novels of German, French, English, or native authors. The legitimate daily newspapers, with genuine Slavic enthusiasm, plunged into the most extreme radicalism. They became, as it were, giddy from the heights which European culture had attained, and to which the youth of the capitals and the denizens of the provincial towns, who had known nothing of the life of Western Europe, were now suddenly carried.

The first question which forced itself upon the thoughts of all was about the education of the people. There were hardly any schools in the land, and the few that did exist were, in the rural districts, wholly in the hands of the ignorant popes. There were no other teachers than the priests of the country towns. At this time, Sunday schools were started, first in the capitals, and then in various parts of the country, and the teachers in these schools taught without pay, from pure enthusiasm for the cause of the elevation of the people. In the various divisions of the army, the officers taught the recruits in similar schools, the officers of the Guard distinguishing themselves as teachers above all others.

It was under these conditions that the great, far-reaching reforms which characterized the beginning of the reign of Alexander II. were begun. The first of these was that which, on the 19th of February, 1861, led to the emancipation of the serfs, and gave to more than fifty million men personal freedom and a share in the ownership of the soil of Russia. As a matter of course, it caused a tremendous diminution of the power of the noble landed proprietors. It was a measure at once democratic and autocratic. And it was carried through at a time when the powers that had hitherto been respected had lost their splendor. The defeats in the Crimea had destroyed the prestige of the army; the shortcomings and the mistakes and the frauds of the administration, which the war had brought to light, had given a death-blow to official authority; the clergy had long been utterly despicable. Now, by one blow the power of the nobility was diminished in an unprecedented manner, at the same time that a large part of their property was taken from them without any proportionate compensation. The hope that there would be a political reform under Alexander II. was greatly weakened, just because the social reform in this form came first. For a long time, the enlightened classes had hoped for a "constitution,"—as it must naturally be in the beginning, an aristocratic constitution. Now political liberalism stood, in the presence of this gigantic advance of the power of the Tsar, without any hope for the future. For now, when all the lofty peaks of society were levelled, the position of the power of the Tsar alone was unaffected and even expanded to a dominion over soldiers and peasants unlimited by any kind of barrier.

The great peasant population was still very far from being satisfied. They had for a long time cherished Utopian expectations, and now, especially since the socialistic agitators had strengthened their illusions, were waiting for the immediate transfer to them, then and there, of all the land which they had cultivated, without any equivalent. This disappointment brought the peasants in the departments of Kazán and the Volga to an armed insurrection. At the same time, disturbances broke out among the students. The abnormal limitation of the number of students at each of the universities to three hundred had been repealed, and the scholar had suddenly attained a prestige almost surpassing that which the officers of the Guard had hitherto enjoyed. Now, with a genuine Russian lack of principle, the execution both of legal reforms and of a new plan of education was intrusted to the old re-actionists. So far as the former reform was concerned, the leading men, like Count Panin, Minister of Justice, accommodated themselves to the demands of the times; but only three months later, when the emancipation of the serfs had set all thought in vibration, a regulation for the government of the universities was published, which deprived the students of all the liberties previously given them, and cut off their hopes of obtaining any of those which they had been led to anticipate. They were deprived of the liberty of holding meetings, forbidden to have charity funds, and, in order to reduce their number, each student was required to pay a fee of fifty silver rubles each semester. In all the university cities, in Moscow as well as in St. Petersburg, in Kief as well as in Kharkof, the young men refused to submit to the new rules. Conflicts with the police and the military followed.

In 1862 the irritation in Russia reached its height. In various parts of St. Petersburg there was a series of fearful conflagrations which indicated the breaking loose of revolutionary instincts. The government interfered, established a summary court for incendiaries, closed the Sunday schools and other institutes and clubs, put restraints upon the press, made the censorship more rigorous.

Thus when the baleful blindness of the Polish demagogues and the indiscreet and cruel measures of the noble Wielopolski against the dangerous spirit of rebellion in Poland brought about the outbreak of the Polish insurrection, it was the event from which all the re-actionary lusts and powers in Russia were to imbibe new force.

Up to this time, Alexander Herzen had been the hero of cultured Russia. He had continually manifested a lively sympathy for oppressed Poland, treated its cause as his own and as that of his friends. He now expressed himself warmly in behalf of the revolt, even after the protecting attitude of the powers of the west and their threatening mien towards Russia (which made the Polish nobility, with Zamoiski at their head, conquer their scruples against an alliance with the popular leaders in Warsaw) had aroused and goaded the Russian national feeling even among the liberal groups of the empire.

Then it was that Katkóf entered upon the scene, and in the course of a very short time won all power out of the hands of Herzen, and rose to the position of the most influential man in Russia. This remarkable man, who died only in August, 1887, represented during twenty-five years the principle of oppression in a land of oppression, promoted during the whole of that time, with all his coarse energy, everything that was inimical to liberty, wrote down everything that was non-Russian, demanded and supported the establishment of complete uniformity in the great empire.

Mikhaïl Nikoforovitch Katkóf is a unique phenomenon in the history of Russia. As long as the empire has stood, it has never been seen before his time that a publicist, without official position and without any external or official authority, has exerted an influence on the acts of the government, saying nothing of what was the case with him, exerting a greater influence than the government itself. To that extent, but only to that extent, can his life be said to point towards a new time. Nevertheless the cause of satisfaction vanishes when we examine into the manner in which he reached this degree of power. He attained it because, with a recklessness which too often disregarded the claims of truth and the demands of justice, he devoted himself to flattering the national vanity and cultivating the national pride in its most detestable forms.

Katkóf made his *début* as professor of philosophy in the University at Moscow with contributions of slight importance to the history of philosophy. He was, from the beginning, an adherent of German philosophy, especially an admirer of Schelling, and then belonged to the same circle as the enthusiastically satirical Byelinski and the celebrated international revolutionist Bakunin. He called himself an idealist and taught the cult of the ideal. As a worshipper of the ideal in 1848 he was removed from his position.

In 1856 he established a monthly periodical, "The Russian Messenger" (*Russki Vyestnik*), and in 1861 he assumed the control of the daily paper, "The Muscovite News" (*Moskovskiya Vyedomosti*). He began his career in both of the journals as an extreme liberal of the English type, demanded self-government, extension of the distribution of power, constitution, etc., until in 1861–2, when radicalism broke out of bounds, when the disturbances of the peasants and of the students frightened timid people, and when it was brought to light that a multitude of men and women in high positions in Russia were in communication with Herzen's revolutionary party in London, the possibility of a complete change in public sentiment was apparent.

Then Katkóf felt that the moment was propitious for a change of front and for setting himself up as the *Savior of Russia*. He broke the silence which had been laid upon the whole press of Russia in regard to his old exiled friends, Herzen, Ogaref, and Bakunin. Although their names could not be mentioned, and their existence was officially ignored by the government, he attacked them openly as enemies of their fatherland, and to blame as the cause of all the disturbances. This was the first shock given to the great influence of Herzen among the cultured classes of Russia. And then in 1863, at the time when the Polish revolt broke out, when Herzen committed the imprudence of offending the Russian national feeling, and the approval with which the uprising was greeted by the Russian emigrants had the result that the liberal Russian newspapers manifested their sympathy by silence, then it was that Katkóf made his master-stroke. He denounced the emigrants and nihilists as *perfidious traitors to their country*, preached the strongest Russian *chauvinism*, demanded not only that the rebels should be put out of the way, but that the independent existence of Poland should be blotted out by changing the kingdom to a Russian province. When the revolt was quelled, Katkóf was one of the most popular men in the higher circles of Russia. It was he who caused Muravief to be sent as "Hanging Dictator" to Wilna. It was under his ægis, under the pretence of the law of self-preservation of the State, that the democrats gave the Lithuanian peasants freedom and land through the unbridled plundering of the Polish nobility, and that the Slavophiles urged religious persecution under the pretence of wishing to eradicate the tyranny of the Catholic Church.

From this time on, Katkóf could only rise and rise in influence in the same degree as the re-action in Russia rose. He had identified himself with it.

The *quondam* philosopher was henceforth the most zealous adherent of the Greek orthodoxy. The *quondam* English liberal was henceforth a worshipper and defender of the national absolutism, more national than the government, more monarchical than his monarch. All his disputes with the Court and the Tsar were only *lovers' quarrels*, occasioned by too much zeal on his part.

His power increased to an incredible degree. When, on one

occasion, the ministry forbade the publication of his newspaper, he nevertheless issued it as usual, only with the comment that it was forbidden, but that the prohibition must have arisen from a misunderstanding. It passed unchallenged; the Tsar sustained him.

The Polish nation, from this time forth, was to the Slavophiles the embodiment of the detested Western Europe and of the detested Catholicism. But the ownership of the soil was given to the Lithuanian peasants, chiefly because the Slavophiles, with Milyutin at their head, hated the Poles as aristocrats. For them the Polish nationality was a peculiarity of the noble caste, and, as such, ought to be rooted out of Russia. Here also the absolute power sought to contract an alliance with the masses against the higher classes.

But to Katkóf personally the uniformity of the Russian state was henceforward the most important principle. He allied himself with the Slavophiles in order through their worship of democracy to bring the government to stir up the Finns against the Swedes in Finland, the Lithuanians against the Poles in Poland, the Esthonians and the Letts against the Germans in the Baltic provinces, because they necessarily insisted on the idea that the strengthening of all these oppressed small nationalities in their relation to the ruling people was only the first step to the final and complete Russianizing of those countries.

Then in 1866 came the attempt of Karakósof to assassinate Alexander II., and it gave to the re-action its last strong impulse. Katkóf shouted with joy, "The pistol shot of Karakósof has purified the air." It is quite true that in a short time the government got frightened at its alliance with democracy. It once more cast its looks towards the nobles, whom it had hitherto mistrusted, because they had wished for a constitution. Even Katkóf's paper was suppressed for two months, as a punishment, because its editor had dared to publish a warning from Valuyef. But soon the reign of terror, friendly to the peasants, conquered under Milyutin in Poland, and the example from Poland could not be defied in Russia proper. The unrestricted, absolute power and the unqualified Greek Catholic orthodoxy, which had been upheld in the western provinces, were necessarily upheld throughout the whole empire. Now, when the glamour of the name of the Tsar has become weaker, we can see the possibility, as a result of the situation, that in times of disturbance a dictator might usurp the power,—a man of revolution, for instance, if such could be found, with a past and a popularity, like Skobelef, the celebrated cavalry general who died under such horrible circumstances.

From 1866 the current of re-action continually increased. Everything helped it on, radical as well as retrograde agitations in foreign lands. Soon at several places in the empire the oppression becomes too strong, produces this revolutionary propaganda or attempts at political murder, and for every political prosecution re-action takes a new stride, with doubled frenzy. Everything strengthens it, everything works to its advantage. The old "Nihilism," which was described by Turgenief, which was substantially an intellectual emancipation, with its whole energy concentrated on the attack on Christianity, and with a love for science, which found its expression in dislike of art as useless and undemocratic, was over about 1870. The insurrection of the commune in Paris, and the outbreaks of the internationals, set the minds of the youth in active ferment at this time. A generation had arisen, which, instead of the individualized radicalism of the older "Nihilists," had socialism for a religion and *the people* for a God.

From all parts of Russia and Siberia young girls streamed to Zürich to study medicine and socialism. In 1872 Prince Kropotkin began to work among the artisans in the suburbs of St. Petersburg. In the beginning of the seventies, young men and women of the families of the highest rank, by hundreds and hundreds, "went out among the people," labored there twelve, fifteen hours a day in the fields, in the workshops, in the factories, in order to propagate modern ideas everywhere among the common people. But in the provincial and country towns, where everything is spread by rumor, the presence of a propagandist could not possibly long be a secret to the police and government. One arrest followed another. Not less than thirty-seven provinces were declared, in a government circular of 1875, to be "infected by socialistic contagion." In 1876 and 1877, the whole of this generation, as it may be called, of youth with their minds in a ferment was mowed down. All the prisons were full of political offenders, and it was constantly found necessary to build new ones. Mere suspicion led to imprisonment. A letter from a friend who had "gone out among the people," an answer from a child twelve years old, who, when interrogated by the police, did not know what he said from fright, was quite sufficient. So also in 1876 to 1878, in the different Russian cities, on the chance occasion of a funeral or a death sentence, there were demonstrations and street revolts, the outbreak of passionate despair, meaningless in so far as they could never reach the proportions of a general revolt, and invariably immediately suppressed by the military. The uselessness of all such demonstrations produced the result that a party of terror was finally formed, which determined to work by single attempts at assassination.

The earlier propaganda made its exit at the end of the seventies with the 193 trial. These unfortunate persons had been in prison for four years, while the slow and thorough investigation lasted. The Russian cell system during this period bore so heavily upon them, that of the one hundred and ninety-three no less than seventy-five committed suicide, became insane or died. A special tribunal had been arranged for the trial of this cause, so that it was not to be expected that the judgment would be against the government. There were sentences of ten, twelve, fifteen years imprisonment, with hard labor, for two or three lectures, privately delivered to a handful of workmen, or for having bought or loaned a single book. And so harshly were political prisoners treated in prison that in the central prison at Kharkof ("house of terror") there were several attempts at insurrection among them for the purpose of obtaining the same treatment as the common criminals. And when the senate of Alexander II., which in other respects was pliant enough, in the form of a petition for pardon, acquitted the larger number of the 193, the Tsar personally set aside the verdict of the senate. Not even in the laws which this government had promulgated did it seek its support against its antagonists. It was, therefore, natural that these antagonists did not regard it as anything else than organized injustice, against which all weapons seemed to be allowable.

In 1877 followed Viera Sassúlitch's attempt to assassinate General Trepof, who had caused a political prisoner to be whipped, and her acquittal by the jury, which aroused the attention of the whole of Europe. In August, 1878, came the bullet from "Stepniak's" revolver, which, in the forenoon, in the open street, killed General Mesentzef, chief of the political police.[1] Among the numerous attempts at political murders which now followed are the four against Tsar Alexander II., of which the first occurred April 2, 1879, the last, which resulted in his death, March 13, 1881.

Nothing has set Russia farther backward than this last occurrence, which was pregnant with misfortune. It immediately prevented the formation of a sort of parliamentary constitution, which had just then been promised. It frightened the successor to the crown back from the paths his father had entered upon at the beginning of his reign, and it seemed to justify the rulers in reprisals and measures of prevention of every kind.

Thus they have reached a point where they now are, reached a policy which is no policy,—a policy of apprehension and irresolution.

Generally, when we speak of the policy of Russia, we mean its foreign policy, and many are dazzled by the extraordinarily large display of the power of the empire. We speak about Russia's great "mission" in Central Asia, about its irresistible advance towards India, etc., and then we admire Russian statesmanship. But what power is there in Russia's subjugating a little larger or smaller number of semi-barbarian tribes in Asia, and what statesmanship is there in involving itself continually with more wars there, when it must concern Russia to collect all its powers and make all its preparations for the great impending conflict! These Russian generals, with their victories won from Tatars and Turcomans, remind us altogether too much of those French commanders who were victorious over Abd-el-Kader and were defeated by Moltke. What else are they doing in Russia now, than once a year to conquer an Abd-el-Kader!

And to pit against a man with Bismarck's genius for managing foreign affairs, Russia has not a single prime minister, not one of any kind whatever. For there is no prime minister in the Russian ministry. The unlimited power of the Tsar does not tol-

[1] Stepniak: *Underground Russia.* Introduction.

erate this at all. When Gortchakof was chancellor it was only a title. Under the present management, Russia, the great exponent of the Slavs, has succeeded in making itself detested to the uttermost by all the Slavic nations. This government has carried it to so great an extent that Russia is now hated by Bulgaria and Servia (nay, by the common people of Roumania) as it is hated by the Poles,—and that means much. Russia liberated Bulgaria from the Turkish reign of terror, and has now successfully, after the lapse of not ten years, by falsehood, violence, hypocrisy, by infamous acts for whose authority the Bulgarians looked to the higher circles of the Russian government, brought matters to the pass that the liberators of that day are more hated than the oppressors were ten years ago.

But the internal policy is still more pitiable. It is certainly not a parliament which is most greatly needed. Only the naïve youth in Russia can think that. A parliament could easily be imagined so chosen that it would be more conservative than the government itself. It would, in all probability, if established now, be such a body as the *Duma* (city council) in Moscow is. That is elected. Yes; Moscow has what Paris has so long fought for in vain,—its own elected mayor. The *Duma* is not on that account the less conservative, and it would not present a different appearance if it had been the government and not the citizens in Moscow who had elected its members. No, it is not a popular assembly that it concerns Russia to get first. Russia needs a *bonâ fide* administration. Yet it is understood everywhere there are no institutions, no provincial home rule, no independent courts, no genuine seminaries of learning, no schools in the proper sense.

During the whole of the reign of this Tsar the enormous Siberia has been denied the permission to found even a single university. It was feared that it would give Asiatic Russia too much independence. Permission has only just been given for the foundation of a university at Tomsk, which, in the present circumstances, is of hardly any importance.

All knowledge is dreaded. The most recent circular (illegal, but carried into effect), which after Katkóf's death was prepared by the curator in Odessa, makes it the duty of the school committees to decide whether the parents are sufficiently well off for the children to be admitted to a grammar school. They are required to ask how the parents live, in what kind of house and of how many rooms, how much money they earn annually, and who their friends are.

The universities are closed at the least sign of a disturbance. This happened to all the universities in Russia proper in the spring of 1888, after the unimportant affair of Brysgalof's box on the ear at Moscow; St. Petersburg, Moscow, Kazan, Kharkof, and Odessa were at once closed for fear of students' pranks.

Since then the curator of the universities in Odessa has prepared a new circular, in which it is said: "Since several instructors have allowed themselves publicly to express their thoughts without the reservations which are due to their position in the educational system, and without feeling themselves bound by the duties of the service when the question turned upon something which had no direct connection with this service,—and since they have even appeared as recognized organs for certain circles of society, have taken part in party debates, nay, have even allowed themselves to be drawn into controversies in newspapers,—the curator requires them for the future to use greater prudence."

It forbids them to take part in the discussion of social and literary questions. It closes with the expression of the hope that for the future they will solemnly devote their leisure hours to matters of instruction and education.

All this was because a poor little teacher in a club had suffered himself to criticise Katkóf.

Upon the whole, we in Western Europe can form no idea of the grade of civilization occupied by these curators. When, in 1884, the students in Kief had arranged a banquet on the jubilee of the old university, one fine day, by a gratuitous regulation of the curator, they were wholly excluded from participation in the festival. When they, mortified and exasperated as they were, hissed at the curator and the well known president of the Synod Pobyedonostsef, as a punishment they were *all* expelled from the university. There was only one single man in Russia with whose principles it agreed to praise this act: it was Katkóf. The students, he wrote, who had not participated in the demonstration are responsible for not having prevented it.

From absolutely trustworthy sources there has been com-

municated to me the following incident, which recently occurred
in the case of another curator, Novikof, who had come to examine (audit, as it is called) a school in Novgorod. He finds at
the teacher's two books: one, a collection of Korolenko's tales;
the other, a volume of Dostoyevski's. Not having any idea as to
who the first author is, he looks for the name of the publisher
and finds the name of the magazine *Russakaya Mysl* (The Russian
Thought), which is published in Moscow and edited by Goltzef
in a moderate, liberal spirit. He says, in a discontented tone,
"Don't read productions from the socialist organ! But," he continues, "what dissatisfies me still more, is that you have Dostoyevski here. He talks about love too much in his books. I know,
indeed, that it is the Christian love; but it doesn't matter, it is
love all the same, and love is good enough in the beginning,—but
look out how it ends!"

Now, if we distinctly conceive what authority such a curator
of universities possesses, especially those who rule over the universities at the capitals, we shall not be greatly surprised at the
monstrosities in instruction to which the press now and then dares
to call attention. Recently *Vyestnik Yevropi* thus called attention
to the oddity of some lectures on psychology which this spring
seriously occupied the good society in St. Petersburg. Vladislavlef,
a professor of Philosophy, gave an outline of psychology, which
contained the following analysis of the sentiment of respect:
"This sentiment," he said, "increases or diminishes in proportion
to the income of its object. A man who has three thousand rubles
a year necessarily has a great respect for a man who has fifteen
thousand. And a man who, for example, has over seven million
rubles a year (in this he seems to allude to the Tsar) necessarily
makes the impression of a colossal greatness. On the other hand,
poverty engenders indifference or disdain." He said all this without irony, and also not even citing many instances of the fact, but
as the expression of a psychical law.

Where such a management and such instruction are possible,
it must be self-evident that the acquisition of higher education
is rendered difficult for the young men. So far as the young
women are concerned, the conditions are even more unfavorable.
Although it has been constantly forbidden them to attend the universities of Russia, to say nothing of passing examinations and tak-

ing degrees, still no young women in Europe crave a scientific education like those of Russia. About ten years ago, some liberal professors in St. Petersburg and others in Moscow, under the leadership of Professor Guerrier, established a kind of university for women in each city. The professors of the universities and men eminent for their literary culture (like Vesselovski and Storosyenko) gave their time without pay, and young girls from seventeen to twenty and upwards came in crowds to hear good lectures on science, mathematics, history, literature, and some other branches. As a matter of course, these lectures were neutral in politics. For some time, a dislike for this course had been manifested on the part of the Tsar. For when the Tsaritsa was asked to allow them to ornament the diplomas not only with medallion portraits of the Tsaritsas Catherine and Elizabeth, but also with hers, permission was refused, so that it was necessary to put the date in the space which was reserved for the portrait of the Tsaritsa Maria Feodorovna. A year ago last spring the universities for women received a blow in a communication stating that they would be closed from and after the month of June, 1887, and that all instruction of that kind would be suspended. The expression that he wished to send all the Russian women back home is, in Russia, generally attributed to a person occupying a very high position.

This is the condition in which the most intelligent part of the youth grow up.

It was from feeling that in such conditions all exertion to attain a higher position must fail, that Gárshin has a novel with the following argument.

A palm, which has been brought from its tropical home to a conservatory in St. Petersburg, struggles towards the clear sky and burning sun of its native land. It grows on in the hope of bursting through the glass roof of the conservatory and gaining its freedom. Finally, the wished-for moment comes. The panes in the roof yield to the pressure of its branches, the curled-down plant stretches itself out into the clear air of the open day. Then it meets the cold wind and the damp snow. It is frozen through, its crown withers away, and the owner of the conservatory has the tree cut down.

VIII

⌇ "The Russian press! I am provoked at this everlasting talk about the Russian press," broke out the editor of the Russian paper having the widest circulation. "There is simply no press in Russia. There are printing-presses and paper, of course, and black marks on a white surface; there are editors and journalists, but a press is not and cannot be found."

From the nature of the case, the Russian press cannot have any political importance, entirely without regard to the question whether, like the newspapers in the departments and some periodicals in the capitals, it has to pass under the supervision of the censor or not.

The best known newspaper, in a foreign language, is a French official journal (the *Journal de St. Petersbourg*); next the two larger German papers in St. Petersburg (St. Petersburg *Zeitung* and the "St. Petersburg Herald"); and a small German sheet in Moscow (the Moscow *Zeitung*), the last being extremely moderate, and at every opportunity only defends and demonstrates the excellent, admirable relations which prevail between Germany and Russia. Besides the official government paper, and a little sheet written in a light and entertaining, and sometimes rather frivolous style, but which has a very large circulation, there are in St. Petersburg two newspapers which are generally read: *Nóvosti* (News), a so-called liberal paper, dignified in its tone, edited by Notóvitch, whose best assistant, in directions which are not political, is the poet P. Weinberg, the well known translator of Heine. Since the publisher is of Jewish extraction, this paper is continually taxed with serving the interests of the Jews. It is sober, serious, earnest, supports the cause of European culture, but is not on that account the less patriotic in its attitude toward England and Germany.

With this paper the *Novoye Vremya* (the New Times) lives in constant controversy. It is a well written journal, but entirely without principle, edited after the pattern of the French *Figaro* (especially as this newspaper was edited in earlier times), by Suvórin, a literary man of business, who in his day made himself renowned in Russia by his open declaration that the time had now come when literature ought to step down from its pedestal, and understand that it is a commodity like other wares, subject to the same laws of supply and demand as everything else, and that there is no disgrace in it. In obedience to this view, *Novoye Vremya* drifts with the wind; in the shortest time possible attacks and defends the same cause and the same person, generally in incisive, entertaining articles. The newspaper is more read than respected. It is known that it is without faith and law (*sans foi ni loi*). From its nature it cannot occupy a leading position, and its political influence is absolutely *nil*.

Since Suvórin, besides his newspaper, has a great publishing house in Moscow, his literary influence is necessarily not unimportant. Many young liberal authors, for the sake of the honorarium, exhibit the weakness of putting their articles or novels into his widely circulated sheet, however little they may sympathize with its standpoint. Suvórin spares no expense in advertising; and, as he has agents in all the large cities, Europe is constantly kept informed through the telegraph bureau of what the *Novoye Vremya* has said about this or that,—a thing in and for itself as unimportant as the barking of a dog or the soughing of the wind in the streets of St. Petersburg, but which at a distance is regarded as an affair of some weight. The *feuilleton* of this sheet is edited by a certain Burénin, who is entirely worthy of his master. The other coadjutors take the tone which is given them by Suvórin and by him.

About one of them, B——of, a foreign author, who had delivered a course of lectures in St. Petersburg, related the following veritable anecdote: "B——of wrote to me several times, while I was still at home, sent me a book, and ended with placing himself and the *Novoye Vremya* at my disposal on the occasion of my visit to St. Petersburg. Immediately after my arrival he called on me, invited me to his house, with so much zeal that he assured me that a plate was ready for me at his table every day. He gave me a very favorable report of my first lecture, after having requested the use of my notes in the preparation of his article. Several times he expressed the wish that I would take his wife with me on a shopping expedition. His manner was so insinuating as to affect me not quite agreeably. I held a little back; and when, at last, after a renewed invitation, I indicated that it would be impossible for me on that day to make any purchases in company with his wife, he inserted in his paper the same evening without any reference to the preceding articles, the boldest attack upon me. 'He had long kept silent, and watched,' said the article, 'but at last so great a lack of talent and conceit must be punished;' nay, concealing the fact, known to him, that I had received one of my lectures back from the censor, so that I was obliged to substitute another, unknown in Russia, but previously delivered, he charged me principally with not being able to hit upon anything new, but with confining myself to the presentation of old and well known stories. 'The Russian public,' it added, 'was not so stupid as I supposed, nor yet so ignorant. It is understood very well that in such circumstances the stranger treats it like a fool in order to get his fingers into its pockets.' " My informant adds, "Even with abundant experience from the press of other lands, even with all the surprises of the past which no one who lives the literary life escapes, the foreigner will be surprised at the shamelessness and corruption, not so much of some Russian as of some particular St. Petersburg newspapers."

Moscow, like St. Petersburg, has two large newspapers. One is liberal, written in the best style, and the most honorable of all the Russian newspapers, *Russkiya Vyedomosti* (The Russian Times), published by Sobolevski, a quiet, honorable, energetic, and scientific man, formerly a professor, but now an editor. This daily paper, certainly the most widely circulated in Russia, has 30,000 subscribers. Next to this is the newspaper hitherto better known in Western Europe, the *Moskovskiya Vyedomosti*, the organ of the lately deceased Katkóf.

Katkóf was a man without much knowledge and of little

reading. In the last twenty years of his life he never read a single book. There was no need of his reading or thinking to support and maintain the general Russification. But he wrote exceedingly well; he was of the first rank among the prose authors. His paper did not have many subscribers; not a third of what the *Russkiya Vyedomosti* has. But it was written for a single reader, who never skipped a single number, his Majesty the Tsar Alexander III. And voluntary subscribers were not wanting when it was supported by the order of the government. All the institutions and foundations of the Crown, the schools, courts, etc., were bound to support this sheet.

When Katkóf died, and the state of his fortune came to light, his name lost a large share of its glamour. He left an astonishingly large fortune, so large that it could not be explained except by gifts from the rich merchants of Moscow. Katkóf had indeed met their views by opposing all reduction of the tariff. It also made a disagreeable impression on the Tsar that he, by an evasion of the law, by a transfer of his property in his lifetime, cheated the State of the succession tax in addition.

Besides the *Moskovskiya Vyedomosti*, which still exists but has lost all importance, there has just been started another newspaper in a similar spirit. The weekly newspaper *Grazhdanin* (The Citizen) has become a daily, and, according to report, the government will grant it a large annual subsidy. It is to be edited by the well known author of poor novels, Prince Meshcherski, a reactionist and tale-bearer, is to have the same drift as Katkóf's paper, only with out-and-out servility instead of talent.

The more important monthlies play a greater part than in any other land, for the rules of the censorship allow much to appear in a periodical that would be forbidden in a book form. Nevertheless in the last ten years several of the best Russian reviews, like the *Dyelo*, for example, have been suppressed. Every month there appears a number of each of the large periodicals, as thick as two numbers of the *Revue des deux Mondes* together.

The best known is *Vyestnik Yevropi* (The European Messenger), edited by Stassulevitch, a stately and finely cultivated man about sixty years old, formerly a university teacher, now occupied with economical and hygienic questions, such as the improvement of the river water in St. Petersburg. His periodical is the organ of correct liberalism. It has a circulation of 7,000. The two great authors, now old men, Gontcharóf and Arsénief, contribute to this magazine, the former at the present time publishing his life, and the latter a clever, scientific critic, affable towards the younger generation. It relies on a circle of men among whom the literary historians Pypin and Spasovitch are well known. The latter has already been spoken of. The former, who originally belonged to Tchernuishevski's group and passed for a radical, but escaped accusation, as author of the great work, "The History of the Slavic Literature," in which the pressure laid on by the censor is felt all the way through, has presented a profound and real representation of the intellectual struggle for existence, and literary productions of the different Slavic races. Unfortunately the most important part, the history of the literature of Great Russia, is still wanting. The two eminent advocates and publicists Koni and Utin are also coadjutors of the *Vyestnik Yevropi*. The former is best known as an author by his interesting treatment of "Dostoyevski as an analyst of crime;" the other, by the series of articles published in the periodical under the title "From Bulgaria," which was forbidden publication in book form by the censor.

By the side of this great St. Petersburg review stands Goltzef's Moscow periodical, *Russkaya Mysl* (The Russian Thought), as suggested above, conducted in the same spirit as *Russkiya Vyedomosti*, and supported by the contributors to that daily paper. It has 10,000 subscribers.

Finally there is the *Severni Vyestnik* (The Northern Messenger), with 4,800 subscribers, published by a lady, Miss Evreïnova, hitherto the most sprightly and most modern of these periodicals, but which has now met with a very great loss, because the celebrated and influential critic Mikhaïlovski has separated from it, and may possibly carry a staff of sympathizers with him. This periodical, on account of the advanced views of several of the contributors, is suspected by the government and placed under the censor. Miss Evreïnova is a lady in the forties, with a stern face and gray hair. She has spent several years on the shores of the Adriatic near Montenegro, in the study of the old Slavic conditions, has copied and published manuscripts written in old

Slavic. Having used up her property in this work, she assumed the publication of *Severni Vyestnik* as a means of subsistence. She is a Russian slave to duty, with a good but not discriminating intellect.

Her circle of contributors has hitherto chiefly consisted of bright literary Bohemians, who in Russia are utterly poor, hungry, and in debt, the older among them generally unhappily married. They live exclusively with each other in a world by themselves,—sadly enough, almost without exception, addicted to drink, and utterly wanting in nervous equipoise on account of their many years of misery and exile. Among them there are still several eminent authors, who have succeeded in passing through the anxieties of a literary life and of exile with unimpaired bodily and mental health.

There was Pratopopof, who long ago contributed to the "Annals of our Fatherland," with great talent and spirit. Then he was exiled, and is now back again. There is Korolenko, who, broad-shouldered and boyish, has returned from Yakutsk. There was Gárshin, who, though subject to repeated attacks of insanity, has published fine and vigorous novels. He was greatly under the influence of Tolstoï, but nevertheless has his own stamp of desperate pessimism. There was the leader *Mikhailovski* himself, in his style inclined to the imitation of the satirical tone of Saltykof, as a critic audacious and wily, who is capable of placing a not inconsiderable store of learning and remarkable ingenuity at the service of the opposition. There is Zlatovratski, who describes almost ideal peasants, and, himself resembling a poor workman of the peasant rank, poor as Job, with a great flock of children, and such a slave to alcohol that he does not any longer dare to go out in the streets alone. Finally there is Glyeb Uspyenski, a great and shining talent, far more important than his brother, Nikolaï Uspyenski, whose *Viesna* was translated into Danish by Thor Lange. In Glyeb, who is familiarly called by his first name, the advanced youth see their apostle. Unfortunately he too has fallen so low as to spend six or seven hours a stretch in the dramshops of St. Petersburg, but his abilities have not been impaired by his irregular life outside of the pale of society. His works, consisting of nothing but short stories, already fill a long row of volumes. At the present time he presents in novels and articles only the woman of the working class, and he works over and elucidates the idea, which haunts him, that this woman has no right to be a mother, since she cannot support her child. He pictures the loose morals of factory life, and the unmerited disgrace which falls upon the woman who errs; but he also writes *for* the working-women, with the design of impressing upon them that they, for the sake of the children, ought not to become mothers.

Glyeb Uspyenski is the genuine literary gypsy. He borrows and gets along without troubling himself about money. He cannot see a needy person without giving him all the money he has with him, and often more; for he borrows of one to give to another. The admiration which is given him in wide circles prevents any one being angry with him for any irregularity. He is forgiven with the words, "We must remember it is Glyeb."

Apart from a few of the most eminent of these authors, it may be said that what is common to all these younger and older authors is propensity to drink, laxity in money matters, lack of fundamental culture, and an every-day dull melancholy. Several of them are utterly ruined by the homeless life, with its debauches of ale, champagne, and women. The loss of all illusions as to the attainment of freedom and happiness, the feeling of boundless disappointment in life, and of a lack of means to do anything for the people or the country, brings them to despair, and to seek to forget the despair in a life of stupefaction.

It is clear that these writers know only a very small part of society, and possess only a restricted and peculiar intellectual culture. And as they have no acquaintance with the higher classes of society, from which they suspiciously keep aloof, so these classes have no acquaintance with them. Towards society in St. Petersburg they occupy the position of pariah. At best their works only are known. The authors as persons have no existence for the fine gentlemen and ladies.

Even the oldest and greatest of them live entirely secluded, and almost every one of them has a wife, who does not understand him at all, and with whom it is only with difficulty that he continues to live; yet the author makes all sorts of concessions from his good nature. When a near friend one day said to one of the most important, an old man, "How can a stupid woman get such a control over a man?" he answered, "*Only* a stupid woman. A man who has something to do has no weapons against stupidity, which tires, nags, always begins over, and never knows when it is beaten. An amiable and intellectual woman would never gain such an influence over her husband."

The old *Saltykof* (Shchedrin), the satirist, the most popular author of liberal Russia, at the present time is lying ill of the gout, and it is hardly likely that he will recover. In the eyes of those who value the tendencies in their poetical works more than that which is essentially poetical therein, he is a greater author than Tolstoï. Of all the authors now living, he is certainly the one who has most consistently made use of irony as the style of prose writing. In his whole form he is the unconscious product of the circumstances. With a passion like his for justice and for civil freedom on the one side, and the government on the other, all criticism of the situation must necessarily assume the character of pleasantry. But what pleasantry! Read as an illustration his book, "Our Pompadours."

By a remarkable change in the meaning of the word, they mean in the daily speech in Russia by the word Pompadour, a man who governs by the aid of the rule of his mistress. In Saltykof's work provincial governors of this kind are characterized by the dozen.

As an idea of his method of representation, take this fragment of a dialogue: The clerk is met in the morning at the office by his superior, an official under the governor, with the exclamation, "Do you know that our fellow has been dismissed?"—"Of whom does your Excellency condescend to speak to me?"—"Of whom? Of our little Pompadour, naturally."—"At this answer," relates the clerk, "my heart stood still in my breast. Little by little, it began to beat again; I thought that we should not be left without a head."—"Does your Excellency know who has been named as his successor?"—"A certain Udarin."—"A general?"—"Yes, a general." [1]—"Of what kind, if I may ask?"—"A mammal."—"We were both thoughtful," continues the clerk. "Then I went out into

[1] In Russia, there are civil as well as military generals, and just as many of them.

the market, and told the news to some muzhiks who stood there. 'Do you know that his Excellency Aufimof is no longer our governor?'—'Bah, what of it!' The peasant had scarcely uttered these words before my hand had given a sound whack on his cheek. 'But a new one is coming! a new one is coming!' bellowed the peasant. I continued to strike—I heard it not. At last, it fell like dew upon my soul: 'A new one is coming.' That was the consolation. I gave the peasant ten kopeks."

Another sketch describes how the clerk one fine morning, when the newly installed governor gives a free rein to his ideas and dreams about his coming administration, allows himself the remark that the law sets certain bounds to these fantasies; as, for instance, as to whipping. There are cases where the law declares it to be useful, and others in which it is forbidden. "You will then have the goodness to inform me when, and when not," said the governor, ironically.—"Not I, your Highness, but the law."—"That is becoming interesting." The governor, it appears further, had long known that there were laws, but he always conceived them as bound books arranged in a case. It was for him the order, —lawful order. When he, on the other hand, saw these same books lying about among others on a table in a room, that was disorder. But what he did not know was that these same laws allowed him certain acts and forbade him others. He regarded them simply as a hymn, composed in the interests of the small pompadours, for their honor, to serve them for recreation. Since he was modest by nature, and blushed whenever he heard any one echo his praises, it can be understood that he did not care to fumble in the laws. When it now dawned upon the governor that the law forbids him to sentence the bigwig Proshorof, whom he was burning to let feel his wrath, to a good sound whipping, he became very uneasy. It soothed him very little that, according to the clerk's disclosure, he always had the recourse of having him flogged secretly and without witnesses. And now his state of mind at this discovery is portrayed. "He had never yet felt such an annoyance. It seemed to him as if he had fallen into a danger, and as if he heard an inward challenge not to be a coward, but to show personal courage." And he shouted with the voice of a commander: "Let Proshorof be flogged on the spot—publicly."

A favorite subject for Shchedrin's satire is the system of patronage, which flourishes in Russia as nowhere else. Every kind of patronage is possible here, if you have connections among the superior officers. A St. Petersburg family of my acquaintance, who were going down to Southern Russia, had a whole railway carriage sent up from Orel, and travelled in it from St. Petersburg down to the door of their country house. It even happened to me that one night on the railroad at Smolénsk a separate carriage, with a bed ready for use, was placed at my disposal by the station-master, who had received an order to that effect from his superior, while the occupants, in spite of my protest, were turned out and placed elsewhere. "You need not say anything against it," said the station-master to me. "You may be sure that there is not one of them who has paid for his ticket." I inquired of some of the bystanders, and it appeared that such was the fact. Thus, on this occasion, the higher patronage did not violate other privileges than those which were acquired by the exercise of inferior authority. Another favorite subject for attack with Shchedrin is the system of bribery, which flourishes in consequence of the low intellectual standpoint and poor pay of the officials. That these men are stupid and servile is chiefly because, as a rule, they must rise in the service from the lower ranks. They are frequently invalids when they approach towards power and influence. As the phrase goes, "My uncle, the general, had a fit of apoplexy, so he became a senator; he lost his sight, and then he was made a member of the council of the empire. If he can only have a new accident he will die as minister." Bribery naturally has its root in the fact that the salaries are so low. They regard the drink money which is given to the officials about as we do the honorarium which is given to the clergy, although the latter also have their salaries from the State. The worst of it is that the relation of the officials to the treasury of the State is often so untrustworthy. From that comes the Russian proverb, "All steal, except Christ," with the blasphemous addition, "and he would if his hands were not nailed to the cross." Or this proverb, "If you are going to talk to an official, you must talk rubles to him." All these customs have one good side, that the officials, just because of their lax morals, sell the common people an otherwise unattainable freedom: tolerance, impunity for the innocent, and free passage for men and books. But it will be understood that this circumstance does not make the government any more worthy of respect.

An administration like this naturally invites a satirical, humorous treatment like Shchedrin's. If you compare his satire with that of a Polish author of the same period, like Svientochovski, you will find that, while the satire of the Pole is almost always anticlerical, and is weakened in its effects upon the masses by the appearance of anything unpatriotic, yet in this direction the Russian satire has its sting unsheathed and its spear-head tempered and glowing like that which was plunged into the eye of Cyclops by Odysseus.

The most important of the contributors to the newspapers and periodicals have now been mentioned. Next comes a whole long list of authors, historical, critical, philosophical, and anthropological,—whose learning is irreproachable, whose style is a trifle professorial, and who as a rule lack inspiration.

Among the historians, jurists, and critics who have already been mentioned, as well as outside of these circles, the foreigner meets many who at first make this impression upon him: They remind him of the German scholars, particularly as they were a generation ago. They have solidity, earnestness, and a little heaviness. A Russian philologian is, indeed, only exceptionally (like Korsh, in Moscow) crammed with learning like a German, but to compensate for this these scholars are usually able to clothe their thoughts in a much more available form. They do not have the boyish innocence, which at seventy unites red cheeks and light blue eyes, as I have seen in the old German philologian Fleischer. But they do have—especially the Little Russians—breadth, good nature, which smiles in great dimples on a brown cheek, roguishness, as a clever woman is roguish. They are impregnated with the modesty of genuine and refined culture. While the German, whether he has a better or poorer opinion of himself, always—and with a certain degree of right—acts upon the theory of the conceded superiority of German science, the Russian often places the information and knowledge of the foreigner above his own. The more he knows, the less contented he is in general with the development of science in Russia.

Among the scientists and authors in Russia there are men of great originality, men whose whole being shows how much originality is suppressed by the Russian rule. Such a man is the naturalist Mikluho-Maklay.

He is not only a distinguished anthropologist, but king of the Australasian island which bears his name. He came back to St. Petersburg with his wife, an Englishwoman from Sydney, to publish a great work. As king he had the right on his island to have one hundred and forty-seven native wives, but, according to his own account, he has not availed himself of it. He is a fine man, with white hair, nearly fifty years old, with a splendid head and young eyes. He is such a sufferer from the gout that he lies all day long stretched out on a deer-skin. He loves as his place of residence only the island Maklay and the Happy Men's Islands, which surround it.

The following little trait is genuine Russian: On his table stands a lamp, made of the skull of a woman he once loved, a young girl whom he nursed in the hospital when as a young man he was studying medicine. Above the skull is an oil-receiver and above this a green lamp-shade. By the light of this lamp he does his work in all parts of the world. Probably it is only a Russian that would rather linger over the skull of his mistress than her portrait, and only a Russian who would turn it to that use. Even the eccentricity of an Englishman would hardly go to that extent.

Maklay detests and despises Giers. He had long sought in vain from the Minister of Foreign Affairs for permission to hoist the Russian flag over his island, without being able to obtain the concession he sought for. Then, one fine day, Bismarck caused the German flag to be hoisted. Maklay telegraphed to Giers. He replied: "We shall protect you, but no violence!" As if Maklay, with his poor uncivilized subjects, could use violence against the German navy. This man has thus become a German subject.

Originality is most strongly marked as a peculiarity among other leading men in science and literature in Russia. What grandiose forms it has assumed in Tolstoï is well known, but in him, as is also well known, it has a religious motive. In old Gontcharóf, on the contrary, who at an early period did his best work in "Oblómof," it has by a comparative barrenness of many years, and by an effeminacy nursed by the great admiration he has received, reached a height which renders social intercourse with him difficult.

During the winter, he had promised to read a novel which he had written for the illustrated weekly newspaper *Niva*, in a house where he is a welcome and honored guest. The sight of a lady whom he did not know, and who had been invited to be present, so upset him that he declared that he would not read at all. A strange countenance, though young and pretty, was enough to make his anger disconcert him. The following little trait shows the irritable passion in him, which seems to be an outcrop of a genuine Russian rudeness at the bottom of his character: Turgenief and he had had a kindred idea of a novel and had talked it over with each other. Turgenief published his novel first. It is the one with the title "A Nest of Nobles." [1] Gontcharóf reads the novel, becomes furiously exasperated, sees Turgenief on the street, and runs after him shouting, "Stop, thief! stop, thief!" Even now, when Turgenief's name is mentioned in his presence, he foams with rage.

It is evidently not easy to characterize the public to which the Russian newspapers and periodicals address themselves throughout the empire. It is too much scattered; and it is far more difficult than in the world of readers of other countries for it to gain an expression and receive examination through "the voice of the people." Nevertheless, by many indications we can conclude that it is docile in a high degree, unprejudiced, and easily acted upon. The quality of a thorough appropriation of that which is read ought to be weaker than in the principal countries of Europe, but the capacity to receive is, without doubt, greater. The enthusiasm of the female sex is especially great.

In the provincial towns a caricature of this peculiarity is very often met with. I saw a lady from Orel, "still young," bedecked and powdered, who passed as the literary oracle of the

---

[1] Also published with the English title "Lisa."

town. She was an enthusiastic admirer of Richepin, and quoted boldly:—

> *L'amour que je sens, l'amour qui me cuit,*
> *Ce n'est pas l'amour chaste et platonique,*
> *Sorbet à la neige, etc.*

It was well meant, and in and for itself did not show bad taste, but was exceedingly unbecoming. Another lady from Kharkof, old and stiff, was, in her own opinion, the source of refinement for the place. She instituted readings of the masterpieces of Russian literature for the common people, was also a writer, was loud-voiced, noisy, knew everything that was printed,—literary to the tips of her fingers and toes.

It is also true that among the Slavic people there is seen more often than in other places that kind of enthusiasm for a poet or author which makes a woman worship him for her whole life. It is hardly an accident that the lady who for twenty years continued in uninterrupted correspondence with Balzac, and at last married him, was a Pole, Mme. Hanska, of the renowned family of Rze-wuski. Her daughter married a Mniszek.

In our time in St. Petersburg, a lady of a good family has been seen to leave her husband and her home to run away with the poet Nadson, then mortally ill, and nurse him till his death; and she now lives only in his memory and for his fame. This lady's feelings for the poet, and her worship of him, were cruelly made sport of in the last years of his life and after his death, although it is, nevertheless, ethnographically significant, because it shows how strong the faith is in the highest literary enthusiasm in Russia.

Some months after Nadson's death, his fair friend published a somewhat comprehensive correspondence between the poet and a lady of distinction, an anonymous countess, who had written to him without ever having seen him or having made his acquaintance personally. The letters of the woman are fine but grotesque. According to all indications, a young, beautiful, aristocratically educated woman, not long married, had apparently fallen in love with Nadson without ever having met him, only from reading his poetry and seeing his portrait. The exchange of letters lasted for seven months. Her letters were full of fire and constantly more passionate. His answers were not without tenderness, yet calm and comparatively cold, although it can be seen he had been much moved by this wonderful love, which came to him so unsought and unexpected. Then he dies. Shortly after, according to the preface of the editress, the fair writer of the letters also died, but not until she had obtained from her husband his word of honor that he would give his consent to the publication not only of the letters which she had received from the poet, but of those which she herself had written.

For several months this correspondence was the subject of the attention and sympathy of the Russian reading world. Then it was discovered, as had been first suggested in the *feuilleton* of a newpaper as a derisive conjecture, that the poet and his fair friend had been the victims of a bold forgery. From what motive it is uncertain, but a lady who frequented the house, at first continually entertained the friend with accounts of a certain countess of her acquaintance, who lived in a state of hero-worship for Nadson. Then she began to bring letters, said that she was willing to carry back the answers, and thus for more than half a year had kept the intrigue on foot. First she was compelled to admit the death of the countess—for the very good reason that she had never lived; then she confessed that she had fabricated all the anonymous protestations of love. It is unimportant whether her motive had been her desire to make herself interesting, a disposition to mystify, or only a mania for romancing and a vigorous imagination. The only thing that is significant about it is that the whole of the Russian public found nothing unusual or incredible in such a personal passion, evoked by black on white, without personal influences.

What is still more remarkable, you will not infrequently find in the men a similarly exalted nature, readily receptive of literary enthusiasm. I think it is in unison with the fact that certain types, among the educated Russians especially, have an uncommonly great inclination to cultivate a life of emotion. Just so far as, by aid of the life and literature, one can comprehend the domain, which it is so difficult to penetrate, they seem to fall more deeply in love and with more reverence than in our time is the rule in other countries. The very young Russian expects a kind of spiritual aid and salvation from the woman he loves. The older man, when in love, tries to supply his wants by sustained homage. It is the same propensity to worship which leads the men of the lower classes in hordes to the religious sects and mystics. And it is this which in the domain of literature becomes an exquisite sensibility.

In spite of the great size of the empire, authorship is not economically remunerative in Russia. Except the two greatest poets, and some journalists without conscience, no one earns money there by his labor with his pen. But in a deeper sense, perhaps, in no other place is it better rewarded to expose one's emotions and thoughts in an article, an essay, or a larger book. The author is understood by great groups of people with a cordiality, and is appropriated with an intensity and devotion which are exceptional elsewhere.

Everything there which can quench the thirst, the burning intellectual thirst, is absorbed like dew-drops on an arid soil.

IX

 We had driven out to a large restaurant outside of Moscow to hear the gypsies sing and see them dance. Accompanied by the male members of the families, they came in crowds, with the chief of the tribe at the head, into the room where people sit and eat in the evening, and sang a series of wild, wonderfully sonorous songs. Several of the young girls dance; a dance which had nothing European in it, a dance for which only the free space of a square between the chair and the table is required, because the dancer, in a contracted place, moves every fiber of her body while in apparent repose. This pantomime, which is a whirlwind within these limits, is Asiatic or African. The song, on the other hand, to which the Russians take great pleasure in listening, barbaric as it sounds, is less original. If several of the melodies are really gypsy tunes, still the mass of them are, in fact, Russian national songs, which the gypsies have appropriated and made their own. And the language which they sing is Russian. Evidently the musical taste of the Russian peasant, the poetic character of the Russian national songs, have set their own stamp upon the spirit of this foreign race so insusceptible to external influences, so that the Russian, who seeks among the gypsies for that which is unlike himself, for the strange and the new, unknown to himself, finds not a little of his own.

These were the thoughts which the grotesque song and dance first awakened in me, and when they were expressed they led by a connection of thought to a conversation about the Russian peculiarity and power of assimilation in architecture and the plastic art. This started many ideas, and now, after the lapse of a year, brings me to giving such an account as I can of Russia's artistic originality in the past and in the present.

The Russians early showed originality in the art of building. While the Scandinavians hewed the tree in order to make their oldest log-houses, the Russians placed the trunks of the trees one above the other, and fastened them at their outer ends, so as to make walls. We do the Russians injustice, therefore, when, without further investigation, we call their art of building Byzantine, for the Byzantine art has in its forms not the least suggestion of a previous log-building. It was only in the eleventh century that the Russians began to erect churches after the Byzantine types, and even then they ornamented them with Asiatic and Slavic elements.

The Scythian burial mounds, which have been opened in the middle of this century, have brought to light a medley of purely Greek and of Asiatic-Slavic objects of art. Many of the antique Russian ornaments which represent the forms of animals or plants, show in themselves a kind of animals and plants which have never existed in Russia, the influence of the East, of Persia, nay of India. But the Russian reproduction, which is free from any influence from Byzantium, has its distinct peculiarities.

It is different with the production of religious images, the representation of saints. In this domain Russia has been and Russia has become wholly Byzantine. On this point it has not separated in any respect from the rest of the Greek Catholic Church of Eastern Europe. But, so far as religious architecture is concerned, there the oldest Russian churches are plainly distinguished from the unmixed Byzantine style, by their slender forms and the endeavor to tower into the heavens.

At the end of the twelfth century Russian art had already become so advanced that it was not behind that of Western Europe nor of Byzantium. The Russian art-craftsmen understood how to work in metal with such dexterity that their fame extended far and wide. In the middle of the thirteenth century, the French ambassadors found them in the Tatar-Mongolian service. The holy Louis of France sent an embassy from Cyprus to the great Khan of Tatary, whose force at that time occupied a large part of Russia. The messengers found a Russian architect and a French goldsmith working for him. And Du Plan Carpin, who in

1246 was sent by Innocent IV. to the great Khan Gajuk, and who described the pomp and wealth if the Tatar Court, speaks of a Russian goldsmith who was a favorite of the Khan, and who had made a throne of ivory, adorned with gold and precious stones and ornamented with bas-reliefs.

It is utterly improbable that the Tatars, in the long time they ruled Russia, should have tried to give a different direction to the artistic taste and style of the people. Nomads as they were, they had no artistic style of their own, and did not trouble themselves about the Russians, except to get money out of them. But the Tatar Khans, in all probability, served as means of communication between the Asiatic races who possessed an artistic style, on the one hand, and the oppressed Russian people, on the other. The Russian artists who resided among them looked deeply into the art forms of the interior of Asia, which were new to them, and they remembered them when they came home. In 1247 the Russian national hero and saint, Alexander Nevsky, celebrated for his victories over the Swedes and the German order of knights, was obliged to pay a personal visit to the camp of the golden hordes, and was thence taken to the great Khan himself, in order to obtain a desired alleviation and mitigation of the conditions of vassalage. The journey took two years, and shows how many points in common there were between the two courts, and how easily impressions must have been received.

In this respect, I am greatly struck by a quotation by Viollet-le-Duc in his work on Russian art, from Marco Polo, the famous Venetian traveller, the first European who (in the thirteenth century) travelled in and described Asia. In this it is shown that a strong influence from Eastern Asia has been effective in the production of the gilded and colored metal cupolas, the variegated roofs and highly colored walls in Russia. He thus describes the palace of the great Khan in the city of Khanbalu:

"La sale est si grant et si larges, que bien hi menuient plus de six milles homes. Il ha tantes chambres que c'en est mervoilles à voir. Il est si grant et si bien fait que ne a home au monde que le pooir en aüst qu'il le seust miaus ordrer ne faire et la covreture desoure sunt tout vermoile et vers bloies et jaunes et de tous colors et sunt envertrée si bien et si soitilement, qu'il sunt respredisant come cristiaus, si que mont ou loigne environ le palais luissent. Et sachiés que cele covreuse est si fort et si ferméement fait que dure maint ans." [1]

Although Russian scholars like Strogonof and Martinof have zealously fought against Viollet-le-Duc's theories about the Tatar and Indian influence in Russian architecture and ornamentation, he seems to me to be right in his view that the Russian art of building is composed of elements which are almost wholly borrowed from the East.

Russian art has been essentially religious, because the religious sentiment in Russia (as in Poland) has been fused with love for the fatherland and the place of birth. The question with the clergy was how to fasten the attention of the people upon religions subjects, and, since the common people could not read, religious painting was employed as a kind of figurative language; and, in order that this language should be understood at all times, all changes were avoided. A hierarchical canon was borrowed from the Byzantine masters, and in the lapse of centuries nothing whatever has been changed in the form and stamp of the images. The holy icon was a national symbol, like the flag in later times, revered and unchangeable as a coat-of-arms; it represented a grave, thin, ascetic person in a long garment, which was the ideal of the stalwart, carnally minded men of the earlier days.

But it was only in this domain that Russian art was stationary. Especially from the moment when Constantinople was no longer a Christian city, but in the hands of the Turks, the Russians ceased to seek there for artistic forms, and in the fourteenth century their original production reached its climax. With a prudent use of their natural materials, they erected churches and houses which exactly answered to their needs; they manufactured leather and ornamented it; they wove cloths and embroidered them in a manner which exactly answered to their sense of beauty. At the

[1] "The palace is so large and broad that it will hold more than six thousand men. There are so many rooms that it is a wonder to see. It is so large and so well built that no man in the world could ask for or do it better, and the roof of it is vermilion and blue and yellow glass of all colors, and it is so well and so skilfully varnished that it shines like crystal, so that the palace glistens far in the distance. And know that this roof is strong, and so firmly built that it has endured for many years."

same epoch that the unity of the empire was worked out, their artistic production took on a homogeneous stamp.

They gave to their church edifices, which were symbolical of the Russian national characteristics, as much splendor as possible. They were intended to attract attention by their size and by the striking outline of the highest parts. They connected a crown of cupolas around a central cupola, gave them the form of a tower, and crowned them with a skilfully worked-out bulb of gilded or colored metal, which ended in a cross furnished and united by chains. They gave to the outer walls, which were covered with tiles, enamelled faïence and paintings, the character of a radiant, cheerful carpet. The predominant colors are red, white, and green, which last color is even specially adapted to the bulb-shaped metal top.[1]

And the Tatar rule was scarcely shaken off before the Muscovites disclosed the greatest talent as artistic armorers, as masters of chasing gold and silver and working in *niello;* and they supplied all the neighboring countries with embroidered linen and artistically manufactured leather. Their embroidery is distinguished, like the vignettes on their old manuscripts, by the harmonious combination of colors. They have, upon the whole, a keener sense of the harmony of colors than for plastic beauty. Since the law for them as painters is not inventive power but fidelity, they sought to atone for the Byzantine stiffness of their figures and the lifelessness of their paintings by surrounding them with gold, precious stones, and pearls, and thus change the images to a kind of gorgeous decoration. And since they did not dare to make any change, and as no kind of originality could be exhibited in the treatment of the head and countenance of the holy persons, they strove, in consequence, to make amends by encircling these heads with golden halos, inlaid with pearls and precious stones, and engraved with the most delicate appreciation of art, and by ornamenting the breast of the image with plates inlaid with gold and silver in blazing designs, and worked in *niello* with arabesques. Some of these halos and breast-plates from the sixteenth century, with small green leaves and small blue flowers inlaid in the gold matte, or with green in different shades, enclosed by white lines,

[1] Viollet-le-Duc: *L' Art Russe*, p. 108.

and with single black leaves and black geometric lines in the gold, are of a beauty, of a fascinating, inspiring loveliness, of which no description can convey any idea.

The common houses, built of the trunks of trees, remind one of the manner of building in Switzerland and Norway. Kindred material has produced kindred forms, even if the peculiar Russian stamp is easily recognizable. Thus even before the time of Peter the Great, Russia had fully developed its artistic peculiarities. In so far as the foreign invasion which ensued did not place itself at the service of these peculiarities, it only succeeded in retarding or stopping their development until the national spirit in this century took a new start in artistic as well as in other domains.

The nineteenth century has brought an art of painting to Russia for the first time. Catharina collected pictures in the Hermitage, and founded an academy of art in order to obtain artists for her empire as other countries have them. But what they painted, they never sold. The rich Russian of her day bought only foreign pictures; and, in order not to make an utter failure, the native artists then began, as well as they could, to imitate the art of painting of other countries. Thus there sprang up several generations of academicians, imitators of David, who painted Spartans and Romans with bare legs and flowing mantles.

The national revival of 1812, which was quickly felt in the literature, had hardly any effect upon art. Nicholas secured two court painters, Beylof and Kotzebue,—the former of whom has become known by a cold academical painting, "The Last Day of Pompeii," and the latter by his battle-pieces, representing the victories of Suvórof and Kutúzof, which of necessity resemble all such scenes of victory of former days. A single artist comes to the front at this time, Ivánof, who is now so celebrated, the painter of a single painting, which, however, was never finished.

It was Gogol, who had formed a friendship with Ivánof, who gave him the idea of this picture from sacred history, which was to be a prodigy, and which, since he was never content with the execution of his plan, made the artist continually begin anew. For twenty consecutive years, Ivánof busied himself with this work, "The Coming of Christ." A throng of men are standing on the banks of the Jordan, about John the Baptist. The looks of all are fixed upon a point in the distance, at which John points with his hand. Here over the highland Jesus appears, a sad man, drawing near to the throng, grazing the ground with his divine feet. He seems to be half beatified.

The characterization in these heads was executed with persistent passion. On the other hand, the coloring is weak. In Tretiakof's gallery in Moscow, a gold mine for the study of Russian art, you can trace a whole series of the attempts through which the painting has attained to its final form.

The unwearied study of Ivánof, prompted by true genius, is the only great protest against the academic art under Nicholas. The Tsar, who would be autocrat over all things and all men in his empire, and who to the best of his ability influenced poetry and poets also,—it was he who made Pushkin busy himself with the history of Russia,—also desired to have a noble and conservative art, partly in a general way as an ornament to his reign, and partly to solve the problem of glorifying his own exploits. He succeeded only in destroying the courage of independent men of talent, and nipping them in the bud.

It is only in the last twenty-five years that there has existed a real Russian school of painting, and that the Russian lovers of art no longer go to foreign countries when they wish to adorn their walls. It was when, with the emancipation of the serfs, which liberated about fifty millions of men, the great blast of freedom spread over Russia, that the artists set to work, and on their canvases—frequently of the greatest possible dimensions—placed important incidents from their national life, very much as the authors at the same time began to write novels in four volumes about society in Russia. And now it became quite the fashion to be interested in Russian art, as it recently had been the fashion to do homage to everything foreign. The artists made good sales, and, among their customers sometimes found a Mæcenas like Tretiakof, who alone has founded a collection of Russian paintings which is many times greater and very much better than that of the Hermitage.

A relationship is now disclosed between the course of development of literature and art. Both move with the same force and speed from an aristocratic romanticism to a kind of realistic rep-

resentation of the people. In literature the path leads from the refined heroes of Pushkin and Lermontof to Tolstoï's and Dostoyevski's dwelling upon the simple-hearted. In art, the path has
taken its course from the expounders of the deeds of the great and
the elegance of the upper circles of society to the bald and sad
pictures of the lot in life of the oppressed and unhappy. So far as
artistic fidelity to reality is concerned, Russia now stands far
above Poland, and close to France.

It is quite true that the academy in St. Petersburg is a sort of
artistic hierarchy. The same *Tchinornisme* (official spirit) prevails there as everywhere in Russia. The chief authorities in this
establishment have no idea of art. At the head, for form's sake,
stands Prince Imperial Vladimir, and an ex-governor acts under
him. The same subjects are constantly given to all students: Priams
who come to sue for Hector's corpse. It is prescribed from which
side the light shall come, what person shall stand in the foreground, etc. It is of no use that the student is much more interested in an old apple-woman at the corner than in King Priam
and his whole court. It is Priam and Hecuba that he must paint.—
"What is Hecuba to him?"

Among the modern artists of Russia there is a group of dec-
orative colorists. The best known among them is not a Russian,
though he constantly exhibits in Russia. It is a Pole, *Semiradski*,
who has been under the influences of Makart. He will be rec-
ollected by the reader from his pictures, of which the photographs have everywhere been widely scattered, "The Living
Torches," "The Sword Dance," "The Girl or the Vase?" That
which is attractive in him and which he can impart is not the
highest art, which paints the sentiment of a scene or the expression of emotion. What he aspires to is the correct representation
of things and the picturesque splendor of fabrics.

Endowed with less dramatic power than he, but otherwise
akin to him, is the Russian *Makovski*, an artist very pleasing as a
colorist, but of little psychological power. He exhibited in 1887,
in St. Petersburg, a great painting, bought by an American: "Tsar
Alexis Choosing a Bride." The subject had a patriotic interest, in
so far as this bride who was sought for was the mother of Peter
the Great. Besides this the artist has availed himself of the opportunity of painting a throng of beautiful young girls in the

costume of the period. Strangely enough, he seems to have used one and the same model—his pretty wife—for all the young women among whom Alexis shall make his choice. The whole does not perceptibly rise above simple costume art. Neither can his later picture, "The Death of Iván the Terrible," which has been much talked of, be regarded as much superior to that style of art. In two of the figures there is expression: in the frightened fool, who is lying at the feet of the Tsar, and in the white-haired Russian dignitary, with a white beard, who, with eyes as if fixed with fear, looks over the game of chess at the drooping man; the other spectators assume theatrical attitudes.

A unique position has also been achieved in the latest Russian art by Verestchagin, just as well known—in Denmark also—for his extraordinary natural gifts and for his abuse of his talents. His biography has found its way into our literature, and a large number of his paintings have been seen in Copenhagen. In connection with this fact, it ought to be mentioned that only too large a number of the paintings which have been seen here were duplicates, which are far inferior to Verestchagin's originals. When he chooses he is able to do great things as a colorist. And among his far too numerous paintings there are not a few which, like his "Field of the Dead," remain ineffaceably impressed upon the memory of the beholder. He who wishes to judge him correctly ought not to be content with studying what he has himself selected for export and international exhibition by electric light, with the accompaniment of hand-organ music, but he should visit the collection of his paintings in Tretiakof's gallery in Moscow. Verestchagin is a genuine Russian, with his bias towards a rambling life of adventure, and with the extraordinary compound in his art of ultra-realism and symbolical mysticism (the allegory of war, for example). There is a certain connection between him and Tolstoï. He would be in his sphere as an illustrator of Tolstoï's works, and "War and Peace" would be specially adapted to his talents. His conception of war, as De Vogüé has correctly felt, is that of the authors who love peace and describe war.[1]

Among the modern artists of Russia there are two who have impressed me above all others, *Riepin* and *Kramskoï*.

The *forte* of Kramskoï, who died in the spring of 1887, was

[1] E. M. de Vogüé: *Souvenirs et Visions*, p. 172.

portrait-painting. In Tretiakof's gallery there can be seen a whole suggestive series of his vigorously conceived portraits of the great distinguished Russians of his day: Herzen, Byelinski, Turgenief, Dostoyevski, and others. After his death there was an exhibition of his works in the academy. There were two religious paintings: "Christ in the Desert," emaciated by fasting, oppressed by the weight of his thoughts; and a huge unfinished picture, "Christ before Pilate," besides five halls full of portraits, the pearl of which, with its peerless expression, is that of the Little-Russian poet Chevchenko, who has suffered so much and written so well.

Kramskoï was born in 1837, in a village in Little Russia, near the town of Ostrogoïsk. His father was a petty tradesman; his mother passed her life in the kitchen. The boy received his first education in the parochial school. At the age of seven, he began to model Cossacks in clay; at thirteen he begged his parents to let him learn the art of painting. Permission was refused, for everybody in the town knew that painters "go barefooted." Having, in the mean time, drawn everything he saw, and copied all the images in the church, a year or two later he was sent to Vorónezh, to the best sculptor there, but remained with him only three months, being only sent on errands about the town, and having no other amusement or recreation than a flogging. From sixteen to twenty he roamed about Russia, in all directions, touching up pictures for a photographer who came through Ostrogoïsk. During this roving life, which brought him an income of two rubles and a half a month, he read everything he could get hold of, and was especially enthusiastic over Gogol and Lermontof. Finally, at twenty years of age, he entered the streets of St. Petersburg, and was so fortunate as to gain admission into the academy. He thought he was standing in the temple of Art.

His disappointment was great. The instruction was simply horrible. The drawing classes were tolerably good, but the higher the student rose the worse was the teaching. No attention whatever was paid to the individuality of the young men, and there were always the same biblical or antique subjects. It was then just twenty years since Ivánof had suffered a similar disappointment in the academy. But it was just in 1858 that this artist came with his painting to St. Petersburg. Kramskoï was strongly impressed by this special picture; he felt the force of genius in the conception, and admired the truth of the expression of the faces. In his letters he puts the head of St. John on a level with those of the Venus of Milo and of the Sistine Madonna, and is scandalized that no one in St. Petersburg has any eye for anything but the mistakes in drawing in this grand painting.

Kramskoï had now obtained his first medals, and lacked only one year of being sent abroad at the expense of the academy, when he with fourteen comrades suddenly left, disgusted at the instruction they received. It is these fifteen men who have extricated Russian art from routine. Kramskoï married early, and his house was the place where the young men met. He himself, who was regarded as the leader of the movement, worked unceasingly, and sought for all sorts of knowledge. His thirst for information and knowledge was so great that it made him regard every student with veneration. His simplicity and kind-heartedness conquered the hearts of all.

At this time, Riepin became his pupil, and soon his intimate friend. In 1868 he also formed a friendship with a landscape-painter Vasilief, who later exerted considerable influence upon him. Vasilief drove him on to independence of authority of every sort, and Riepin enchanted him by his bold style. From 1868 Kramskoï was celebrated. He, the old enemy of the academy, was himself appointed a member of the academy. Gradually he became more and more of a colorist. In 1876 he writes from Paris, that he had hitherto worshipped form alone; that now he was beginning to understand what the art of painting is. He becomes an idolizer of Velasquez: "Everything is pale and insignificant in comparison with him. He paints with his nerves. The impression is *crushing;* there is no other word for it."

Kramskoï died in his vocation. While, in 1887, he was painting the portrait of Rauchfuss, the imperial physician in ordinary, he dropped his brush, and, stooping over for it, fell dead on the spot. No one else has painted the Russian race in so many different physiognomies as he.

His pupil, Riepin, the greatest living artist of Russia, has gained special reputation by some historical paintings: one of the Tsaritsa Sophia after Peter the Great has driven her from the throne, and the much-talked-about Iván the Terrible, throwing himself broken-hearted over his son, whom he has killed by a blow from his iron-shod cane. The latter is a masterpiece, and admirably painted. You can almost smell the pools of blood.

Still, these are not the paintings which are the most characteristic of Riepin's talent. They are those in which he has represented his own age. There is a simple strength in them, a profound and genuine earnestness, and a fascinating heartiness. He has caught upon his canvas what, in the strict sense of the word, may be called modern Russia. His pictures, on that account, are regarded in certain circles as paintings with a purpose,—radical paintings. You will find in his works the types of the intelligent young men of the day, of the female students with short hair and wise expression. He has painted the *burlaki*, who drag the boats on the Volga up against the stream. The expression in the depraved or resigned countenances of these bent, sweating laborers, with the tense muscles under their tatters, is admirable. He is fond of subjects like the departure of the recruits, the simple, every-day scene frequently met with: the young man's departure from family and home; or like "The Return of the Exile," a picture which never ceases to be thrilling from its very simplicity. The look cannot be forgotten which the mother and sister, astonished and half frightened, not yet glad, cast upon the emaciated young form, in the sorry clothes, which silently glides in through the door.

The profound sympathy in this art veils the remorselessness of the realistic representation.

There is in Russia at present only one eminent sculptor, who is of equal importance with these painters, and that is Antopolski, one of the few men of Jewish descent who have made themselves known in the history of sculpture. He passed his youth in great poverty, and was learning the trade of shoemaker in St. Petersburg when his talent was brought to light. Baron Günzberg, the rich and genial banker of St. Petersburg, took an interest in and supported him, until, quickly enough, he was able to support himself by his art. After having been a long time in Rome, he is now a resident of Paris and enjoys a European reputation.

Antopolski's "Christ" may, perhaps, be remembered from

Julius Lange's "Art of Sculpture." Bound, with his feet joined close together, Christ is presented to the people in a form executed with a melancholy realism, in the costume of the time, with broad sandals under his feet, his hair fast bound to his brow by sweat under the burning sun,—an earnest and truly Jewish type. He looks a little down before him, but the look is contemplative; he accepts with manly firmness the ignominy that the cry of the populace prefers Barabbas to him. There is a Russian stoicism in this look.

Another celebrated statue of Antopolski, representing the dying Iván the Terrible, is not less interesting. The Tsar sits in his arm-chair, awaiting the coming of death. The position has unquestionably been affected by Houdin's "Voltaire:" the hand of which, groping, anchors itself on the arm-chair. There is something in the look as if he saw, in his dying glance, the thirty-five hundred men whom he has condemned to death pass slowly before him. Lange has the phrase, "It is like a soliloquy of Macbeth."

In Baron Günzberg's house, rich in works of art, there is a very admirable bust which Antopolski has made of Peter the Great, of large size, idealized into a hero, with royal beauty and the stamp of immense power of will. In the same place, there is also a captivating bust of a lady, the likeness of Baron Günzberg's deceased wife. Among his other works, a statue of Spinoza, smiling and contemplative, deserves special mention.

But if the art of sculpture thus has at present only one great name to point to, yet there is, nevertheless, great ability in this field in Russia, and a great deal of plastic talent finds employment in the service of art industries. It is one of the peculiarities of Russian society that all the anniversaries, all the jubilees, which fall to the lot of persons of high position are celebrated by the presentation of one or more pieces of silver or gold artistically designed. Not infrequently a jeweller receives an order from a society or corporation with permission to go as high as twenty-five thousand rubles, provided he can produce a real work of art. The Russian taste for color is employed in a more pleasing manner in such small works than in large architectural designs. The jewellers in Moscow understand how to combine both high and pale colors with gold and silver matte with extraordinary beauty. Unfortunately, the most that we had the opportunity of seeing at the Scandinavian exhibition in Copenhagen was less characteristic of the Russian people, because the workman in part had often been carried away by French designs and patterns, and in part because, as a whole, this art came rather from the mountaineers of the Caucasus than from the Russian people proper. They seem here to have preferred to work with elegance rather than with individuality, and especially to have preferred to present proofs of the talent of the Russians in imitation, rather than their remarkable gifts of compelling the foreigners on their own soil to create artistic effects in the Russian style and spirit.

IMPRESSIONS OF
RUSSIAN LITERATURE

I

◄§ Even if the Russians of our day are not the descendants of the races which in remote times ruled the countries north of the Black Sea, they are at least their heirs, and he who is much interested in modern Russia gladly turns to the Greek and Roman authors for their descriptions of these countries and their climates, and for their accounts of the people and their manners and customs.

What made the deepest impression upon the classical authors is without doubt the cold, the eight month's winter, which Herodotus describes (iv. 28), and which is followed by a cool and rainy summer. That whole arms of the sea and broad rivers are frozen, so that people can drive and ride over them, is a terrible prodigy to them. We read in Ovid: "They protect themselves against the cold by skins and sewed trousers, and of the whole form only the face is to be seen. The hair often rattles from the ice which hangs on it, and the beard shines with the frost which covers it. The wine keeps the shape of the bottle, when the bottle is broken in pieces, and they do not pour it out, but divide it up. Why should I say that all the brooks are stiffened by the cold and that they dig water out of the sea that they can break into pieces? Even the Ister (Danube), which is not less broad than the Nile, and which, through its many mouths, mingles its waters with the sea, freezes, when the winds harden its waves, and steals out into the sea under a covering of ice. Where the ships went before, people go on foot. The horse's hoof stamps on the frozen plain, and over these new bridges, above the flowing waves, the Sarmatian oxen drag the barbaric vehicles. You may hardly believe me, but, since I shall gain nothing by telling a falsehood, I ought to be believed: I have seen the immense Black Sea hardened into ice, which like a smooth shell lay upon the immovable waters. And I have not only seen it, but I have trodden on the hard ocean plain and walked with dry feet over the sea." (*Tristia*, iii. 10.)

In the next place, the lack of trees in these regions made a great impression on those who came here from Greece and Italy. Of the country of the Sarmatians, Herodotus says that it is entirely bare both of cultivated and wild trees; of the Scythians he relates how for want of wood they cook the flesh of their sacrificed animals in the stomachs of the latter, with fire which is made of their bones (iv. 21, 61). Ovid turns back again and again to the melancholy want of vegetation in the region. "No trees, no vines in the Getian land. Rarely in the open fields is there a bush, which even then does not flourish." (*Tristia*, iii. 12; *Ex Ponto*, iii. 1, 7.)

In remote times, as is well known, all the races on the plains which became Russia were mingled together under the names of the Scythians, Sarmatians, Getians, and some others. It is impossible now to determine how far they were the ancestors of the Slavs. But that the latter generally had ancestors among them, is evident from the character of the bones which have been found in the old burial mounds (*Kurgans*) in Southern Scythia.[1] Several places in Herodotus have already drawn our thoughts in this direction. Thus the place (iv. 75) where he relates of the Scythians that they never wash their bodies in water, but use steam baths instead. (Comp. Nestor's Chronicle v.) But the chapter in Herodotus (iv. 5) where he speaks of their myths is far more remarkable. How Slavic it is even then, that the common ancestor of their race was a son of the supreme God, whom he had from a daughter of the river Borysthenes (Dnieper). Here already is the personification of the rivers which is so common in the old Slavic epics. But still more surprising is the resemblance between the myths about that Kola-xais, the youngest son of the common father, prince of the ploughshare, and Mikula of the *bîlinî* (the epic poems), the son of the peasant. Herodotus relates that, while Kola-xais and his brothers reigned, there fell a plough, a yoke, an ox, and a bowl, all of gold, down into Scythia from

[1] Elisée Reclus: *Géographie universelle*, v. 299.

heaven. When the eldest brothers, one after the other, approached, they were burned by the gold and driven back by its glow. But when the youngest came up, the fire was extinguished, and for that reason they gave him the whole kingdom. Also Mikula, the child of a village, the agricultural hero, has a wonderful plough. When Volga, the bold warrior, with his guard, rides from place to place to collect taxes from the Slavic towns, he suddenly hears out in the country the sound of a plough. He hears the creaking of its woodwork and the grinding of its ploughshare against the stones. Volga and his men take a course in the direction of the ploughman, and ride a whole day without finding any one. Yet the sound of the visionary plough, and the striking of the iron against the stones in the furrows, constantly ring in their ears. Volga rides another day without meeting any one. As Orestes Miller has remarked, the picture is developed in this direction, so that it assumes huge proportions. It becomes a poetic representation of the boundless plain of which the Russian land is made up. The farmer draws his furrow in this plain with such a wonderful skill that they only see in him a divine workman, the representative and protector of Russian agriculture.

It is only on the morning of the third day that Volga reaches the countryman who is ploughing up the ground with the mighty plough, tearing up the roots of trees and breaking off fragments of rock. He greets him and congratulates him. Mikula tells him, in return, how one day, when people from the neighborhood came to him and demanded taxes, he gave them all taxes with his staff. When Volga begs him to join his body guard (*Druzhina*), Mikula consents on condition that one of Volga's men shall pull his plough out of the furrow and throw it into a bush. But not five, not even ten, of his brave men can stir the plough from its place. Then Mikula comes up alone, and with one hand seizes the plough and flings it up in the clouds, from which it falls down into a bush.[1]

As we saw, the plough thus fell down from heaven. Over and over again, as ethnographic studies make progress, scholars have occasion to admire the scrupulous trustworthiness of old Herodotus.

[1] A. Rambaud: *La Russie épique*, p. 39.

To read Ovid after Herodotus is to be transported five hundred years in time and from one world to another. But the poetical lamentations of the over-educated Roman poet and his letters from Pontus are still one of the oldest sources of our knowledge of how the regions which to-day lie on the southwestern frontier of Russia were inhabited in ancient times, and of their natural conditions. Poor Ovid! The knowledge we now have was bought by the misfortune which befell him,—a misfortune so great and complete that it is incomprehensible how any one has ever been able to speak of his lamentations in a careless tone. No author in the Roman literature had a more original or bolder talent, and no one met with a more cruel fate. It was so long before the days of the Russian empire, an actual exile for life to Siberia. The illegal judgment strikes him, the finest, most sensuous, most petted poetic nature of Rome, tears him, even then growing old, out of the pleasures of home life, away from a wife whom he loves with the most heartfelt tenderness, after having been twice unhappily married, away from the circle of his friends and admirers, away from the city of the world which is all in all to him, from his fatherland (nay, from civilization), and drags him over the sea and the salt waves to the end of the known world. He is landed solitary and alone in a place where the air itself is painful to him; where he can endure neither the drinking water nor the food, cannot protect himself sufficiently against the climate, cannot find a physician when he is ill, nor a single man with whom he can exchange ideas when he is well; where few understand Greek and none Latin; where he must live in perpetual fear of attacks from hostile tribes, who swarm about the town and often enough break in, in constant anxiety lest there should be attacks from the inhabitants of the town, who were little less than barbarian; finally, where he cannot once move outside of the poor strongholds of the town, or own even the least bit of a garden, of which he so bitterly feels the want, because there are no gardens in the town, and personal safety is wholly wanting outside, so that the land for miles distant remains uncultivated. When the guards on the towers give the alarm, he, the refined foreigner, lays hold of his weapons. The coast is inhabited by Greeks and Getians mixed together, the latter being the more numerous, and even those who speak Greek have the Getian accent. Getian and Sarmatian horsemen ride through the streets in crowds, clothed in skins, with long and loose trousers, with long beards and hair which hangs down over their faces, with knives loose in their sheaths, their bows in their hands, and their quivers full of poisoned arrows rattling on their backs. The hostile Getians also use only arrows which they have dipped in poison; they live by robbery alone, come driving on their horses with the fury of a storm, very little dismayed by the slight walls of the town, and many a time their death-bearing shots fly in over the walls, so that the houses of the town were as if larded with arrows. Grant that there is a little poetic exaggeration in his description of his continual danger, there is wretchedness enough left. And in this condition Augustus and his successor let the most original poet of Rome pine away, year in and year out, always cherishing delusive hopes of a milder place of banishment, separated from everything he loved and had a taste for, and for a fault which was not a fault; for having got on the scent of a court secret, which he did not dare to mention, and which is unknown to us. It is no wonder that he, with his gentle and timid character, begs for mercy from the powerful father of the land, with continual humble adulation. But when we read these prayers for liberation we feel an involuntary admiration rising up for the Russian authors who, exiled in our day in similar circumstances, live and die without a prayer or a complaint, much less a word of flattery or adulation for him who exiled them, falling from their lips.

Putting Ovid's "Elegies" back on the shelves, and taking down Nestor's chronicle in its place, we are fully a thousand years later in time. The great national migrations had driven the Slavic races in broad waves in over Russia. Kingdoms have been founded in Novgorod and Kief. Together with legends and naïve conjectures about the more remote times, we have here a history becoming more trustworthy as we approach the period of the narrator's own life, ending with the year 1110. And even from a period concerning which Nestor has only exceedingly doubtful traditions to depend upon, he possessed treaties and agreements, genuine documents of the highest importance, which he incorporates in his book. He is Russia's Saxo-Grammaticus, but a hundred years older than the Danish monk, and his work has the greater literary value, given to it by the use of the mother tongue.

What especially attracts the attention of the Scandinavian reader is everything which relates to the rule of the Norsemen in Russia, the statesmanship of the Varings and their campaign. In the Danish translation of Nestor's chronicle, there are given in learned notes all necessary criticism of the old chronicles and information as to the present condition of investigation. The explanation of the Scandinavian words by Gislason, at the end of the book, is also very instructive.

In historical and psychological respects, a comparison between the style and descriptions of Nestor and of the Icelandic sagas is of great interest, especially in those cases where the chronicles and sagas treat of the same persons and events. An essay by the Russian scholar Senkovski on the Icelandic sagas and their relation to Russian history, which has been translated into Danish, awakens the attention and sharpens the reader's capacity to recognize Nestor's peculiarities and limitations.[1] Senkovski compares, as an example point by point, *Eymundar Saga* with the chapters (forty-eighth and following) in Nestor. The worthy monk here falls far behind. The saga was composed from the verbal narrative of Icelanders who had been participants in the events described, and have the trustworthiness of eyewitnesses. Nestor, credulously, with many oratorical embellishments and pious remarks, gives an account of martial exploits, victories, and defeats, concerning which he has only an indistinct and unintelligible tradition. The Icelanders had political talent and ability, in addition to the skill of the Vikings in tactics and war. While the monk from the cave-cloister in Kief, without considering the material difficulties of keeping forces in the open field, makes the armies of Yaroslaf and Sviatopolk stand full three months face to face in battle at Liubetch; and while he, in biblical fashion, reports the threatening speeches of the leaders of the armies to the enemy, and the impatient expressions of the troops at this derision, the saga shortens the time from three months to four

[1] Annals of the Society of Northern Antiquities, 1847.

days, shows what lot and part Eymund, the chief of the Varings, had in the battle, describes his flank movement, his attack on them at once from front and rear, and gives, without any fabrications, embellishments, or pious reflections, an intelligible picture, even if it seems as if the author of the saga had mixed up the reports of two different battles.

The greatest difference between the cloister spirit and saga style is felt in the account given by Nestor and in the saga of Sviatopolk's (Burisleif's) decisive defeat in the revolt against Brother Yaroslaf (the Jarisleif of the saga). In Nestor it is said, "But towards evening Yaroslaf conquered, and Sviatopolk took flight. And, as he fled, the devil came upon him, and his joints were loosened so that he could not sit on his horse, and they carried him in a litter, and brought him in his flight to Berèstije. But he said, 'Fly with me, for they are pursuing us.' And his servants sent a messenger back, and said, 'See if any one is coming after us;' and there was no one who followed them. And they fled farther with him, and he was then lying in delirium, and started up, and said, 'They are coming after us! Hasten!' He could not stay in one place, and flew through Liachland, pursued by the wrath of God, and came to a desert place between Liacher and Czecher, and there in a pitiable manner he ended his life. The unjust and godless man now had his deserts, when the judgment came upon him, after his exit from this world, given up to torments in the next. This was plainly shown by the mortal pangs which came upon him, and mercilessly drove him to death; and after death he is suffering everlasting torments in chains. This has God done as a warning to the Russian princes," etc.

In the saga the extract is less theological. It is told there how the practical Norse chief lays before Yaroslaf the necessity of letting his rebellious brother be slain. "For there will never be any end to this misfortune so long as you both live." When the king gives the answer that he will not call upon people to attack his brother, and then afterwards prosecute them in case they killed him, Eymund interprets the answer as it suits him, sallies forth with eleven others, hides himself in a forest, by the borders of which the hostile army is encamped, murders the king's brother, and brings to the king his severed head. "See here, my

lord, if you know this head." Yaroslaf turns red. "This deed we
Norsemen have done," says Eymund, "but now let your brother
be buried in a becoming and honorable manner." Yaroslaf answers, "You have done a rash deed, my friends, which weighs
heavily upon me. You have killed him; then bury him also."
About condemnation of the event, even on the side of the injured
brother, not a word is said. Senkovski properly notices the im-
probability of attributing to the Varing-Russian heroes of that
age the aversion of the Christian monk to bloodshed. It was only
cowardice that was despicable in their sight. For the perfidious
and bold wrong-doer they had a respect which was not denied
to him even when they were in arms against him.

The language, as well as the peculiarities of race, of the ruling
warrior caste of Scandinavian Russians was speedily absorbed by
the great Slavic people, largely because the Varings seldom married any other than native-born wives; therefore no traces of
the Norse mythology are to be found in Russia. On the other
hand, we meet (especially in the only written epic poem of Russia) not a few reminiscences of the old Slavic worship of God
and nature. Still, what we know about the mythical beings is
very little. The Slavs worshipped the heavens by the name of
Svarog. The sons of the heavens were Dazhbog, god of the sun
(and wealth. From *dazh*—day, and *bog*—god), and the god of
fire, Ogon (Indian, Agni). The god of the sun had other names
besides: Hors and Volos, who like Apollo was god of the flocks
and of the poets. Perun corresponds to Thor as the god of thunder. Stribog is the god of the winds. In addition they worshipped
"the damp mother earth;" the spring season, Vesná; and Morana,
the god of death and of winter. The souls of the dead were
called Rusalki. In Russia, as everywhere else, on the introduction
of Christianity, the heathen forms and ceremonies were not
rooted out, but named anew, and consolidated with the festivals
of the Church. Thus, for instance, the holy Elias, with his chariot
of fire, appears in place of the thunder-god Perun. There are
many songs, which it is the custom and usage to sing on anniversaries, over the whole of Russia, which have a mythical
origin.[1]

[1] See Alexander von Reinholdt: *Geschichte der Russischen Literatur*,
bk. 1.

But an entirely different, copious and valuable source of knowledge of the old Slavic intellectual life is to be found at the present time in the *bîlinî*, which were first collected and published in this century,—that is to say, the old Russian epic poems. The first collection of these appeared in 1804, consisting of songs which had been collected among the iron-workmen in the department of Perm. In 1818 a new edition of the collection was published, with sixty numbers in place of twenty-five. It was then found out that there were a large number of epic songs in circulation among the peasants in Northern Russia. From 1852 to 1856, Sreznevski published *bîlinî*, which were recited in these northern departments; yet it was only in 1859 that the investigations of Rybnikof, in the regions about the Onéga Lake, made it plain that Russia had an enormously large unknown national literature in the form of popular poems, which it was simply necessary to collect from the lips of the people. The isolation caused by the severe climate about the Onéga Lake, the simple manner of life and naïve mode of thought of the inhabitants, the superstition and ignorance, the inability to read and write, have made these regions a sort of oral Iceland for old Slavic poetry. Rybnikof was followed by Hilferding, who, in the same wild provinces, collected more than three hundred new songs or new variations. Next comes a garland of poems published by Kirievski, collected from almost all parts of Great Russia and Siberia. And in all these songs the same persons appear, the same adventures happen, and the same poetical expressions are found.

The best of these poems, and the most of them, turn upon the oldest memories of the Slavic countries, and range themselves into two principal circles, the Kief circle and the Novgorod circle. Sometimes they point straight back to the heathen Russia and the oldest Aryan mythology, which lies back of the Slavic religions. Thus they also present points of comparison with the holy books of India, and even several, and for a Scandinavian reader more interesting ones, with the Edda and the Norse myths.

Maïkof succeeded in fixing the eleventh and twelfth centuries as the period of the most important song-circle: the Vladimir cycle, whose centre is Kief. He has proved that in all these poems there is no other Russia known than that which lies about the Dnieper. The capital is Kief; there is no mention of Moscow.

The subordinate places are Chernigof, Galitch, Murom, Smolensk, etc. The Russia of the *bilinî* has already been converted to Christianity, and obeys one prince, but is in continual war with the nomads in the south and east. We find ourselves in the period between the introduction of the orthodox faith and the rule of the Tatars. Closer examination gives the circumstance that there is mentioned in the German "Otnit," from the twelfth century, an "Ilias of Riuzen," plainly the Russian national hero Ilia of Murom, and that in like manner in the Icelandic Thidrek saga of the thirteenth century, which is composed from Saxon songs or traditions from the twelfth century, there is mention of a Russian King, Vladimir, and his brother Jarl Ilia from Greece, which means Russia.[1]

Now and then, as already stated, we hit upon a passage in the *bilinî* of the Kief circle which call to mind Norse myths and popular traditions. Thus it is said of Sviatogor, one of the oldest heroic figures, a Titan with supernatural strength who is sometimes mixed up with the Bible Samson, that when, one day, he was lying stretched out on a mountain, Ilia of Murom, the national hero, the son of a peasant, in whom the saga figure Mikula seems to have been born again, wished to challenge him to single combat. But the most vigorous blows from Ilia's club were hardly able to awaken Sviatogor from his dreams. He thought it was pebbles that were falling on him. At the third blow, he says to Ilia: "You are strong among men; remain strong among them; with me you cannot compare yourself. The ground could not bear me, so I lay down on this mountain." Who does not recall the scene between Thor and the giant who, at the most vigorous blows of the hammer of the god, thinks that he was hit by a falling leaf or acorn!

Another adventure also reminds us of Thor and Utgardloke. It is an account of how Ilia disappears in the pocket of the sleeping Sviatogor. (The wife of the latter hides him there to escape the anger of the giant.) In just the same way, Thor passes a whole night in Skrymer's glove. Both Ilia and Thor here are the lightning which conceals itself for a long time behind the clouds, and

[1] A. von Reinholdt, above cited, p. 49. Rambaud: *La Russie épique*, p. 155.

very significantly Thor, immediately after coming out of the glove, strikes the giant on his head with his hammer so that the blood spurts out.

Among other things, Ilia also fights with the robber Soloveï, who blocks his way to the mountain of the Sun-prince. This Soloveï has a face of a bird and utters a horrible bird-cry, whose shriek works such destruction that the roofs in Vladimir's palaces fall in. He is, therefore, the spirit of bad weather and storm, and by his bird-form calls to mind that giant in the guise of an eagle who, in Vafthrudnismál, sitting at the end of heaven, with his wings which are those of an eagle, sets the winds in motion; or the giant Thiasse, who, in the guise of an eagle, carries away, conceals, and later pursues Idun, until he meets his death in the fire which was kindled for him behind Asgaard's wall. Bird-forms everywhere are symbols of storms and bad weather.

There is still another little incident of Ilia's battle with the giant which recalls a Norse tradition. As Ilia finds gold and silver in great quantity in Soloveï's nest, so Sigurd finds the red gold under the dragon Fafner. It is one and the same symbol of the shining beams which the dark clouds hide under or behind them.

Among Sviatogor's adventures, in the next place, is one which greatly reminds us of Thor's when the giant plays a trick upon him, and lets him drink out of the horn the other end of which is in the sea, raises a cat which is the Midgaard-serpent, and is troubled by an old woman who is old age. When the giant Sviatogor one day is riding over the plains, he meets an old man who asks him to help him put his sack on his back. The hero would lift the sack with the end of his whip, with his finger-tip, with his strong hand,—he cannot do it. Then he alights from his horse and tries with both hands, with tremendous efforts, to lift the sack which is so heavy, while the sweat drops from his forehead. Finally, he thinks he has got it up to his knee; but it is he himself who has sunk down to the knees in the ground. In the little sack, God had put the weight of the whole earth.

We finally find a characteristic incident, which reminds us of one of our national traditions, where Sviatogor and Ilia, after having formed a foster-brotherhood, visit Sviatogor's old father together. The old man is blind and apparently impotent. He asks to be allowed to press Ilia's hand to see if the Russian *bogatyrs* (the generic name of the national heroes) still have strong limbs and warm blood. At a nod from his friend, Ilia grabs a huge iron bar glowing in the fire and hands it to the old man. "Good!" says he to the young hero. "I feel that you have a strong hand and hot blood." This is the story of Holger Danske and the peasant.[1]

There is no one among the heroes of these *bîlinî* who is more characteristic and typical than this Ilia of Murom. He belongs to the cycle which has Vladimir, *the beautiful sun,* for its centre; but he is treated by the poets as the son of a peasant, with even more sympathy than the prince. Regular geological layers can be found in all the epic poems of Russia; we can see, more or less plainly, how certain conceptions of nature which are common to all Aryan peoples about the eleventh century began to assume a constantly more decided Slavic stamp. The mythical heroes, which were at first like those of other countries, like those of the old North, for instance, become decidedly Russian and decidedly Greek-orthodox. They are born in a definite Russian village; they are slain on a definite Russian field. The celestial mountains, streams, and seas, which, in the oldest mythological language, indicated clouds, rain, and air, become Russian mountains like the Ural, Russian rivers like the Dnieper, and Russian seas like the Caspian Sea. In like manner, we see Ilia also individualized. It is related of him that, before he makes his appearance as *Bogatyr*, he sits for thirty years (the constant expression for a very long time) immovable and lame. Then two celestial old men who come to Murom call him up from his sleep of death. It is in vain that he answers that he can move neither hand nor foot. When they call to him again, he is able to raise himself and open the door to them. They give him a strengthening drink, and he feels an immense power suddenly rippling through his limbs. Here Ilia is evidently the same thing as nature, which is awakened from its long winter sleep.

Ilia is thus roused to action, and his first exploit is to cultivate the Russian soil; with superhuman strength he tears up a whole oak forest and transforms it to arable land. After that he

[1] Rambaud: *La Russie épique,* pp. 41, 50, 111, and following.

sallies forth to free peasants, as a hero of the fields to protect this Russian earth against monsters, robbers, and heathens. We have seen how in these conflicts he appears as the God of Thunder. He shoots an arrow from his bow against an oak, and the oak is entirely split to pieces as if struck by lightning; he swings the club like Perun, the hammer like Thor.

But then we see him like a true Russian hero travelling from Murom to Tchernigof to free the land from robbers who were exhausting it. We see him reject the money and the sovereignty which the *muzhiks* of Tchernigof would confer upon him, and hasten to Kief to Vladimir, to aid the national prince against his many enemies. And he becomes chief *Ataman* over Vladimir's forces. In some of the *bîlinî*, at this point, he develops in entire consistency with the popular ideal. When Vladimir, one day, offers him an insult, he gives his men a sound thrashing, runs down into the courtyard, batters the gold tiles down from the roof of the palace and the gold crosses from the churches, and with the gold he entertains all the *muzhiks* and beggars of the region at a feast, where mead and spirits flow freely. In other *bîlinî* he is suspected by Vladimir, because he is slandered by the Prince of the Boyárs at his court, and he is thrown into prison to starve to death. He remains there for three years, secretly supported by Vladimir's young daughter. When Kief was attacked by a huge Tatar host, and Ilia was bitterly missed, Vladimir, led by the advice of his daughter, finds in the underground prison the hero, "the old Cossack," who is sitting at a plain table, reading the Evangelists. Vladimir, on his knees, begs him for help, not for himself, but for the churches of the Blessed Virgin, and for the widows and the fatherless in the holy Russia. Then Ilia discloses himself as the Christian knight, who protects the defenceless and has the churches near to his heart. Nay, he travels straight to Constantinople (Tsargrad) and liberates the Tsar from the heathen army.

It is now peculiarly Russian that, before this great military hero starts out into the wide world, he makes the vow that he will never soil his hands with blood. The few incidents of wildness that are met with in his history are plainly mythical elements, as when he kills the robber Soloveï, and afterwards the terrible

Amazon or *Polenitsa* (who at last shows herself to be his daughter), tearing them both into small pieces, and scattering these upon the earth to make it fertile. Otherwise he performs all his exploits with the greatest calmness, and, while he despises danger, he is fond of making derisive jokes after the manner of the Russian peasants. Like a good son of a peasant he began by helping his old parents. Everywhere, as at Vladimir's table, he compels the persons of position to give place to those of low degree. Like a genuine *muzhik* he sometimes drinks deeply and sleeps out his drunkenness; but he is openhearted towards his prince to the last degree, and when the latter has taken it ill and punished him cruelly for it, he is ready to forget the injury as soon as he hears that there is any question about the cause of the defenceless. He never brags of his victories, wishes that honors may redound to the glory of Russia, and, in his aversion to soiling his hands with blood, spares his enemies when he can do so, and sets his captives free.

It is a very remarkable instance of Russian imagination that a well-known *bílina*, with the title "Why there are no more heroes in holy Russia," for the purpose of increasing the impression of the power there is in this national hero, represents Ilia of Murom as stronger than Fate itself, to which this people otherwise so patiently submit, and which conquers all the other heroes.

Ilia had become fully three hundred and fifty years old, but his powers were less impaired than Stærkodder's as an old man, when, one day, while riding through a forest, he read on a stone the inscription, "If you go to the right you will become rich, if you take the middle road you will be married, if you go to the left you will be killed." The old Cossack, as he is called here, after considering it, concludes that it does not become his age now to seek for wealth or marriage. It is more becoming for him to ride in the road in which death is found. After riding a short distance he meets with a band of robbers, but disperses them, turns back and writes upon the stone, "I rode to the left and was not killed." By the middle road he comes to a splendid castle. A king's daughter, dazzlingly beautiful, first waits upon him, and then asks him to share her couch on a bed of silk and eider down. But the old hero, suspecting treachery, declares that in his country it is the custom for women to lie down first, seizes the princess by her belt and throws her on the bed, and then rushes down into the vaults of the palace. He liberates the forty princes she has held imprisoned there, causes the enchantress to be broken on the wheel, and writes a second time on the guide-board at the cross-roads, "I rode by the middle way and was not married." By the road to the right he finally finds an iron cross and under it a great treasure. He divides it into three parts and builds three churches with the gold: one for the merciful Saviour, one for St. Nicholas from Mozhaïsk, and one for the bold St. George, so he can properly write on the stone: "I rode to the right and did not become rich."

From this *bílina* we can perhaps best learn with what strength the Russian imagination has felt obliged to endow its heroes. His most extraordinary trait of character, nevertheless, is in the exhibition of self-sacrifice. He does not, like the heroes of the West, perform the act from a feudal devotion to his prince nor from a feeling of duty to him; still less, like the Norse heroes, from ambition, but from a magnanimous tenderness for children and the abandoned, or to protect the country and its religion. It is the common weal, not the happiness of the prince or his own honor, which lies near to his heart. While Achilles never pardons Agamemnon for the insult he received from the king, Ilia forgets on the spot what Vladimir has done to him. On that account the Russian scholars, like Orestes Miller, seek to show that Ilia's feeling of duty is conclusively significant in relation to the idea of community, which is the Russian fundamental idea for the Slavophiles. They see in Ilia's indifference towards mere personality, and his willingness to serve the common cause, a symbol of the original tendency of the Russian spirit to community in family, society, and state.[1]

Besides this popular epic poem, moreover, the Russian literature possesses in "The Story of Igor's Campaign" an old epic of art of very high rank, corresponding to what the "Song of Roland" is for the French, and the *Niebelungenlied* for the Germans, but which, nevertheless, has the fault, which would be

---

[1] Rambaud, above cited, 62, 113. A. von Reinholdt, above cited, p. 69. Reinholdt has extracts from the *bílinî* translated in the original metres.

very serious in the eyes of the Germans, of being much shorter.

This was written a very short time after the event which it describes: the campaign which Igor Sviatoslavitch, one of the princes from Novgorod-Sieversk, in 1155, undertook against the pagan Polovtsians, a nomadic tribe of Turco-Finnish descent, who lived on the banks of the Don and were continually attacking the careless Russians. Igor was a cousin of the Prince Imperial of Kief, who the year before, with other princes, had conducted a victorious expedition against the Polovtsians. Now, for his own part, he wished to cover himself with honor, and therefore sallied forth with his brother Vsevolod, "the wild bull," to whom he was greatly attached, and his son Vladimir. But his expedition was unfortunate; he was himself taken prisoner and with great difficulty escaped from captivity by the aid of a trusty esquire. We have the same incident related in the old Russian chronicle of the monk Ipat, one of those who wrote a continuation of the chronicle of Nestor, and we can see from that the endeavor of the unknown poet to confine himself to the historic truth. It is quite true that we find in the "Story of Igor" many traditions or mythical stories incorporated with the principal event, while the monk who is the author of the chronicle has carefully eliminated every heathen expression and element, but still there is a more evident attempt in the chronicler to endow the heroes with fine qualities. When the battle is lost the princes are advised to fly. In the chronicle they refuse to do so; they will not desert their men, their common soldiers, but will live or die with them. The story has nothing of this. And when Igor is taken prisoner according to the chronicle he refuses for a long time to escape from captivity, because he has given his word to the princes of the Polovtsians, until at last the regard for Russia, now so exposed to the enemy, moves him. In the story he is at once ready for flight.

When we mentally compare the "Story of Igor" with the heroic lays of the Edda, which are probably of greater antiquity and, at any rate, describe a rougher and wilder form of national life, the Russian poem, no doubt (in contradistinction to the Niebelungennôt), has the inequality and lyrical form as well as the predilection for a vivid dramatic representation in common with the Norse poems, but the essential feature of the Slavic epic is still entirely distinct. In the first place, the latter possesses an individuality. We do not know the author's name, but his entity stands out very distinctly before the reader, rich as it is in enthusiasm and piety. He speaks in his own name, stands as an individual responsible for his words, is conscious of a personal style of composition which is less flighty and fantastic than the style of the older seers and bards, whom he in other respects admires. In the next place, you feel that his love for the poetic art is not less strong than his admiration for the deeds of the princes of his day. He is an enthusiast for poetry. It is, as he expresses it, his intention to free himself from the poetic traditions; he does not wish to borrow from his predecessors "the old words." From the *bílíní* we can see what he meant by this. There is found in them, just as in the Homeric poems, a standing supply of descriptive epithets. The mountains are always *gray*, the sea always *blue*, the sun always *red*. The earth is *our mother, the damp earth*. They always run on their *swift* feet, always take another by his *white* hand, etc. The unknown poet has plainly wished to adopt as little of that as possible. Nevertheless, we meet in him certain constantly recurring expressions which are evidently inherited, as, to drink the Don dry with his helmet, to set ten falcons on a flock of swans, to sow the earth with human bones, and certain constantly recurring epithets, as, Vsevolod, *the wild bull*, the *falcon* Igor, and his son the *young falcon*, and others.

As a man, the author of "Igor's Campaign" is far milder in his emotions than the author of even the mildest of the heroic poems of the Edda, "The Songs of Helge." The style in which, in his poem, Yaroslávna expresses her longing for Igor during his absence in the war, and her fear for the life of her lover, is more like Ingeborg's languishing lamentations in Tegner's poem than it is to Sigrun's loss of Helge in the Edda. And the whole life of emotion and nature, which the nameless poet has spread out before us, makes an entirely characteristic impression, by the grand, childlike simplicity with which the association between man and nature is interpreted and described. The whole of nature is alarmed when Igor starts upon his unfortunate ride to the Don: the sun is darkened, the night groans, the beasts howl in anticipation of the impending danger. Both Yaroslávna and Igor, on their part, address winds and streams as if they were men; nay, give them titles and complimentary words just as plainly as it is done in the Iliad two thousand years before. And the river Donyets gives Igor an answer. The living naturalism, the transfer of human qualities and emotions to nature, is so prominent here that it is noticed as the expressive personal naïveté of the characteristic poet.

Finally, the patriotism of this epic and of its author is characteristic in the highest degree. Patriotism permeates and constitutes its motive; a love for the Russian land, which breaks forth not only in mourning over the triumph of the heathen Polovtsians, but even more vehemently in wrath and laments on account of the discord between the Russian princes who, at the close of this pregnant period, rent the land asunder with civil war. When the defeat is sustained, the singer exclaims:—

"The grass bowed down in pain. The crowns of the trees bowed down to the earth in sorrow. For the cheerless time was already come, brothers, when it was void of power, when injustice spread itself in the ranks of the descendants of Dazhbog [princely power]. Quiet, like a young girl, it stole into our land, and, as if with the wings of a swan, dabbled in the waters of the Don and of the blue sea. It awakened the hours of disaster. Then the contests of the princes against the heathen were broken off; brother said to brother, 'This is mine, even this also is mine.' And the princes began to say about small things, 'This is great.' But the heathens from all sides fell down upon the Russian land."

The old poet is a skilful battle-painter. Like the authors of the old Northern ballads, he embellishes his poems by descriptions of many battles which he has seen or in which he has participated; for example:—

"The Russians fenced round the wide field with their purple-colored shields, sought honor for themselves and glory for their princes. At daybreak on Friday, they crushed the heathen host of the Polovtsians under their feet, carried the beautiful Polovtsian girls away with them, and with them gold and veils and costly velvet garments. With the ribbons and capes and furs and finery of all sorts they began to build bridges over pools and swamps. But the red standards, the white banners, and the spears with the silver points fell to the lot of the brave Sviatoslavitch."

Or read the description of the battle on the following day:—
"On the next day the blood-red light very early heralded the dawn. Black clouds swept in from the sea; they would cover the four suns [the four Russian leaders of the army], and the blue lightning trembled in them. There was heavy thunder. The arrows flew like rain from the great Don. Then the spears were splintered; then the swords struck against the helmets of the Polovtsians, by the river, by Kayála, near the great Don. O Russian land! thou art still protected. But behold the winds, Stribog's offspring; they blow a sea of arrows against Igor's brave warriors. The earth trembles; sadly flow the rivers; the field is covered with dust; the banners rustle; the Polovtsians come from the Don and from the sea, and from all sides surround the Russian army; the children of the devil beset the shrieking battle-field; still the brave Russians enclose it with their purple-colored shields."

But the pearl of the poem is Yaroslávna's lamentation and Igor's flight.

"Listen, the voice of Yaroslávna! Like a cuckoo she complains alone early in the morning. 'I will fly,' she says, 'like a cuckoo over the Danube; will plunge my beaver-skin sleeves in the Kayála's stream; will dry the prince's bloody wounds on his stiffening limbs.' Yaroslávna weeps early in the morning on the wall at Putivl, and thus she speaks: 'O wind, thou mighty wind, why, oh, Lord! dost thou blow so hard? Why dost thou bear Chanen's arrows on thy light wings against my lover's men. Was it not enough for thee to blow the mountain waves out from under the clouds when thou didst rock the ships on the blue sea? Why does the breath of thy spirit waft my joy away over the grass of the plains?' Yaroslávna weeps early in the morning on the walls at Putivl, and thus she speaks: 'O Dnieper, the famous! thou hast broken through the rocks in the country of the Polovtsians, hast rocked Sviatolaf's ships against Kobyak's [1] hosts. Lord, bring my lover back to me, so that I no longer shall send him my tears over the sea!' Yaroslávna weeps on the wall at Putivl, and thus she speaks: 'Thou clear and thrice clear sun! thou art warm and beautiful for all. Why dost thou aim thy burning beams on my lover's men? Why hast thou in the arid desert dried

---

[1] Prince of the Polovtsians.

their bows together in their hands? Why hast thou tortured them with thirst, so that the quiver became heavy on their backs?'

"Towards midnight the sea became disturbed; whirlwinds raised themselves among the fogs. God shows Prince Igor a way out of the country of the Polovtsians to the Russian land, to his father's golden throne. The glow of the evening is extinguished. Does Igor sleep? No, he is awake; he measures in his mind the plains from the great Don to the little Donyets. Listen! the sound of his horse at midnight. Ovlur whistles on this side of the river, gives information to the prince: Igor must not remain longer. The earth roars, the grass whistles, the guards of the Polovtsians draw near. Then Igor leaps up like a weasel in the rushes; like a white sea-duck, he leaps into the water. He jumps on his fleet horse. Soon after he leaps down again, and, like a wolf, with light steps he hastens to the meadows of the Donyets; flies like a falcon in the fog, killing geese and swans for his meals morning, noon, and night. While Prince Igor flies like a falcon, Ovlur runs like a wolf, both dripping with cold dew in the grass of the steppes. For they have broken the wind of their fleet horses.

"Donyets said, 'Prince Igor, thou shalt have no little honor now, and Kontchak no little wrath, and the Russian land no little joy.' Igor answers, 'O Donyets! no little honor hast thou now, thou who borest the prince on thy billows, made him a bed on the green grass on thy banks, and covered him with warm fog in the shade of green trees; thou who causedst him to be guarded by the sea-duck on the water, by the gull on the rivers, by the wild-duck in the air! Not such,' said he, 'is the river Stugna, whose stream is so dangerous when it has swallowed foreign brooks, and which has broken our barks against the roots of the trees on its shore. Nor is the Dnieper such a river. That thrust our young prince Rostislav back from its sombre banks. Rostislav's mother now weeps over the young prince. The flowers wither, consumed by grief; the tree bowed its crown down to the earth in sorrow.' " [1]

[1] Wenceslaus Hanka: *Igor Svatoslavitch.* Prag, 1821. (Text, Bohemian and German translation.) Wolfsohn: *Die Schönwissenschaftliche Litteratur der Russen.* Leipzig, 1843, pp. 182-226 (the best translation in German). Rambaud, above cited, pp. 192-223.

From these extracts we can form a conception of the style and tone of the Russian epic. We see that they are very different from those of the heroic poems of the Edda. This written epic is unique in Russian literature. It differs from the *bîlinî* of the Kief-circle by its purely historical character, since none of its leading actors are demi-gods, but all the heroes who figure there are men, who conquer or suffer in a purely human manner. In the next place, this epic is characteristic from its stamp of aristocratic culture, since it was evidently written with the purpose in view, like the old Norse laudatory poems, of being recited before the body guard of a prince. Therefore it does not extol the masses in the person of a popular hero, but sings of the chiefs and leaders of the army as the leading men. Still, however patriotic the poem is, it is nevertheless inspired by the patriotism of the princely power and of the highest culture.

II

⊸§ The Russian national literature, like the Danish, dates from the eighteenth century, and it is even a little younger than the latter. The foundation was laid by Lomonósof, thirty years after Holberg became the founder of ours. But between the ancient literature written in the Church Slavic together with the *bíliní*, which date from a period before the reign of the Tatars, and the modern Russian book-world there lie the popular ballads, the short lyrical poems, Little Russian as well as Great Russian, rich and attractive from their tenderness and their sadness.

Little-Russian and Great-Russian popular ballads, each written in its own dialect, sung by widely different people, belong, in fact, to two different literatures, of which one, in later times, by despotic command, has been suppressed; but, in spite of the differences, the two groups present so many points of resemblance that they influence the mind in a cognate manner.

The Little-Russian ballads treat exclusively of the life of the Cossack people in older and later times. The Ukraine steppes are the theatre of this life, but the ballads also follow the Cossack in all his bold excursions away from home for centuries. They present picture after picture of the dangers in the martial life on horseback, in eternal conflicts with enemies in the east and west. There is the mortal hour of the wounded Cossack longing for home in a foreign land; the corpse which is washed by the cold rain and whose eyes are picked out by the birds of prey; the lamentation of the Cossack girl when the signal for the departure is given, and her lover rides away; her ardent regret for him when he is absent on a military expedition in a foreign land; the lamentation of the old Cossack over the young men who have disappeared; the young Cossack's self-reliance and confidence in victory; the sorrow of the lovers at the gossip about them, and the ignominy which they who would separate them heap upon the loved girl,— all this in short lyrical poems different from the more narrative form of the Cossack *duma*, which is fond of describing a definite historical person or exploit.[1]

The Great-Russian ballads are of several kinds: partly being the more stereotyped wedding and Christmas verses; partly the so-called ballads of men of adventure, that is, of highwaymen,— the semi-pathetic, semi-humorous, always humble ballads of those who are under sentence of death, which open the perspective to the gallows, and to that extent have a certain resemblance to several poems of François Villon; and partly (the great bulk) of genuine popular ballads, nearly all of which are about the longing and sorrows of lovers.[2]

The Little-Russian and Great-Russian popular ballads agree in two principal features: in the comparison between a display of nature and a mental condition, which is continually evoked by companionship with nature and a poetic view thereof, and in the richness of expression for the most varied moods and shades of a love upon whose multifarious sorrows they dwell with ineffable sadness.

The natural parallel is of this sort:—

Little Russian: "A hop vine alone in the garden—hurled itself down to the earth.—A young little girl among men—wept very bitterly.—'O green, blossoming hop, say—why do you not twine?' —'Oh, dear young girl,—why do you grieve over your fate?' " etc.

Great Russian: "Between two mountains, two high mountains, —grew up a slim white birch tree—a slim birch tree, a branching —where the sun warmed it not, and the noon and the starry host shed not their light,—where only the blasts shook it,—where only violent torrents of rain fell upon it—so among our neighbors— grew up a sweet little girl,—praised for her beauty and neatness,— her slenderness and plumpness and daintiness," etc.

So far as richness in expressions of love is concerned, it may

[1] Comp. Fr. Bodenstedt: *Die poetische Ukraine, Sammlung Kleinrussischer Volkslieder*. See G. Brandes: *Indtryk fra Polen*, 220, 227.

[2] See the poems in Wolfsohn: *Die schönwissenschaftliche Litteratur der Russen*, 227-272.

be regarded as scientifically proved that, of all living and dead languages, there is none so rich in expression as the Russian in both of its dialects. The philologist Carl Abel has written an essay which gives a vivid impression of the peculiarity of the Russian language in this respect. ("The Conception of Love in some Ancient and Modern Languages.") They have, for the expression of love as a pure, simple emotion, as an involuntary attraction, the noun *liubov* and the verb *liubity* and the adjectives *liubezni, liubeni, liuboï, liub* (loved for superiority, by voluntary choice, by taste, from interest); next, *zaznóba*,[1] which indicates the growing love with its sweet apprehensions and its tender hopes. *Milost* is the active love in endless shades: preference, good will, partiality, grace. *Blagost* is especially grace in all its goodness, warmth, and inexhaustibility. The study of languages shows that, while love among the Romans in particular was love for the family, for kinsmen, and regarded as a duty, among the Hebrews love was for the whole tribe, and, at the highest point, for the whole of mankind, and was regarded as a religion; the Russian sentiment, according to the derivation of the words, is caressing and full of charm, exclusively a natural instinct, far less conscious, circumspect, and trustworthy, always wholly involuntary.

The domain of Russian love is the tender flattery which expresses itself in innumerable ingratiating diminutives. *Of liubov,* love, as a woman's name, the common people make use of the names Liuba, Liubka, Liubkascha, Liubaschenka, Liubashetchka, Liubotchka, Liubutchka, Liubushenka, Liubushetchka, Liubenka, and even many others, each with its different shade of tenderness and caressing. And, however numerous the linguistic expressions for the sentiments and moods of love are, naturally just as numerous are the sentiments and moods themselves.[2]

Here is a short erotic poem, which is typical:—

"Thou ash tree, oh, thou full of branches!—when didst thou sprout, when didst thou grow up?—Thou ash tree, oh, thou full of branches!—when wast thou in blossom, and when didst thou ripen?"

[1] Passion, "flame."
[2] See Carl Abel: Linguistic Essays, pp. 23-78.

"I sprouted in spring, shot up in summer—I was in blossom in the spring, became a tree in the summer."

"Under thee there grows, under thee, thou Ash!—no poppy flowers and no grass,—there grows no grass, there burns no fire.—There burns no fire, yet a heart so warm.—Yet the heart so warm in a youth's breast—it burns, burns, nay, boils like pitch—boils in longing for my little swan—my swan, my dove, my little soul,—my charming dove, my dearly beloved.—

"Oh, thou soul, my soul, my beautiful maid—in the hour of daybreak, when the morning was red—when the shining sun rose up in the heavens—without leave of thy father and mother—without even once seeing thy friend—thou left life, thou went away from here.—

"Oh, ye winds, ye warm winds, ye!—warm winds, ye who waft towards autumn—blow ye not here, I need ye not.—But come only thou storm, oh, thou roaring!—From the regions of the North fly only thou hither!—Split only with thy breath the moist earth—split the wide field, split the broad field!—Oh, open for me, storm! open for me here my grave.—And ah, let me, let me for the last time—here take leave of my loved friend—of my loved friend, of my dearly beloved.—Only a tear-kiss amid weeping so bitter!—Then I expire and die with her."

When from these tones of nature you come to the lyrical in the founder of the later Russian literature, the transition is abrupt, so abrupt that for a man of the present day it demands a very great interest in the historical development of a great people, not to put Lomonósof aside with disgust. For he, who, moreover, was a far greater philosopher than poet, belongs absolutely to that tendency of taste in the eighteenth century for which the inartistic poetry of the people was no poetry at all, and which saw the end and aim of lyric poetry in the strained pathos of the style of the ode and its artistic form of regular combination. The modern artistic poem, in various parts of the country, begins in this eighteenth century by separating itself as far as possible from the ballads of the people and from everything which belongs to them, so as for the first time at the beginning of the new century to seek backwards for simplicity, unity, and nature.

Lomonósof, whom Byelinski has called the "Peter the Great of Russian literature," was obliged to shape the modern Russian language, as a literary language, entirely anew. Before the time of Peter the Great they wrote in Church Slavic, after that a mixture of Church Slavic and Russian. As a boy, Lomonósof had drawn the language of the people from the purest fountain, had heard it as it fell from the lips of the Russian fishermen in Archangel, but he had studied Slavic at an early age in the old church books. He was thus able to mould his language with the confidence of a man of intellect, and created the newer prose style and the Russian metre and wrote the first sonorous verse existing in Russian, composed by any poet whose name is known.

Lomonósof's importance for Russia is, as already stated, closely akin to that of Holberg for Norway and Denmark. He had a wonderfully many-sided genius, developed by a career which is almost marvellous. Mikhaïl Vasilyevitch Lomonósof was born in 1711, in a village in the department of Archangel. His father was a royal serf, who earned his living as a fisherman, and who used to take the boy with him out in his boat. From his tenth to his sixteenth year the intelligent boy thus sailed about every summer over the White Sea and the Arctic Ocean, receiving impressions of a great and wild nature, experiencing the poor man's hard fight for bread, seeing salt-works, cloisters, religious meetings, and among the people of the region he acquired a knowledge of the character of the Russian people in its purity.—He learned to read and write from the village priest, devoured one or two old church books, which were the only reading available to him, discovered that Latin must be learned in order to acquire knowledge of a wider scope, and therefore ran away from home at the age of seventeen and went ten miles on foot to catch a wagon-train of frozen fish which was going from Archangel to Moscow. There he was dropped in the market-place, and by the accidental kindness of a monk a few days later was taken to a cloister school, which indeed only received the sons of the nobility, but where his ancestry was overlooked. Here, and for a short time in Kief, his progress in Latin and Greek, in the Slavic language, in philosophy, physics, and mathematics, is that of a genius. When he had completed his courses at Moscow and Kief, he obtained the privilege of being sent to the Academy at

St. Petersburg and to Germany, where at Marburg he attended Chr. Wolf's lectures on philosophy, and at Fribourg he studied practical metallurgy and mining.

He had previously made attempts at writing verse in St. Petersburg, and now he showed his enthusiasm for the poet Johann Christian Gunther, forgotten in our time outside of Germany, by transferring his metres to the Russian language. His first ode to the Tsaritsa Anna, a memorial ode celebrating the conquest of Chotin, is an exact imitation of a poem by Gunther in honor of Prince Eugene. Lomonósof, perhaps, surpasses his German model in spirit, and is possibly his equal in the domain of the ode in bombast; but he does not at all succeed, like Gunther, in writing bold and audacious verses about his personal experiences or his erotic inclinations.

In 1740 he is secretly married to the daughter of a poor tailor in Marburg, runs in debt, and, when he is threatened with the debtor's prison, flies secretly from the town without even telling his wife, and begins to beg his way on foot with the intention of getting to Holland. On the way he falls in with a Prussian recruiting officer with recruits, who gets him drunk, gives him the bounty money, and receives his promise. The next morning Lomonósof wakes up in uniform, and, in spite of all his prayers and protestations, is a Prussian cavalry soldier. He is taken to the fortress at Wesel. He deserts, hotly pursued, amid dangers and anxieties, crossing the Westphalian boundaries, and arrives at Amsterdam, representing himself to be a poor student from Saxony. In Holland the Russian minister takes charge of him, and sends him back to St. Petersburg.

From the Hague he wrote to his wife for the first time since his flight; but in St. Petersburg, where he did not feel that he was in a situation to support his wife and the child she had brought to him, he allowed two whole years to pass without any communication, until she, through the Russian minister at the Hague, finally learned where he was, and with his consent came to him.

From 1745 Lomonósof labored at St. Petersburg as professor of chemistry and experimental physics, and from 1755 began to advocate a plan for the re-organization of the Scientific Society, in which he fought against the encroachments of the Germans, hitherto the sole masters of the situation; and, as the passionate, nay, fanatical exponent of Russian nationality, was soon guilty of no less scientific and personal encroachments.

Here at home he developed his whole genius as a scientist. He was the first Russian naturalist who, on the foundation of the scientific results of Western Europe, which he laid before his pupils, was an independent inventor of machines and apparatus, and an independent discoverer of hitherto unknown laws of nature. The great mathematician Euler gave the most appreciative praise to his work on the phenomena of electricity, light, and air. Euler publicly declared that "this talented man did honor to the academy and the whole people." In physics, Lomonósof, independent of Franklin, explained the principles of electricity in the air and of the Northern Lights, which accords in many points with Franklin's, and which in some other respects he is even more advanced. In mineralogy he was the first to point out the vegetable origin of amber and the production of coal from peaty soil under the influence of subterranean gases. In astronomy he was the discoverer of the atmosphere of Venus. Finally, as a chemist and geologist, he distinguished himself by his popular descriptive powers.

His studies in the Russian language, literature, and history made an epoch. His Russian grammar has controlled education in his native land for half a century. He wrote books about Russian style, rhetoric, and metres at the same time that he himself was working as a poet and orator. Finally, he is Russia's pioneer in mosaic art. There still exist from his hand a well executed portrait in mosaic of Peter the Great, and a large work representing the battle at Poltava.

It is this man of genius who, for the first time since the introduction into Russia of the intellectual and in some directions material foreign ascendency by the Tsar Peter, gave an organ to the old Russian national feeling, while he at the same time made himself its poetical exponent and its practical champion,—the latter being carried out to the most infatuated *chauvinism*. His great reputation in this generation, when his poetry is no longer read, depends on the fact that it was he who gave the first impulse towards the liberation of the Russian intellectual life and of

Russian science, then just dawning, from the foreign and especially from the German yoke.

When Lomonósof was admitted to the Academy of St. Petersburg, there were two illustrious Germans, Gerhard Müller and A. L. von Schlözer, who had laid the foundation for all historical investigation in Russia, who were the influential persons in the Academy, where, moreover, they found themselves surrounded almost exclusively by their countrymen. At the request of the Tsar Peter, the founder of the Academy, Leibnitz, had prepared a plan therefore, expressly designed to "bring the culture of the west into Russia, and to be instrumental in teaching the Russians to know and appreciate it, and in thus causing them to cease to be regarded as barbarians." It was in his spirit that only books of instruction of the Academy were printed in Russian, while the purely scientific publications, which, moreover, would not have found many readers if printed in Russian, were issued in German or French. But, naturally, this condition, when the national feeling first grew strong, could not long continue.

In 1741, Elizabeth, by the aid of the party of the native nobility, annulled the rule which Münnich, Ostermann, and some other aristocrats of German birth in the regency of Anna Leopoldovna, had established for the minority of Iván VI. Elizabeth had banished Münnich and Ostermann, "bravery and wisdom," from her empire, and was now everywhere greeted as the person who was to bring about an age of reform in Russia, only on account of the agitation in the direction opposite to that which was due to her great father. She had inherited Peter's sensuous instincts, but not his genius. In the mean time, simply that she dreamed about again making Moscow the capital of the empire, that she had only native-born Russians about her and continually took the part of protectress of the orthodox clergy, who had long been repressed, was enough to make her generally regarded as the liberator of the people from the oppression of Western Europe. She was especially so regarded by Lomonósof, whose lyrical poems have hardly any other subject than his sovereign; and she was celebrated as "the Astræa who had brought back a golden age," "the Moses who had brought Russia out of the darkness of Egyptian thraldom," etc. Under her guidance, Russia was to show that, without foreign teachers, it was in a situation to bring forward "profound Platos and intellectually endowed Newtons"—a manner of speech which sounds strangely in the mouth of Lomonósof, who had himself been so thoroughly grounded in the schools of foreign lands, and who, without the instruction in Marburg and Fribourg, never would have attained the level of the European culture of his day.

His general enthusiasm for science was beyond all doubt, but in the domain of history and language the rabid national feeling handicapped him as to the results within reach. In his contests with Müller and Schlözer he maintains, for example, that they derived the Russian word *kniaz* (prince) from the German word *knecht* to dishonor the Russian people and stamp them as a nation of thralls. (*Kniaz* seems to be cognate not only to the word *knecht*, but also to the English word knight, and other appellations of rank of the highest repute. Nevertheless, the comparison, by Anatole Leroy-Beaulieu, of *kniaz* with *king* [*La Russie*, i. 214] is certainly misleading.) An address of Müller, which was to be delivered on the name-day of the Tsaritsa, "About the Scandinavian Origin of the Russian Race and Name," struck Lomonósof as insulting to the honor and prestige of the Russian people. He was so reckless in his passion that one day he burst into the audience-room of the German professor, and began to scold and abuse him. When he was summoned before the consistory in regard to it, he fell upon his associates with such abusive terms that they refused to place them upon the record. He was condemned to be punished with the knout for this, but, "out of consideration for his services as a scholar, and his superior intellectual qualities," the sentence was commuted to a reduction of his salary.

At this time it became established as an article of faith that the intention of Peter the Great had been to drive foreign culture out of the land as soon as it had done its work; and as they now contended that its mission was already accomplished, they succeeded in being able to honor Peter also among the great national rulers. Lomonósof, therefore, compares him in his speeches with God himself. To the speaker's servility to Elizabeth, one of whose favorites he was, there is naturally even less limit.

Lomonósof's lyrical poems were at first didactic, like the antiquated, naïve "About the Use of Glass," which, on account of the insight of the author into the natural sciences, stands a little above the didactic poems of this kind of the eighteenth century, and rather reminds us of the cognate poems of Hans Christian Oersted. In the next place he wrote religious poems, observations on the greatness of God and on similar themes, in the same style as Johannes Ewald among us, and finally hymns in laudation of Elizabeth and her husband, which remind us in the highest degree of the flights in the first ode of Victor Hugo in *Odes et Ballades*.[1]

The strongest impression which the foreigner receives of this great figure, planted at the entrance to Russian literature, is its typical Russian stamp. We notice, in the next place, its quality of appropriating the results of a foreign civilization, with such remarkable rapidity and in so many different directions, and how the imitative tendency has taken root and become productive. We remark the universality which reminds us of Peter the Great, and which, as in the case of the latter, takes its starting-point in mechanics and technics. Lomonósof is a real *muzhik*, the ingenious serf who, in the space of one generation, goes through the development which we trace back to the natural gifts of the Russian peasant in the main, but which his class of society as a whole will take a thousand years to travel through. Lomonósof is a genuine Slav by nature, flighty and gentle. Several years in succession he vanishes from his wife's range of vision without sending a word to her; but when she reminds him of her existence and of his child, he bursts into tears, and exclaims to the man who brings him the letter, "My God! how could I have left her! Circumstances have prevented me from calling her to me.

[1] About Lomonósof, see Wolfsohn, above cited, 305-340, with excellent metrical translations; Reinholdt, above cited, 304 and following, with translations by Bellinghausen; and the anonymous work, *Aus der Petersburger Gesellschaft, Neue Folge: Wassily Ostrov und die Akademie der Wissenschaften*, pp. 194-245.

Now I will send her a hundred rubles for the journey." Like a genuine Slav, he is above everything else, at the same time, a rationalist and mystic. On his journey back to Russia he had seen in a dream his father's corpse cast up by the waves on an uninhabited island in the Arctic Ocean. The strong mathematician could not escape from this vision. He had scarcely reached home before he inquired of people from Archangel about his father's fate, and learned that now for four months after he had gone out a-fishing on the Arctic Ocean, nothing had been heard from him. He then sent his brother with a letter to the fishermen of the region, and directed them to seek for his father's body on the island seen in his dreams, whose situation he exactly described; and, since the body was found, was for the rest of his life obstinately convinced that it was found exactly on the spot shown to him in his dream.

Finally Lomonósof is Russian in his rambling propensity, and his thirst for foreign knowledge; very Russian in his adoration of the Tsaritsa; Russian in his coarseness and violence towards his foreign colleagues; but Russian especially in the way in which, a pupil of the Germans, he goes *to the end of his rope* in his hatred of and opposition to the intellectual sway of the foreigner.

From Lomonósof it is a direct descent through Derzhavin and Zhukovski down to Pushkin and Lermontof, the literary geniuses of this century.

Derzhavin (1743–1816) represents in lyrics the period of Catherine II., as Lomonósof does that of Elizabeth. He was born at Kazán, learned German early, read Gellert and Hagedorn, Herder and Klopstock, was compelled to pass twelve hard years from 1762 as a soldier of the guard. The day when Catherine ascended the throne, he stood as a soldier of nineteen on guard at the Winter Palace. No one could then have imagined that in the future his name would be mentioned in connection with hers.

In 1773 he took part in the campaign against Pugatchef on the Volga, which he afterwards tried to describe in verse. In 1777 he published his first collection of poems, which contained among others a translation of a number of the poems of Frederick the Great. He obtained a civil appointment by his well-known "Ode to Feliza, Tsaritsa of the Kirgiz-Cossacks" (viz., Catherine). He attracted the attention of the Tsaritsa, received a snuff-box and some ducats for his poem, and then one important office after the other, since on account of his passionate, fiery temperament, which was strangely united with the most methodical pedantry, he was generally very soon obliged to leave his posts. His ode on the occasion of the taking of Izmail by storm inspired Catherine anew just when his affairs were at a low ebb. In 1791 he was appointed private secretary to the Tsaritsa, but tired her excessively in this capacity. Under Paul he became the leading officer in the home department of the empire, and under Alexander minister of justice, without being of any use in either of these offices. He was obliged to leave the former on account of "licentious language;" in the latter he showed himself to be ultra-reactionary, and, among other things, set himself with might and main against the plan, which had even then been proposed, of emancipating the serfs. Derzhavin had some other traits as an official; he was disagreeable and pedantic, and at the same time possessed a vigorous conscience, a combination which reminds a Dane of Schack Staffeldt.

He passed that part of his life which fell to the nineteenth century almost wholly as a private man, surrounded by the admiration and piety of the rising literary generation. His figure inspired veneration, his eye was full of fire, and the expression of his countenance was mild. When, a year before his death, he was present at the final examination of a grammar school in Tsarskoye-Sielo, a pupil recited a poem composed by himself. This pupil was Alexander Pushkin, and his verses made such an impression on the old poet, that, after having heard them, he exclaimed: "My time is past—you will now be a second Derzhavin." Pushkin, in his *Yevgeni Onyégin* (viii. 2), recalls, with emotion, these encouraging words which his predecessor in the poetic art gave him by the way.

Derzhavin began as the imitator of Lomonósof's bombastic style with the broad, cold pathos. His ode "God," admired and celebrated in its time, corresponds to the import of the religious odes of Baggesen in the Danish literature. It must be owing to the subject that the poem has been translated into a great many different tongues, and last of all into the Japanese. It contains everything which such a hymn must contain of gratitude and humility, on the part of the very small towards the eternal greatness, but no genuine emotion and not an idea. The long-winded poem which won Catherine's favor is far better. It surprises us agreeably on coming from the Klopstock bombast of earlier days. It keeps to the earth, is jocular and sportive, adopts a tone like that which Horace assumed towards Mæcenas, in the broad description of the worldly-minded laziness of the poet in comparison with the life full of responsibility of the regent. The poem "The Great" has no longer any poetic, but a historic and psychological interest, because, without mentioning any names, it contains a disparaging description of Potemkin (pronounced Patyómkin) in contrast to other unappreciated but really great Russians. Our respect for the poet is, however, somewhat diminished, from the fact that he himself was indebted to Potemkin's energetic protection for his escape in a lawsuit brought against him by some bitter enemies, so that gratitude ought to have restrained him from giving utterance to his ill humor. He also, at a later period, commemorated Potemkin's solitary death in the middle of the steppes in his poem "The Waterfall."

Constantly changing influences from Western and Southern Europe, from the contemporary age and from the past, had their effect upon this poetry, which just escaped mediocrity. The influence of Horace and the Anacreontics, perhaps through the influence of the Göttingen lyric, follows that of Klopstock. When the ballad style prevails, Derzhavin begins to write ballads and to imitate, at second-hand (after Zhukovski), Bürger's "Leonore." At the close of his poetic career he was influenced by Ossian, who was then making an impression everywhere.

The influence which Ludwig Holberg exerted even here in distant Russia at this period is specially interesting to a Dane. The author who laid the foundation of Russian comedy, Denis von Wízin (1742–1792), received the impulse to his dramatic attempts from Holberg. French and German companies had found an audience in Russia before the Russian theatre was established, and it was a German manager, the distinguished actor

Ackerman, who, so to speak, introduced the entire comedy of Holberg into Russia. When a permanent Russian stage was opened in St. Petersburg and Moscow (1756–57), a long list of plays of the favorite Danish author, translated from the German into Russian, was produced upon it. "Don Ranudo" and "Henry and Pernilla" gave the most satisfaction, yet they could not compete in power of attraction with the lyrical tragedy of Metastasio, "Artaxerxes," translated by Holberg, which was regarded as an original production of Holberg and always filled the house to the last place.

Von Wízin saw "Henry and Pernilla" in St. Petersburg when he was a student, and felt, to use his own expression, "an indescribable fascination" in this comedy. His first celebrated comedy, "The Brigadier-General," is greatly influenced by Holberg, especially by "Jean de France." The General's son Iván (that is, Jean), who has been educated in a boarding-house of a French coachman, has returned from his journey to Paris with the "Francomania." How great the resemblance is between this figure and the Hans Frandsen of Holberg, a brief extract will make plain.

THE GENERAL: "Listen, Iván, I have seldom blushed since I got out of leading-strings; but to-day, in spite of my gray hair, I was so ashamed of you that my cheeks burned."

IVÁN: "*Mon cher père!* Can it be agreeable to me to be told that I must marry a Russian girl?"

THE GENERAL: "Are you a Frenchman, then? I thought you were born in Russia."

IVÁN: "My body was born in Russia; that is true. But my spirit belongs to the French crown."

THE GENERAL: "Then you owe Russia more than France, for there is more coherence in your body than there is in your spirit."

IVÁN: "See here, papa, now you are beginning to say civil things to me, since you understand that you cannot make any progress by severity."

THE GENERAL: "You are a regular fool! I have called you a blockhead, and you think that I am paying you compliments. What an ass!"

IVÁN: "Ass! *Il ne me flatte pas.*—I repeat to you, papa, *je vous le répète,* that my ears are not accustomed to such expressions."

It is no slight honor for Denmark that the man who laid the foundation of our national literature and created the Danish stage has also been instrumental in the foundation of the Russian theatre. He died without seeing anything of this; he certainly never suspected how large a portion of the world his genius would affect; but it is a curious idea that even in the last years of Holberg's life, when his countrymen were turning their backs upon him, the inhabitants of St. Petersburg and Moscow were jubilant over his comedies, and that only ten years after his death his influence could be traced as predominant in the first Russian comedies that gave any pleasure to their hearers.[1]

Von Wízin, "the Russian Molière," was also influenced by several other foreign authors besides Holberg. But, upon the whole, down to the present time, it has been a law of Russian literature and intellectual life that no progress and no new form of development has been attained except on a foundation of foreign influence in its most emphatic and unequivocal form.

This is again to be seen in the author who shows the next advance, and who, in Russia, is regarded as the Columbus of romanticism; namely, Vasíly Zhukovski (1783–1852). A man of subtle talent; a character tender as a woman, but pure, with A. W. Schlegel's gifts as a translator, but without Schlegel's wealth of ideas,—an honest visionary and upright lover of the good, the beautiful, and the true, as three venerable, conservative powers, well fitted to develop as court poet under the Tsar Nicholas, and to end, as Slavic men of talent like to end, in mystic pietism. He is the author of the Russian national song, the hymn to the Tsar.

Zhukovski was the illegitimate son of an elderly Russian country nobleman by the name of Bunin and a young Turkish woman whom Bunin had brought home to his residence as booty after the conquest of Bender. The boy grew up with Bunin's legitimate daughters, who were much older; early developed, and

[1] See Alexis Wesselofsky: *Deutsche Einflüsse auf das alte Russische Theater, von* 1672-1758, p. 107. Reinholdt, cited above, p. 358 and following.

spoiled in a purely feminine atmosphere. While yet young, he read Diderot, Voltaire, Young, Bürger, Herder, Wieland, and Schiller. At the age of nineteen, he translated Schiller's "William Tell;" some years later, "Don Quixote;" also wrote original epic poems, ballads, and tales, yet without close connection with the Russian popular spirit, because, in almost every one of his poems, you can point out the foreign models.

In 1812 he participated with distinction, as an officer, in the campaign against the army of Napoleon, and became celebrated by the poem, "The Singer in the Russian Camp," and by a metrical homage addressed to the Tsar Alexander from Paris, which for the first time brought him in contact with the ladies of the imperial family. He suffered the heartache of youth when some one, on grounds of orthodoxy, refused to give him his niece in marriage. In order to enjoy the young girl's society, he accompanied the family to Dorpat, passed an instructive year in the little university town, and then, in 1816, in St. Petersburg, joined the literary society "Artasamas," composed of persons similarly educated, of which Pushkin, Nicholas Turgenief, and the later re-actionists, Minister Bludof and Uvarof, were members; a society which, as a league of the Phosphorists in Sweden of that time, started the opposition of the new century against the French classicism.

The romanticism which the society advocated as an offset did not and could not have that relation to the past, especially to the Middle Ages, possessed by the German romanticism, of which it was a product. For the Russian antiquity and Middle Ages were, at that time, still a sealed book. They only brought forward a new and, in its essence, a tolerably inexact æsthetic doctrine: fantasy should have freer flight than before; deeper psychological insight is of more account than local color. Still, like all other nationalities during the reign of Napoleon and after his fall, the Russian nation turned its attention to its national peculiarity, and the problem of describing the nature of the Russian land and people, and of representing the domestic world in poetry, was now presented for the first time, and for the first time solved by Pushkin in his way. Here, as everywhere else, Shakespeare made his influence felt on the nascent romanticism, and here, as in Poland, Byron soon became the poet of the romancing youth. The little circle of romanticists was broken as soon as the political question entered it. On occount of his liberal tendencies, Pushkin was sent for a six years' exile to Southern Russia. Bludof became a legation attaché. Zhukovski, after 1817, became a courtier, because he was commissioned to supervise the instruction in the Russian language and literature of Alexandra, the German-born wife of the Prince Imperial Nicholas. Very soon also the Tsaritsa Elizabeth, the somewhat neglected, sentimental and fragile consort of the Tsar Alexander, became interested in the gentle, bland poet, and dipped alternately into his elegies and into Tiedge's "Urania." From this time Zhukovski assumed a position which for Hans Christian Andersen would have been the realization of the ideal of happiness. He read aloud with never-failing applause his ballads and odes, his poems on grand birthdays and on the occasion of the birth of little princes and princesses of the royal family, in a circle of ladies of the family of the Tsar and of the court, whose real life he neither understood nor wished to understand, but who to him were supernatural beings,—"angels," "guiding stars," as he called them in his festal poems.

As he had already translated a number of notable European poems, among them Gray's "Elegy in a Country Churchyard," existing in all languages, and Bürger's "Leonore" (Liudmila), he now displayed to this circle of hearers an incredible productiveness as a translator: a large number of the poems of Goethe and Schiller, whole plays of the latter, like *Die Jungfrau von Orleans*, Byron's "Prisoner of Chillon," Moore's "Lalla Rookh," the Indian poem, "Nal and Damasjanti," Fouqué's "Undine," and Hebel's Allemanic poems, Homer's "Odyssey," and Rückert's "Rusten and Sohrab,"—all these different kinds of poetry with his subtile talent he transmuted into flowing Russian verse.

In 1821, on a journey to Germany, he contracted a friendship with Justinus Körner, whom he resembled in superstitious mysticism, and made a visit to Goethe, but without winning any favor from the old man. He was more agreeable to "the romanticist on the throne," Frederick William IV., who introduced him to Tieck, and also to other leaders of the German romanticism.

Some years after his return to Russia, a re-action towards all the youthful desires of Alexander I. for an enlightened despotism in the aid of progress ascended the throne in the person of Nicholas. Soon the tender Zhukovski, with painful astonishment, saw the best of the friends of his youth banished; others, less prominent, but still strong characters, leave the vicinity of the court, and isolate themselves in obscure silence on their estates. Nevertheless, when at this time a genius of Pushkin's rank turned around and extolled the victories of Nicholas over unhappy Poland, it will not astonish any one that Zhukovski issued from this crisis with firm faith that whatever the Tsar regarded as right is right.

After Pushkin's early death (1837), Zhukovski occupied the position of Russia's leading poet, distinguished at the imperial court in every manner, even appointed as the civil tutor of the Prince Imperial Alexander (afterwards Alexander II.). If he is now remembered with gratitude in Russia, it is, significantly enough, more on account of the humane influence he exerted on the young prince, who was admirably endowed by nature, than on account of his literary services. He dared to put in a word for many a political offender, whom a man who was not in so good standing or less courageous would never have dared to name, and he thereby accomplished a great deal of good. We see from Alexander Herzen's "Reminiscences," that he procured a considerable diminution of the burdens of exile for this great man, who as a youth was languishing in Viatka.[1] When Zhukovski, after 1840, took up his residence in Germany, where at the age of fifty-seven he married a girl of nineteen, who worshipped his talent, he had the affliction of finding out how the rule of his dear native country was hated and despised by all thinking men in the foreign land. The intellectual agitations of young Germany, and still more the revolution of 1848, shook him fearfully, and gave him the most melancholy pietism in all its force. He lived in Frankfort for some time in company with Gogol, in whom the re-action had already been accomplished which converted him from the wittiest and most caustic mocker of the Russian situation to a poor, sick admirer of absolute power and a mystic obscurantist, who lay for whole days prostrate before

[1] *Le Monde Russe et la Révolution. Mémoires de A. Hertzen*, ii. 154.

shrines. The two men constantly filled each other more and more with universal hatred of liberty and the personal feeling of their boundless sinfulness. They both ended as insane mystics.[1]

Zhukovski's life spans the whole of that of the epoch-making Russian poet. He prepares the way for Pushkin, becomes his friend, and ascends his vacant throne without being able to cause his predecessor to be forgotten. Zhukovski was sixteen years older than Pushkin, whom he survives for fifteen years. His importance vanishes by the side of the younger man, who began life as his and Derzhavin's imitator.

[1] *Aus der Petersburger Gesellschaft. Neue Folge*, p. 106 and following: *Litteratur und Press unter dem Kaiser Nikolaus.*

III

◆§ With Alexander Sergeyevitch Pushkin, Russian poetry becomes an independent power, just as it is with Goethe, Oelenschläger, or Victor Hugo. It no longer does duty for inculcating noble emotions or useful instruction; it is—in principle, at least—the handmaid neither of morals nor of patriotism. It stands erect, wild, and free.

Like the other leading Slavic poets of this period, Pushkin was greatly influenced by Byron, and had to go through this experience in order to become himself. He is very peculiar from the beginning from his violent temperament. He descends, on his mother's side, from the negro Hannibal, whom Peter the Great bought and educated in France as a civil engineer, and who died with the rank of general, possessing a good landed estate. The face of the author as well as his poetry plainly betrays the African blood in his veins. His father was a man of the world, educated in France, who had never spoken any other language than French, and who, in the fashion of the aristocracy, also caused his son to learn that language. Puskin was indebted to his nurse alone, a good Russian peasant woman, for his early and so fruitful acquaintance with popular ballads, *bilinî*, and fairy tales of Russia.

Precocious, dissolute at an early age, and then and for a long time a "dandy," he belongs to the not small number of artistic geniuses from the beginning of the century, whom an inner power, which no depravity destroys, preserved sound and capable of production in circumstances which would undermine and shatter weaker minds. What harm he suffered in his soul did not come from the wildness and irregularity in his life, but from the pressure of the political situation when his character was not developed, and even from the personal attempts of the Tsar Nicholas to win him, which the young aristocrat could not resist.

When he was only ten years old, Pushkin had devoured his father's French library, including Voltaire, Rousseau, and the Encyclopedists. From his twelfth to his eighteenth year, he went to the imperial school in Tsarskoye-Sielo, where the instruction and spirit were French—even the French language was taught to the pupils by Marat's own brother—where the instruction was very bad, and where the older students saw their ideals in the lieutenants of the Guard in the garrison, after whose example they kept mistresses, gambled, and played mad pranks. The young Pushkin was regarded as one of the worst madcaps of the school, but at the same time enjoyed a certain reputation for erotic and epigrammatic verses. In 1817 he got a position in the office of the Minister of Foreign Affairs, which he neglected, and plunged headlong into the whirlpool of St. Petersburg social life, apparently desiring no other honor than that of being a fully developed man of the world and aristocratic lion. How much importance, almost to his last days, he attached to the refinements of foppery is best seen in the description which he has given of himself under the name of Tcharsky, in his posthumous novel, "The Egyptian Nights." Like Byron, he did not wish in any manner to be regarded as a poet "by trade," very reluctantly spoke of literature, and, on the other hand, with great pleasure of horses, cards, and dinners, "although he could not tell a mountain horse from the Arabian, never remembered what was trumps, and, at heart, preferred fried potatoes to all the dishes of the French cook" ("Egyptian Nights").

In spite of all his dissipations, in 1820 he published his first poem, "Ruslan and Liudmila," which made an unusual sensation, although this fairy tale in verse, founded on a Russian legend, reminds one of Ariosto, of Wieland, and of Zhukovski, and has no other originality than that which depends on great skill in story-telling and careful composition. The poem passed for pure romance; it was interesting from a certain archness in its tone and a strong sensuousness in its color, but was otherwise without any psychological interest.

At this time, Pushkin fell into disgrace for the first time. As a young man, he had been a political revolutionary poet. An ode written by him, "To the Dagger," was sung in all the garrison towns of Russia, but probably without knowledge of the author's name. He detested the despotism which they were compelled to endure at the close of the reign of Alexander I., hated the idiotic censorship, which then weighed heavily upon poetry, and the rough rule of the police, to whose arbitrariness the young men beheld their welfare intrusted; and, witty as he was and with cutting sarcasm, he pierced the ruling persons and prevailing conditions with epigrams which circulated through the land. In 1820 the Governor-General of St. Petersburg complained of him to the Tsar for an "Ode to Freedom;" but Alexander read it without indignation, and only asked the young poet to let all his other manuscripts be laid before him. Unfortunately, among them there was a lampoon of the Tsar's favorite, Arakcheyef; and, indignant at this scornful treatment of a man whom he had treated with distinguished consideration, Alexander exiled the sinner first to Siberia, and then, on the intercession of many, to Kishenef in Southern Russia, as assistant secretary of the general-governor there. During his sojourn here, after an illness, Pushkin obtained leave to visit the Caucasus and the Crimea. The epoch-making impression of its natural scenery is plainly visible in his poetry. In the Caucasus, he became acquainted with Byron's poetry, and the impression of it became fused in his youthful mind with the impressions of the Caucasus, and the Byronic impression was even the more radical of the two. In Kishenef and Odessa, he gave offence by his wild life and his Byronic manners, and was already in bad odor with his superiors, when a private letter from him to St. Petersburg was intercepted, which described a young Englishman, a friend of Shelley's, with whom he had become acquainted, and in which he defended Shelley's so-called atheism. The result was a new exile. Pushkin was directed, under the supervision of the police, to reside on his estate Mikhaïlovskoye, in the department of Pskof.

As is well known, the six years' exile from St. Petersburg saved Pushkin's life. He would, no doubt, have taken part in the revolt of December, 1825, on the accession of Nicholas to the throne, if he had been on the spot. After the fearful result of the revolution and the annihilation of his nearest friends, when he resolved to petition the Tsar for the termination of his exile, he nevertheless humbled himself no more than to admit, in answer to the direct question of the Tsar, that his sympathies, on the 25th of December, had been on the side of the rebels. Among the few points of the Russian literary history which have become public property is the poet's promise of future loyalty to the Tsar, the embrace with which the Tsar responded to the pledge, and his own promise to Pushkin that he would protect him from the stupidity and chicanery of the censorship by being himself his censor in the future. Pushkin, who was confronted with the choice between reconciliation with the Tsar and his system or a lifelong persecution and exile, had not the strength of character that would have made compromise impossible.

His position in society as well as in the literary world was soon assured. The Tsar gave him a pension of six thousand rubles a year, with the task, which bore lightly on the poet, of writing the history of Peter the Great, and, at the same time, appointed him gentleman of the imperial bed-chamber. This appointment was regarded as very slight honor by the poet, who thought the title absurd and degrading for a man of his importance and reputation. He took part anew with *brio* in the "high life" of St. Petersburg, but was, in fact, secretly and heartily ashamed of the court favor he enjoyed while the friends of his youth were languishing in the casemates of fortresses and in Siberian mines, or living in exile in foreign capitals.

He stupefied this sentiment by taking refuge in the feeling of pride at the extent of Russia and its strength as a military power, which is not uncommon among eminent Russians. The former radical enjoyed the presentation of the Russian power of beating down resistance of every kind which came from the Poles, who had rebelled from their longing for independence, or from the nations of the West who sympathized with them in their love for freedom. It is thus that his "Ode to the Slanderer of Russia," written in 1831, must be understood.

However, he was too unlike his worldly-minded associates, among whom he was placed, too thoroughly original, too peculiar, proud, and sarcastic, too much admired and appreciated

by those who understood his genius, not to live environed by
irritated envy and hate. It was this hate which gratified itself
by defending the advances of the Franco-Dutch adventurer
Dantés de Hecheren to his wife, and which thus drove Pushkin
to an early death. The outburst of anger was, therefore, justi-
fiable, with which the younger generation in Russia, through the
voice of Lermontof, greeted the tidings of Pushkins' death in the
well-known duel.

Pushkin is the first modern person in Russian poetry; or, as
it could also be expressed, the first illustrious man in Russia who
had the courage to express his personality fully in poetry. In
contrast to his predecessors, he at once makes his appearance
while a youth, asserting himself without respect for tradition and
authority in literature, and he has, even when young, the stamp
of greatness on his forehead, style and power in his aspect as a
poet, which compel his contemporaries to greet him as a chief.
There is something manly about him, which even his opponents
do not fail to recognize. He belongs to the number of those who
are vituperated, assailed, envied, and hated, but whom no one
puts in the second rank. The combination of power and grace in
his language surpassed, in a very high degree, anything that had
been known before.

To a foreigner, much of his poetry now seems antiquated.
The overwhelming influence of Byron, under which he ripened,
can be seen too plainly in his shorter epic poems. Of the four
which he wrote between 1821 and 1824, "The Prisoner in the
Caucasus," "The Fountain in Bakhchisaraï," "The Brigand-
Brothers," and "The Gypsies," the first is the most pleasing from
its pictures of nature, the next two from a genuineness in the
poet's personal emotions, which is not affected by the close imitation of Byron's "Giaour," "The Prisoner of Chillon," and "The
Corsair." Pushkin's brigands certainly do not feel at all like real
brigands, but he has naïvely allowed his emotional life to find
free expression through them. "The Gypsies" stands the highest.
The fresh wildness with which the figure of the gypsy girl appears makes a very strong impression in comparison with the
lack of moral force in Alyeko, who flies from civilization and
brings one of its most disgusting vices with him: jealousy which

regards another being whom it has once loved as its own property. Probably, this fine poem has given Prosper Mérimée, who
has translated it, the idea of his masterpiece, "Carmen."

Like the Prisoner in the Caucasus, Alyeko suffers from the
Byronic spleen and scepticism. The poem "Count Nulin," which
assumes a lighter, more frivolous tone, again reminds us of Byron,
especially of "Beppo." In 1823, Pushkin, entirely under the influence of the English poet's "Don Juan," began his chief work,
"Yevgeni Onyégin," without any plan; and to it he constantly
returned for seven years, in order to express there a constantly
more characteristic poetical delineation of himself, and, above
all, a far more complete autobiography than is found in his other
poems. Finally, his great epic poem, "Poltava," is evidently inspired by Byron's "Mazeppa," although, regarded in and of itself,
it far surpasses the youthful poem of Byron in its power of picturesque description, and in the historically correct representation of the appalling character of the old hetman, which forms a
striking contrast to the romantic stamp Byron has given to the
figure.

With the exception of short lyrical poems and prose novels,
in which Pushkin stands independent, hardly a poem of his can
be named for which he did not have a model. His tales in verse
in the popular style, like the "Song of Oleg" (pronounced
Aleeokh) and his fairy tales are modernized *bîlinî*. Pushkin was
one of the first in Russia who made collections from the epic
songs of the people. His only great drama, "Borís Gudunóf,"
treated in such a masterly manner as to give great promise, is an
imitation of Shakespeare's historical plays, especially of Richard
III. and Macbeth. That this play is widely celebrated and greatly
admired, while Prosper Mérimée's *Les débuts d'un Aventurier*,
which with infinitely more originality and truth treats the same
theme, the rebellion of the false Dmitri, is almost wholly unknown, shows with how little justice literary fame is often
awarded. Finally, so far as Pushkin's ballads are concerned, they
are not only strongly inspired by Mickiewicz, but two of the
best known and most frequently translated, "The Three Budrys-
ses" and "Voyevods," are verbal translations from the Polish
poet, without expressly naming the latter. It may possibly have

been stated in some of the earlier editions of Pushkin's works, but in the edition for the people it is not mentioned, and in Bodenstedt's translation of 1855 the ballads are treated as Pushkin's, as a matter of course.

Necessarily a vigorous independence permeates the best of these metrical works, and even more the prose novels in which Pushkin took up and developed the Russian prose style created by the great historian Karamzín. In so far as Pushkin, himself sick, attains the high point of presenting the healthy, he possesses, in an extraordinary degree, the characteristic of a great artist. The artist is generally an outlaw, a living irregularity, a watch which goes now too fast and now too slow,—this may even be said of Shakespeare and Molière,—but his surprising quality therefore is that the product is healthy, obedient to law, a watch which goes right. So it is with Pushkin. As a man, he was only in too high a degree a child of the St. Petersburg civilization, a victim of society culture, a slave of fashion. As a poet, the more he is developed, constantly the more plainly does he show the nascent Slavic re-action against St. Petersburg and the hatred of all society culture, as well as of the foolish dominion of fashion which forms the fundamental passion in "Yevgeni Onyégin," and which has its clearest expression when Onyégin kills his best friend, the young Lensky, in a duel demanded by the conventionalities of society.

Intellectually Pushkin is far behind Byron, in whom no satiety exhausts the glowing enthusiasm for freedom, which was his life, and which led him to death, while Pushkin's youthful faith in freedom, when he came to man's estate, surrendered to a brutal patriotism. But he surpasses Byron in his ability to draw figures. His fine historical tale, "The Captain's Daughter," is the precursor of Gogol's "Taras Bulba;" and his admirable novels pave the way for the realistic representations of the coming generation in what is called by a Russian critic "the sentimental, naturalistic style."

How much nearer to my heart is Pushkin's successor, Mikhaïl Yuryevitch Lermontof! How much deeper, more intensively, does he act on a receptive mind! Never shall I forget the

impression his "Hero of Our Time," in Marmier's French translation, made upon me as a schoolboy. It was Byronism in its
strongest, most delicate essence, the greatness in this Caucasus to
which Lermontof was again and again banished,—greatness in
nature, greatness and frigidity in the hero's soul. It was the
Prometheus of the newer time, chained to the rocks of the Caucasus. It was courage, modesty, thirst for pleasure, feeling of
superiority, bound up in banishment, tortured by the eagle's
beak of a world-weary passion for scepticism.[1] How I loved and
admired this book, the first which I understood as a grown-up
man! How I sympathized with the poor Tscherkesserine Bela,
with the passionate and morbid Viera, and with the little Princess
Mary, all those women who love the hard and proud Petchórin;
and, in the next place, with the good old Captain Maxim Maximitch, whose admiring attachment Petchórin rewards with corresponding coldness! And in the preface to the book, the admirable
poem contributed by Marmier, which is so descriptive of Lermontof.

> *"Je te rends grâces, O Seigneur!*
> *Du tableau varié d'un monde plein de charmes,*
> *Du feu des passions et du vide du cœur,*
> *Du poison des baisers, de l'acreté des larmes,*
> *De la haine qui tue et de l'amour qui ment,*
> *De nos rêves trompeurs perdus dans les espaces,*
> *De tout, enfin, Mon Dieu! Puisé-je seulement*
> *Ne pas longtemps te rendre grâces!"*

Bodenstedt has given a description of Lermontof as he saw
him, the winter before his death, in a restaurant in Moscow: "A
young officer of middle height, with a stately, unconstrained
demeanor, and unusual elasticity in all his movements. He had
his neckcloth carelessly tied about the neck, his uniform was not
wholly buttoned up nor wholly new, but under it dazzling white
linen could be seen." He stooped down to pick up something
which he had dropped, says Bodenstedt, "with a suppleness as if
all the bones in his body were broken, although from his breast
and shoulders you would conclude that he had a reasonably

[1] Comp. Geo. Brandes: *Soeren Kierkegaard*, p. 120.

strong frame." And he describes the contrast between the great, sedate, expressive eye, and the mocking expression about the finely cut mouth, paints his cynicism in the use of language, his pleasure in showing himself superior to those present, and his sincere desire for reconciliation when he had offended any one.

What we admire in this description is that it not only vividly recalls Lermontof's own description of the "Hero of our Time," but that every single expression and turn corresponds to the place where Petchórin is introduced in the section, Maxim Maximitch. It reads thus: "He was of middle height, elegant and delicate; but his broad shoulders augured a strong frame, and, when you observed, you readily saw that nature had furnished him with power to endure the toils of a roving life, the influences of varied climates, the whirlwinds of life in the world, and the storms of the soul. His velvet jacket, carelessly buttoned, betrayed perfectly white linen, one of the criterions of a man of good taste. . . . When he sat down on a bench, it seemed as if his frame folded itself up, just as if he had no backbone. His whole bearing thus showed a kind of nervous weakness."

This parallel shows in what a high degree Lermontof had himself in mind in the representation of the person of Petchórin, and any one familiar with the whole work will easily see how much of Petchórin there is also found in the distracted leading characters in his two greatest poems, "The Demon" and "Ismael-Bey."

Lermontof [1] was born in Moscow. While yet a boy, he visited the wild, picturesque mountain regions of the Caucasus, absorbed Byronism, studied at the university in his native city, went through the school for gentlemen's sons at St. Petersburg, and left it as cornet in the hussar regiment, and while only a young officer was already known for wanton and indecent verse. The poem Hadji-Abrék, written in his early youth, is strong and harsh as a fantasy of Mérimée written in verse. In 1837 the twenty-three-year-old poet was for the first time exiled to the Caucasus and for a reason possible only in Russia, for his elegy on Pushkin's death, which simply expressed what everybody felt, the Tsar included, but in which Lermontof had shown the bold-

[1] Of the Scottish family of Learmont originally.

ness to call on Nicholas for vengeance on the murderer, who was one of the favorites of the Imperial Court—as he afterwards in the reign of Napoleon III. was one of the courtiers, best known for his shameless appearance in the Senate as the leader of Orthodoxy against Sainte-Beuve.

At the end of a year Lermontof was pardoned, and then lived for some time in St. Petersburg, where he was already highly esteemed as a poet. He published his "Song of the Tsar Iván Vasilyevitch, of his young chief of the life guard, and the bold merchant Kalashnikof." Pushkin had already tried his hand at giving the keynote of the old *bîlinî*, yet only in purely romantic poems. Lermontof reproduced the spirit of the historical and heroic *bîlinî* in a graceful little epic, sustained in the most correct style, which breathes the whole spirit of the age of Iván III., expressed with pure native simplicity. What an artist he was, this demon in human form, who as a boy was man, and who died in his youth after having produced works of undying importance.

And at the same time he wrote a host of short lyrical poems, in which his proud soul unreservedly exposes his stubbornness. Pushkin could yield, allow himself to be won over, compromise, become a patriot of brutality,—he, never! His friends disappointed and betrayed him. He continued faithful in friendship. Others were reconciled to what they hated. He continued faithful to himself in his hate. The greatness and elevation of his inner being exposed him ever and again to a fall. He continued to experience great emotions and to think freely. He was surrounded by spies, suspected when he was silent, accused when he spoke, denounced, slandered, hated, abandoned. He was always far greater and stronger than his fate. He never bowed the knee to Baal.

They reviled him for being a poor patriot. He answered: "I do indeed love my fatherland, but I can feel no enthusiasm for barbarity. I do not value that fame which is bought with blood, nor that proud confidence which relies on bayonets, and least of all in the glory of the heroes of antiquity." (The poem "My Fatherland.") And a similar outburst of contempt and dis-

gust for bloody honor ends the masterly battle-piece "Valerik."
How conventional does not Pushkin appear in comparison!

The most hidden emotions of Lermontof are revealed in the
collection "Little Conceits and Fancies." "They tortured him because he dared to think, stoned him because he dared to speak;
they could make no answer, and that was the sole cause of their
frenzy." "But he did not envy them their decorations, nor their
servility by which they were won. They robbed him of everything except his pride and his courage. He was on fire for the
beautiful, fought for the true. The others found that to be bad
and dangerous. When liberty is taken from him, long, solitary
contemplation changed his hate to boundless contempt. He knew
that a single prayer for mercy, a single repentant word, would
open to him all paths, but he would rather fall down in his chains
than say the one lying word which could save him. He does not
grudge the others their pleasures; he allows the others to deplore
his condition; he would rather suffer everything than be like
them."

In 1840 Lermontof was a second time banished to the Caucasus, for a duel with a son of the French minister, the historian
of literature, Barante. In principle he was opposed to duels, but,
as a nobleman and an officer, he could not free himself from the
laws of society which were honored about him. Shortly after he
left the capital, his romance, "The Hero of Our Time," appeared.
In this book several characters are found, the prototypes of
which could be found in the higher ranks of society of his day.
A comrade of Lermontof, Martynof, felt that he was insulted
in several places in the book. Probably he thought himself portrayed in the person of Gruzhnitski. When the poet, one day,
made a joke about him, the latter embraced the opportunity for
a challenge. In the duel which followed, Lermontof was killed,
on July 15, 1841, pierced through the heart. A memorial to him
was raised at Pyatigorsk, in the vicinity of which he fell.

There was a demon in him, a ruling spirit, hot and cold,
good and cruel, wild and tender; cherishing independence in defiance of everything above him, and to emancipation from everything which would cling to him. Young as Lermontof was, he

was often obliged to ask himself if he was not possessed of an evil spirit,—one which gained him women, who soon became a burden to him; one which laughed disdainfully at him, and mocked him, where others were moved pathetically. If he had lived more than the twenty-seven years which were vouchsafed to him, this question would not have troubled him more. He would then have felt that his powers were sound, his right secure, his nature rich and great, and that the source of his being was situated beyond the contrast between good and evil.

We have from him only the above peerless prose romance and several volumes of poems, in which there are several erasures, which are real gaps, made by the censor.[1] Of his "Stories for Children," we see that what we, for example, possess of the "Demon"—this poem which is so popular in Russia that the illustrations to it are to be seen on every wall, and that Rubinstein has made it the text of one of his operas—is in reality so little that, in the opinion of the poet, "there is not left a trace of the demoniac nature of the spirit." Nevertheless, how high does not this "Demon" stand above De Vigny's celebrated "Eloa."

The whole romance of the Caucasian country lives in this poetry,—nature and man saturated with a wild, heroic spirit, illuminated by youthful defiance, like lightning in lightning. No one describes so fascinatingly as Lermontof the solitary ride of a young Circassian prince through the mountain-paths of the Caucasus. No one like him has pictured a battle between the Cossacks and the Caucasians. Pushkin's battle picture in "Poltava" is powerful and pompous: it is a poet's fantastic reconstruction of a past. In Lermontof's "Valerick" every little trait has been experienced, seen, and reproduced in so striking and admirable a manner, that no other poem brings us nearer to him. We see him by himself, as he lies there before the battle begins, with the white tents of the camp stretched out before his eyes, while the Cossack horses, small and thin, stand with hanging heads by his side. We feel the sun burn, catch a glimpse of the Cossack sentinels, two by two, in the distance, hear the first bullets and

---

[1] The same imbecile censor who forbade all representations of women in statuary which "were not fully dressed,—that is, from the chin to the knees."

the first cries. And the more thoroughly we become acquainted with Lermontof as a man and as an author, the dearer he becomes to us.

It is emblematical that his life was a series of slights and exiles in a land where, as he himself has somewhere said, "no one comes forward, except those who go backward." His poetry produces its effect by its strong personal originality. He began, like all Russian authors, under foreign influences, particularly the German romanticism of terror,—a work of his youth has the title *Menschen und Leidenschaften;* afterwards, like the Poles and Pushkin, he looks up to Byron as the great poet of the age; but, although he dies so very young, younger even than Shelley, his manly and proud face stands out before us with pure and distinct features.

He was too much occupied with his own thoughts and his own affairs to be able to unfold the broad Russia to our gaze; he was a revolutionary romanticist, but still a romanticist. Shortly after him, or at the same time with him, new influences had begun to exert a force in Russian literature and intellectual life, which were destined to displace him and Pushkin.

IV

&§ With Gogol a new inspiration came to Europe from Russia. With him, authors ceased to describe themselves. He was wholly absorbed by his subject, and the reader no longer received the impression of the spiritual life of a man of the world and a cosmopolite, but of the national peculiarities of the subject as it was displayed in the soul of a genuine Russian. Gogol possessed an extraordinarily artistic talent, which two or three times rose to genius, but which speedily declined, because it was a genius without moral views, which was supported neither by culture nor character.

Nikolaï Vasilyevitch Gogol (1809–1852) was by birth a Little Russian, and as a child grew up in the midst of traditions of the bold and eventful Cossack troopers in the Ukraine. His father, an impoverished landed proprietor, possessed no mean capacities as a narrator and actor, which the son inherited from him. As a boy, he had already displayed a considerable power of observation of human stupidity and weakness.

In St. Petersburg, he tried without success the career of an actor, and then that of a government official, when, by the aid of Pushkin, he obtained a position as professor of history in the university. He utterly failed in this, on account of a lack of preparatory knowledge and defective education, and abandoned it for the profession of an author.

He made his *début* as a humorist,—a strong and confident humorist,—who used his talent on subjects of small compass, taken at first from the country life of Little Russia, which he knew so thoroughly, and then from the lower, poorer, gay, disorderly life in St. Petersburg. In these tales, he weaves into his pictures of real life a free imagination. That he starts from romanticism is shown by such tales as "King of the Spirits of Earth," "Notes of a Lunatic," or "The Nose." This last story, which is essentially a study after E. T. A. Hoffman, is the wildest *capriccio* on the theme: a suddenly lost and then regained nose, an ingenious and humorous story for children of an older growth, but without any deeper meaning. The celebrated history of the "Quarrel between Iván Ivánovitch and Iván Nikiforovitch" is a humorous, amusing story, well carried through in style, on the all-consuming spirit of frivolity and conceit in Little Russia, written in much the same style as Gottfried Keller later wrote his humorous stories about the faults and vices of the Swiss.

With the historical romance "Taras Bulba," which, in Russia, is of repute as an heroic epic, Gogol entered upon a new path. The narrative describes the heroic period in the Cossack world during the struggles for liberty against the Poles. But in spite of the greatness of the style and the realism with which this picture of a wild, extinct past is painted, the book has the common defects of historical romances. The idealism which, as a rule, has dictated them weakens their effect. That which is most beautiful in them is not true; we feel behind the whole description that he started out with the intention of glorification; we notice how the author puts opportunities in the way of this heroism, which in the middle of the battle displays itself in a single combat, and fastens upon it the gaze of all.

Among the longer and shorter stories in the first three volumes of Gogol there is not one which is out and out worthy of admiration, except "The Cloak." It is the simple story of a poor St. Petersburg official who through half his life has needed a Spanish Cloak, which he finally obtains, and from whom it is stolen. De Vogüe quotes a saying of a Russian author, "We have all grown out of Gogol's 'cloak.'" There is this truth in it, that the whole of the modern emotional Russian naturalism descends in the direct line from this little story. Dostoyevski's first book, "Poor Folk," may be named as having had its germ here.

Nevertheless, even this classical story does not give to the Western European reader the standard of Gogol's high rank as a modern author. That is done only by his play, "The Reviser," and the first part of the romance, "Dead Souls." It is the stinging satire and the bold fidelity to nature, expressed in a vigorous style, which here first betrayed Gogol's great superiority to the circumstances in which he was born, and which showed that Russian literature was ready to launch out into an entirely new field, which demanded boldness and originality to enter, and which this literature silently, as it were, pointed out to that of several other countries lost in romanticism, as the path which alone emerges from the world of dreams.

However Aristophanic the satire is in "Dead Souls," the theories on which this comic epic rests are so peculiar that they appear to the foreign reader like a story from another part of the world or from a remote age. Outside of Russia, even the cunning conceit about which everything in the story revolves can hardly be understood: the idea of the audacious speculator, of buying up dead serfs, who were still nominally counted as living, carrying them to a worthless tract of land, and then mortgaging them to a bank.

The drama, "The Reviser," on the other hand, is perfectly intelligible everywhere, and is as pointed as it is simple in its plot. More than twenty-five years were demanded to raise the Norse drama, under Henrick Ibsen, to this height; the German drama has not yet attained it.

It is said that it was Pushkin who gave Gogol the idea of "The Reviser." If so, he deserves just as much honor for it as for any finished work of his own of any kind whatever. For there is hardly a single play in modern literature which can compare with it in wit. But it is improbable that Gogol is greatly indebted to Pushkin for this. For a careful examination shows that his two great modern works, "The Reviser" and "Dead Souls," notwithstanding all the differences required by the forms of drama and romance, are alike in all essential points. In both, the fundamental defects of different ranks and types of a whole community are subjected to a test, in which all these men are brought in connection with a single person, a rather common but shameless sort of a being, before whom they stand as before a mystery they are not sure of having penetrated. In the play, this person makes, directly or indirectly, unusual claims upon them, because he is regarded by them as a superior officer sent by the government to inquire into their conduct, and whom, with their guilty consciences, they meet with bent backs and full hands. In the novel, this person makes an unusual proposal to them, because he offers them a bargain never heard of before,—the disposal of their dead souls; but in both cases he compels them to unveil their true characters and disclose their weakest points.

Nowhere else in the comic literature known to me is there found a more vigorous comic *dénouement* than that which is presented just after the disappearance of Khlestyakof with all the spoils he has secured and the recollections of the favors he has enjoyed from the ladies, when the coming of the real reviser is announced, and we feel that a day of judgment is breaking in upon the sinners who have just bought their freedom in the wrong place.

As is well known, the government had serious misgivings about allowing "The Reviser" to appear. Finally Nicholas gave his consent, and at the first performance burst into such laughter that he called the author to his box and said to him: "I have never laughed before as I have this evening."—"I had really aimed at another effect," was Gogol's manly answer.

And yet he did not himself comprehend the scope of his comedy; it was the product of a satirical genius, not of a conviction. With his deficient culture he was a Russian patriot in the sense that all the Russian institutions and peculiarities were good, viz.: absolute power, bureaucracy, suppression of all individual independence, and above all Greek Orthodoxy. When he became melancholy with his advancing years, it came over him that his principal satirical works were wicked, traitorous to his fatherland, and he bitterly repented of them. In 1846 he surprised the Russian reading world by the publication of his "Selected Correspondence," in which he declared war against the civilization of Western Europe, glorified re-action and obscurantism, nay, furnished a defence for serfdom.

In this condition of mind, to make amends for the first part of "Dead Souls," he wrote an unreadable second part, with purely virtuous persons. He became absorbed in theological meditations.

His friends in vain sent him abroad to travel to liberate him from his conceptions of the decadence of the heathen Western Europe. He journeyed from St. Petersburg to Wiesbaden, from Wiesbaden to Paris and Rome, and undertook a pilgrimage from Rome to Jerusalem. The revolution of 1848 finally made him an unconditional supporter and admirer of the system of government of the Tsar Nicholas and brought him to the highest degree of Orthodox fanaticism. Four years after he was found one winter day in Moscow, starved to death before a shrine, before which he was accustomed to lie for days in silent prayer.[1]

We pay little heed to the fact that a man like Gogol was a Little Russian. The reason for this is that, as soon as his son manifested a turn for poetry, his father gave him the decided advice to write only in Great Russian, and that Gogol followed his advice. Almost all the authors born in Little Russia, in view of the contempt with which their language has been treated as a peasant tongue, good for common people, in which they could only address themselves to a public of schoolteachers and popes, have written in one of the great neighboring languages, Russian or Polish. The Little Russians Padura, Tchaikovski, Groza, have thus in the beginning only written in their mother tongue and later in Polish. The same thing is also true of Bogdan Zabski.[2] For, however much the Polish language is set aside and suppressed, the suppression it endures is not like that which is used towards the Little-Russian tongue, against which a real war of extermination has by degrees been finally reached.

No single person has been hit harder in this war than Gogol's contemporary Taras Grigorovitch Shevtchenko (1814–1861), the greatest poet whom the Little-Russian people have ever produced. While the other poets in the Little-Russian dialect have built wholly upon the popular ballads of the Ukraine, appropriated them and carried them farther by adding individual personality, European culture, and artistic style, Shevtchenko alone,

---

[1] "Taras Bulba," "Dead Souls," "St. John's Eve and Other Stories," including "The Cloak," have been translated by Isabel F. Hapgood. (T. Y. Crowell & Co., N.Y.) Prosper Mérimée has made a masterly translation of "The Reviser" in French.

[2] See G. Brandes: Indtryk fra Polen, pp. 227.

although he is poet of the people above everything, has raised himself high above the level hitherto attained by the Little-Russian literature.

Shevtchenko was born in a village in the department of Kief, and was the son of a serf peasant who belonged to a rude German landed proprieter, Engelhard. At the age of eight he had a step-mother who tormented him, and at eleven he lost his father. He was sent to school to the parish clerk, a drunken scamp, who flogged the boy and treated him cruelly, for fear that he, by his rapid progress, would soon outshine him in knowledge and de-prive him of his bread. The boy ran away, roamed about homeless for some time, and then came a second time under instruction, this time under a servant of the church who painted shrines, in order to learn the art from him. This one also whipped him so inhumanly that he ran away and took a place as a swineherd in the village where he was born. Here his master's attention was drawn to the remarkable swineherd who could read and draw, and he took him into his personal service as bootblack and pipe-cleaner. When he was caught copying pictures with a stolen pencil, on paper also stolen, Engelhard had him punished with the knout; that was at least suitable for a serf. Nevertheless, when it became certain in many ways that the boy had talent, he sent him to a painting master in St. Petersburg, in hopes of getting the money he laid out on him richly repaid in due time. Here Shevtchenko began to draw with his own hand, awakened the interest of an artist, who recommended him to Zhukovski. The latter, ready and humane as he always was, took the young man's cause in hand. The first thing to be done was to buy his freedom. Engelhard asked twenty-five hundred rubles for this "soul." Zhukovski had his portrait, which the court-painter Brylof, who has been previously spoken of, was going to paint, sold by lottery and obtained the sum needed. In 1838 the emancipated serf began his studies in the Academy, and, having served his time, left it in 1844 to go to Little Russia to find there subjects for pictures and poems.

In the mean time, he had begun to write verse. In 1840 he had already published his first collection of poems, *Khobzar* (The Singer),—lyrical tendency poems, which with deep national feeling dwelt on the heroic memories of the Little-Russian people, their sufferings in the past and their hopes for the future. His anxiety for everything which could operate for the breaking-up of the monotony in the empire, manifested in this collection of poems, made the government withdraw all support from Shev-tchenko, and place him under the supervision of the police. The year after, he published his largest work, the Little-Russian epic poem, "The Haïdamáks," and still later several different smaller poems in the almanacs. In a poem called "Caucasus," he com-memorated an unfortunate friend of his, Count Balmén, who on account of his liberal views had been sent as a common soldier to the Caucasian army. For this imprudence Shevtchenko, in spite of his reputation, was condemned in 1847 to be whipped, and, after the execution of that sentence, to go as a common soldier to Orenburg. He was also most strictly forbidden to write.

At first he remained for some time in Orenburg itself, then in the fortress of Orsk; then he took part in an expedition to Lake Aral, and at last he was transferred to fort Nev-Petrovsk on the Asiatic shore of the Caspian Sea.

While still in Orenburg, he had again followed his irresistible impulse to write. Thousands of copies of his poems of freedom and vengeance, which then issued from his pen, were distributed in the Ukraine, and, during the time of the revolt in 1848, were printed in Galicia. A second time he was punished by the lash. It did not crush him. But in Nev-Petrovsk, whither he was last taken, and where the garrison was made up of the most worthless dregs of society, while the duty was the most arduous that can be imagined, and where neither a human being in whom the poet could confide, nor even a book or newspaper, could be found, he sickened, and slowly grew stupid.

When, after the lapse of seven years (1857), his admirers in St. Petersburg, especially Countess Alexis Tolstoï, at last obtained his discharge from the military service, the commander of the fort was able to support the petition by the statement, "The man is harmless." He went to St. Petersburg, and there wrote, with powers flaming up anew, a bitterly scornful poem, "The Brothers' Mission," against Russian Panslavism, which would free other people, but cruelly oppress the Slavic races in Russia, published several works anonymously, and wrote a short autobiography.

He was cured of the uncritical enthusiasm of his youth for the Cossack part of the Ukraine. "Hetmanship" had lost its romantic halo for him. Against the traditions of its nobility he now placed the idea of the amelioration of the peasants; and against the literary world of the Slavophiles, he proposed what they forgot or overlooked,—the severe distress of the people of Little Russia, the misery which thraldom and ignorance had brought upon them.

He died in St. Petersburg in February, 1861, and, according to his wish, he was buried in Kaniof in the Ukraine. However much ill he had personally suffered, however great was the persecution of the Little-Russian nationality to which he had been a witness, still he did not live to see what would have afflicted him more than any personal torture to which he had been subjected, —the prohibition issued in 1875, and constantly enforced down to the present time, against printing or publishing in the Russian Empire any kind of book or newspaper in the Little-Russian language.

Shevtchenko's poetry is thus not only the highest and richest expression which the race to which he belongs has attained in literature, but it is for the present its last expression. His gifts are varied; he wrote political lyrics, idylls, love poems, short sketches of society in verse, and a great historical epic in the spirit of the elder Dumas, which among the modern Slavic epics is surpassed only by Mickiewicz's incomparable "Pan Tadeusz." "The Haïdamáks" (that is, the Cossack warriors) treats of the last independent revolt of the Little-Russian popular spirit, the Cossack insurrection of 1770 under Gonta. It was directed against the nobility of Poland, who in those days oppressed the Ukraine in a cruel manner, and who, when it came to the point, were too imbecile and disorganized to defend themselves. But the Russian government, which was alarmed lest the disturbances should spread within the confines of Russia, determined to interfere. The leader of the Russian army, Romanzov, proposed to Gonta an alliance against the Poles, lured him and the officer next in command into an ambush, and immediately delivered them to their enemies. Then the Cossack army, which had been deprived of its leaders, was surrounded, captured, and fully eight thousand men were divided in crowds among the cities of Poland for execution. Gonta and the other chiefs were broken alive on the wheel, and all the common men without exception were executed in different ways. They generally preferred suffocation to hanging, on account of its convenience, and to save the trees. This is the subject which Shevtchenko, without going out of his way for horrors, has presented, describing the cruelties the oppressed were guilty of as fully as those which were inflicted upon them, even to the extent that his historic scene furnishes the background for the fate of a pair of lovers.

His little pictures of society, which are usually idyllic and emotional, are not wanting in marks of an energy which sees life as it is at its worst. In one of the best, "The Drowned," he tells the story of a mother and daughter who lived in a country village, and whose ghosts now on moonlight nights are seen hovering to and fro over the steppes along the banks of the streams. The mother was a Russian, proud and sensual, rich and beautiful, a young widow, who held a court for her admirers. She gave birth to the daughter secretly, and put her out to nurse in a poor Little-Russian peasant family. The daughter grew up, became an extraordinary beauty, and when the mother finally took her home, she received more attention in the rich house than the mother. When the latter became possessed with jealous hate, she gave her daughter poison, and when the poison did not result in death, she went with her to take a bath, seized her by her long braids of hair, and hurled her out into the eddies of the stream, where she met with death.

There runs through this poem the attempt to show the coarse and cruel traits of character in the Great-Russian race, without sparing the poet's own countrymen. But the vices he upbraids them for are the vices of the oppressed: self-abandonment and cowardice. Thus in the poem, "Taras's Night," the singer narrates for the Little-Russian youth of the country the achievements of the great hetman, Taras Triasylo. The circle listen with tears in their eyes. But immediately after the listeners begin to sing and dance with happy recklessness. Then the singer shouts to them, "Lie behind the stove; it is warm and safe! I will go to the inn and make jokes about the Poles and Muskovites. Will you go with me? That you can still do. But you can no longer have any spirit." [1]

The history of Russian literature counts martyrs and apostles in great number. The life of Shevtchenko is a prolonged martyrdom; among the other great men of Russia who bore their part of the martyrdom is the apostle of activity who first attracted the attention of posterity. A long time imprisoned, twice exiled, and finally banished, Alexander Ivánovitch Herzen (1812–1870) is the apostle of the new times for Russia.

He is, as a spirit, among the Russians of this century, what the year 1848 is among the years of the century. He is the year 1848 in human form, an incarnation of all the ideas which that year came to the front, and of all the noble struggles for liberty which were then set in motion.

Herzen's father was a rich Russian *grand seigneur*, Yakovlef, a retired captain of the Guard, with a colossal fortune, who had received his whole culture from his journeys in Western Europe, —a disciple of Voltaire, who read only French and spoke it better than Russian. His mother was a young lady, the daughter of a tradesman, Louise Herzen, from Stuttgart, who, at the age of seventeen, consented to accompany the rich Russian gentleman who had won her heart to his home in Moscow, and who was always treated as his wife, although no marriage ceremony had taken place between them. The son was born a few months before the French troops marched into Moscow, and it was the great event in his father's life that Napoleon, who was in want of a messenger to the Tsar, sent for the Russian nobleman, who was of old known to his Marshal Mortier, and gave him a letter, "To my brother, the Tsar Alexander," and gave him safe conduct out of the burning city.

His father developed constantly more and more into a bitter, reserved, aristocratic eccentricity, wholly absorbed in a boundless contempt for the human race. His mother was an unhappy, soli-

---

[1] Pypin: *Geschichte der Slavischen Litteraturen*, i. 480 K. E. Franzos: *Von Don zur Donau*, i. 85-126. Selected pieces of Shevtchenko have been translated into German by J. G. Obiest.

tary creature, with intellect and heart. In the son, the qualities of parents and ancestors were so mingled as to amount to genius.

He has written his life,—reminiscences in three volumes,— and his work ought not to be neglected by any one who takes an interest in the struggle for the development of modern Russia. There is no better insight accessible to us. With artistic clearness, with the unreservedness of an author of memoirs, Herzen has told, not only the life of his boyhood and youth to his thirty-fifth year, but he has given the description of a superior, incisive, and penetrating observer of the social, political, and literary conditions of Russia between 1812 and 1847, and especially of the reign of Nicholas. The observer of the conditions is also the victim of them; yet he has no pity for himself, and when he can he uncovers the humorous side of his misfortunes. But with withering scorn, with an indignant, harrowing contempt for the throne, with a heart which moans and bleeds, he spreads before the eye of the reader the heartrending cruelty which proceeded from the throne of the Tsar, and all that spirit of thraldom, corruption, and stupidity which made such a rule possible.

He never dwells upon the horrible, and yet it is a question if even Dostoyevski's Recollections of the Dead House in Siberia contain pictures which fill one with a deeper sense of terror. (See, for example, about the torture in the prisons.) [1]

With Herzen and his friends, modern knowledge and modern philosophy force their way into the Russian Empire. He and his fellow-students were first inspired by the languid liberalism of Lafayette and Benjamin Constant, and then, after the suppression of the Polish revolt of 1831, went through a rigorous course of Saint-Simonism. At the age of fifty, Herzen writes in his reminiscences on this subject, "A new age knocked at the door; our souls, our hearts were opened to its coming. Saint-Simonism laid the foundation for our convictions, and constitutes, even at the present time, an essential part of them." The young men were inspired by the two fundamental ideas: the calling of woman to share in the common duties, and what they at that time called "the justification or the honorable satisfaction of the flesh." An idea, says Herzen, to which people with an imagination which

[1] *Mémoires de Herzen*, i. 290 and following.

reminds one of the imagination of lewd monks have wanted to give a low and cynical interpretation, but which, in reality, only means dethronement of Christianity, the religion of beauty and life, which supplanted the religion of asceticism and death.[1]

From the fact that some other students, with whom this group of young men had no connection, late one evening, at the instance of a member of the secret police, had sung a song in which some abusive language could be taken as pointing at the Tsar, Herzen, his friend and late companion-in-arms the poet Ogaref, and many others equally innocent, were first kept in prison for months, and then sent away. Herzen was first exiled to Vyatka, on the Siberian frontier, where he happened to fall under a governor by the name of Tiufayef, who most resembled a wild and malignant beast, and afterwards to Vladimir, only a day's journey from Moscow. On the way to his exile, he became thoroughly acquainted with the Russian situation in its worst aspects, among other things falling in with a convoy of eight wagon-loads of small Jewish boys, the most of them between eight and ten years of age, who were sent to military colonies; a third part of them had already died on the way.[2] From Vladimir, Herzen eloped with his young cousin, whom he had loved for many years, and whom they had endeavored to prevent from marrying him. In her society, he passed the fifth and last year of his exile, and lived happily for many years, until their marriage relations came to a tragic end in London. George Herwegh here, for a short time, won the heart of the young Russian; but she died of a broken heart in consequence of her infidelity to her first and, in reality, her only love. A letter of Turgenief to Saltykof, dated January 19, 1876, shows that there exists an unprinted account, written by Herzen, of the bitterest catastrophe of his life.

On his return to Moscow, Herzen found the youth filled with Hegel's philosophy. When he saw that he was regarded as outside of agitations, he devoted himself to the encyclopædia, logic, the science of phenomena, æsthetics; studied and canvassed them paragraph by paragraph; at last, he devoured every single Hegelian writing he could obtain, from the nearest disciples of

---

[1] *Mémoires de Herzen*, i. 236.
[2] Comp. G. Brandes: *Indtryk fra Polen*, p. 67.

Hegel to the liberal Hegelian Arnold Ruge. Herzen interpreted the teachings of the master entirely in the spirit of the young Hegelians. While others, as, for instance, the great critic Byelinski, Herzen's intimate friend, accepted in a purely conservative spirit the well-known sentence from the preface to the "Philosophy of the Right," "That which is reasonable is real, and that which is real is reasonable," so that they only found in it the justification of the Russian absolute power, with all the crimes which flourished in its bosom, Herzen saw in it only the simple expression of the principle of *the adequate cause*, broke with Byelinski, until he—for that matter very soon—gave up his quietism, and, on his side, found in Hegel's philosophy an algebra of revolution, which freed the spirit by not leaving one stone upon another of the Christian world of tradition. And when Ogaref brought him Feuerbach's "Spirit of Christianity," on reading this work, he felt himself at once wholly emancipated. And in his first philosophical enthusiasm he wrote the series of articles which he published in 1842, with the title, "Dilettantism in Knowledge," by Iskander (that it, Alexander).

Shortly before Herzen's return from exile, Tschaadayef had published the celebrated "Philosophical Letters" about the insignificance of Russia to European culture, its everlasting coming too late. To punish him for this, he was declared and treated as insane by the Tsar. Byelinski, "the Lessing of Russia," already far gone in consumption, which carried him off when only thirty-eight years old, now began his impassioned literary campaign with the official world and the official literature. When "The Annals of our Fatherland," appeared on the 25th of each month, the whole cultured youth were in a fever to get hold of the thick volume. They were continually asking during the whole forenoon, in the cafés, if the number had come; as soon as it arrived, they tore it open with the question, "Is there anything of Byelinski's in it?" If only one page was found of his, it was devoured eagerly and debated in endless discussions.

His fire, his sarcasm, his sneers, his unmaskings enchained all, and people flocked together where he swung his whip, as if to see an execution. Almost on his death-bed, he attacked his disciple Gogol for his back-sliding. As the disciple of the culture of Western Europe, he cut down pedants and Slavophiles. When he died, his friends were forbidden to place an epitaph at his grave. The newspapers were forbidden to mention his name, and the prohibition has remained in force for full eighteen years.

It fell to Herzen's lot to carry Byelinski's literary purification and reformation into the political arena. He was admirably consituted for such a contest, which was to endure for many years. He was not spindling and weak like his friend, but large and broad-shouldered, a powerful frame, and not poor and therefore dependent, but after his father's death he was in possession of what, even by Russian standards, would be regarded as a large fortune. Thus, all that was needed was that he should obtain leave to pass over the Russian frontier, so that, with solid ground under his feet, he could use his great talent as a writer in shaking up Russia in all its joints.

He was the creator of a public sentiment in the Russian Empire.

In Paris, where he first took refuge, he formed a league with the party of the French socialists and the Polish emigrants. What he felt when the great storm of insurrection burst over Europe, and when one popular revolt after another was suppressed, all the promises of kings and pope were broken, and contra-revolutions were victorious along the whole line, is shown by his two books, written in the most fascinating style, "From the Other Side of the Stream," and "Letters from Italy and France." They were published anonymously in 1850, and first in German, having been translated by Frederick Kapp, who subsequently became the well known German-American historian, and who at that time was a tutor in Herzen's house. It is sixteen years since I read these books, and they are not now at hand, but the impression is as vivid now as when I first read them. Never has manly political enthusiasm found a more elegant or more lucid expression, and never have disappointment and contempt spoken in more energetic language.

From Paris Herzen went to London, and there, during the

Crimean War, established his liberal "Russian Press," and published in London from 1857 to 1865, and in Geneva from 1865 to 1869, his celebrated weekly paper, *Kólokol,* whose overwhelming influence in Russia has been previously spoken of, as well as the manner in which this influence was destroyed by Katkóf.

The same year in which Alexander Herzen went into exile, he published a novel, which is still worth reading, less for its literary value than on account of the movements to which it gave rise in Russia. It is the romance "Who Is to Blame?" (1847), an indirect attack on marriage as an institution, dedicated to the author's wife "with hearty devotion." The book is written without any regular plot, with a long-winded introductory historical sketch, several digressions, and without style; but the characters are living as in the better novels of George Sand. The theme is substantially as follows: The peaceful, happy marriage between the calm and amiable teacher Kruziferski and his elegant wife Liubonka is disturbed when the young, talented but idle man of the world, Beltof, comes within the sphere of these two married people. Without any guilt on the part of either, Beltof and Liubonka are irresistibly attracted to each other, understand each other, need each other, and cannot do without each other. They strive to conquer their passion, but Beltof tears himself away in vain; he drags himself off on journeys to no purpose, Liubonka wastes away, Kruziferski takes to drink and is ruined.[1]

The idea embodied in this book grew luxuriantly, since, in 1863, the man who may be regarded as Herzen's great intellectual heir, and for a time as inheritor of his influence, published his celebrated novel, "What Is to Be Done?"

Nikolaï Gavrilovitch Tchernuishevski was born in 1829, the son of a pope in Saratof on the Volga, and was first destined for the clergy, but soon gave up theology for the study of ancient and modern languages, and, in 1846, began his career as a philologist in the university of St. Petersburg. After passing his examinations, he became Professor of Literature in the Cadet School in St. Petersburg, but soon after, at the desire of his mother, who could not bear to be separated from him, he accepted a position

---

[1] *Vom andern Ufer: Briefe aus Italien und Frankreich,* Hamburg, 1850. *Wer ist Schuld?* Reclam's *Bibliothek.*

as teacher in the grammar school in his native town. Here he was married at the age of twenty-two. After his mother's death in 1853, he returned to the capital, wrote a thesis on the relations of art to nature, but in his oral defence gave utterance to such radical ideas that the minister of education refused him his diploma.

From 1853 to 1862 he wrote for Niekrásof's newspaper, *Sovremennik*, a large number of articles and discussions of an economical, critical, and historical character, which, from their way of treating the problems, and by their ironic, satirical tone, awakened the greatest attention. Tchernuishevski presented and criticised John Stuart Mill's "Political Economy," the æsthetic criticism of the Gogolian period, the party quarrels in France during the Restoration, Lessing and his age, etc., treated with the same superiority subjects of widely different kinds, but had his principal interests centered on the solution of certain great social problems,—the arrangement of the relations between the sexes, the abolition of serfdom, the abrogation of all individual property in land for the good of the community.

Everything that he wrote was passed by the censor. But in July, 1862, to the astonishment of all, Tchernuishevski was arrested, and kept in custody in the Petro-Pavlovsk prison, on the island of Neva, until May, 1864.

On the 24th of May, 1864, about eight o'clock in the morning, in a pouring rain, a great crowd of men was collected in St. Petersburg around a scaffold with a pillory surrounded by soldiers in a hollow square. Presently the wagon which was expected drove up, escorted by gendarmes on horseback, and out of it alighted first a general and then a pale man, dressed as a civilian. The latter ascended the scaffold, where two men with red caps took him by the arms, hung a black plate over his neck, on which his sentence was written in white letters. Then one of the executioners took his hat off his head so that he should listen reverently to what was to be read to him.

It was his indictment. It was long enough; closely printed, it fills over six hundred lines; it took more than an hour to read. But it would be difficult to find a legal document with less foundation for its charges.

"Several circumstances," it says, "have pointed out to the government the said Tchernuishevski as an agitator dangerous to the State." These circumstances are: first, an anonymous letter sent to the Third Section (the secret police). This letter, which is quoted at length with all its vulgarity and stupidity, calls upon the government to free the people from Tchernuishevski. In the second place, an intercepted letter from the exile Alexander Herzen, in which is found, "We intend to publish *Sovremennik* here or in London with Tchernuishevski." For these two things Tchernuishevski was imprisoned. Now follows in the indictment the list of the papers "belonging to the case," that is, a letter from the accused to his wife, in which he says that they both belong to history, so that their names will be known for centuries, and the production of a newspaper article from 1853, which was now in 1862 found to be dangerous.

In all this, however, there is no foundation for any legal proceedings. But while the accused is in prison, in March, 1863, they were fortunate enough in the Third Section to obtain possession of a letter from a certain Kostomarof to one of his friends, in which it is said that "Tchernuishevski had written the appeal to the serfs." As proof of the truth of this contention, a note found in the pocket of Kostomarof is read, which, observe, was when he had already been a long time in prison, sentenced, ready to be sent away to exile, and in which he is asked to correct a misprint. The note is signed "Tcher." The secretaries of the Senate, before whom this letter was laid, were not able, it is true, to find any resemblance to Tchernuishevski's handwriting as a whole, even admitting that, when the letters are taken separately, twelve of the twenty-five letters resemble his to a certain extent; but the Senate *in pleno* found the resemblance striking. With incredible ease it is said, in the next place, that a *copy* of Tchernuishevski's proclamation to the peasants has been found in the possession of Kostomarof, although no original is forthcoming, and although the style bears no resemblance to that of the great author. And, in conclusion, a letter is read, full of scratches and erasures, which comes from the Third Section, and which is presumed to be from the accused, since it is signed "Tsch," and directed to one Alexis Nikolayevitch, who is presumed to be the poet Pleshcheyef, whose Christian name has the same sound. Tchernuishevski firmly denied having written this letter, which, moreover, would have been entirely innocent in any other place than Russia and modern Germany. Pleshcheyef denied before the court not less firmly that he had received it; but they were not believed. It was regarded as a proof of the attempt of the accused to stir up the serfs, and his culpability is increased by his obstinate denial.

"As guilty of participation in a conspiracy for the destruction of the present political arrangements, N. G. Tchernuishevski, thirty-five years old, is sentenced to fourteen years' hard labor in the mines, and then to exile to Siberia for life."

Immediately after it was announced to him that the Tsar in his mercy has commuted the fourteen years' hard labor to seven. Then he received an order to kneel down. They broke a sword over his head, and chained him for some minutes to the pillory. A bouquet of flowers falls down at his feet. The bouquets which follow are thrown into the air by the police. He is taken to the wagon, and vanishes. . . .[1]

He vanished, never more to be seen among those who admired him, and who were indebted to him for the best part of their intellectual culture. He passed his seven years among the criminals in the mines underground, then fifteen years more in solitary exile in one of the most distant points of Siberia, without books, without men with whom he could exchange ideas, cut off from all communion with Europe. A year or two since they at last found the prisoner sufficiently subdued by his martyrdom of more than twenty years. They transferred him to a milder place of banishment, and allowed him to occupy himself in a harmless manner by translations and similar things.

He is now and then visited there by some faithful admirers, who dare to expose themselves to the odium which follows upon such visits; and I know of nothing more significant of the contentment into which public opinion has sunk in Russia, than the satisfaction with which those who have seen him express their

[1] *L'économie politique jugée par le science. Critique des principes d'économie politique*, de John Stuart Mill par N. Tschernuischevski. Bruxelles, 1874, i.–xxxvi.

impressions on their return: "Tchernuishevski is well," they say generally; "he is not entirely broken down intellectually; *he translates from the German.*" It has gone so far in Russia that when a genius, who was the honor of the nation and the pride of the youth, after having been abused for a quarter of a century with the coarsest cruelty, has, nevertheless, not become an idiot, they then do not think much more of what has happened; they feel entirely satisfied with the result,—feel about as if they had made a bet with the government, and, in all probability, had won it.

Even one who is not competent to judge of the value of Tchernuishevski's economical work will read with pleasure his critical treatise on Mill's "Political Economy." The urbanity of the tone, the crystal clearness of his description, and the richness of his pertinent psychological observations, enchain an outsider. But the three-volume novel of Tchernuishevski, which was written in prison (finished April 4, 1863), "What Is to Be Done?" has had a far more important influence.[1]

It is not that the book is a fine poetical production, nor even poetical at all in the true sense of the word. It is highly intellectual and liberal, a thorough and free development of the man's views of life, so far as he could develop them in a manuscript which must pass under the inspection of the prison authorities and of the censor before it could reach the printing-office.

Strange as it may seem to the reader, a radiant good humor pervades the book, which only towards the end becomes long-winded and tiresome, partly because everything must be expressed so indirectly, frequently in a far-fetched manner, partly because the poor prisoner at the last felt far too great need of light and air and freedom and men.

The work was intended and was received as a gospel for the modern Russia. It was intended to point the way out of the conflicts which are occasioned in one direction by the regulation of the sexual relations, and in another direction by the whole economical disorder of society. "What Is to Be Done?" is a sort of bastard between a novel and a treatise on political economy; it

[1] In French, *Que Faire?* In German, *Was Thun?* (Brockhaus, 1883). In English, "A Vital Question" (T. Y. Crowell & Co.).

descends on the female side from George Sand and on the male from Karl Marx.

Books of this kind have apparently been written before. In tendency it has a resemblance to the "Jacques" of George Sand, in its story it also reminds one strongly of a much older romance, namely Jean Paul Richter's *Leben, Tod und Ehrestand des Armenadvokaten Siebenkäs*. But still there is no book of this kind in the literature of the world, and no work in the whole Russian literature is more Russian.

The argument can be stated in a few lines: The medical student Lopukhóf marries Viera Pávlovna for love. They live happily together for a long time. After the lapse of some years she falls in love with his comrade, Kirsánof. Lopukhóf, with whose notions it does not agree to stand in the way of two lovers, apparently commits suicide and disappears; he travels under another name to America, returns home some years later, marries another woman, and continues to live in friendly relations to his former wife and her husband.

There are many most excellently drawn subsidiary characters, who take part in the story, who are grouped around the leading persons. The form of the narrative is personal to the highest degree. Every moment the author addresses himself directly to the reader, humorously makes the ordinary excitement of a novel impossible, by telling far in advance everything which is going to happen, pokes fun at the reader's consternation at the immorality of the narrator, telling him that it is even far greater than it appears to be. But in truth this is not at all a story, but is in all respects a treatise on social morals. Much which wearies a modern reader, the description of Viera's sewing establishment, where every sewing-girl shares in the receipts, and much more of the same kind, is for Tchernuishevski only the means of proclaiming that socialism which he regards as right and promising for the future. He cannot proclaim his ideals directly. A careful reading will show that all the Russian ideas of progress and all the Russian Utopias are contained in this book.

On a hasty reading one understands nothing at all of this. The book was not written for the superficial reader. By an artistic circumlocution the poor prisoner must inform the reader of his ideas of how the world of the future will come to look. When he cannot do it any other way, he lets his heroine fall asleep and tells us her dreams in regular dream pictures, with symbolical meaning in great poetical visions, the description of which sometimes fills over thirty pages in succession.

Thus everything is combined in this book which is most thoroughly characteristic of Russia: the broadly constituted nature, the proud frankness, and the radical disposition to go to the end of the rope; strong influences from foreign lands, and independent originality, lively sense of reality down to the dry prose and penetrating fanatical mysticism.

When the foreigner in Russia, after repeatedly asking if this or that person is prominent, gifted, remarkably interesting, or the like, and after continually receiving a negative answer, at last demands impatiently, "Who, then, in the whole world is gifted?" then it will happen to him again and again to receive from the most different directions the melancholy answer, "Tchernuishevski was."

He will understand this answer when he has read attentively all that is accessible from the pen of this great man, whose name they do not even dare to print in Russia.

V

~§ October 28, 1818, there was born in the department of Orel, in an old noble (originally Tatar) family, the man to whom, down to the very latest time, the cultured classes in the German and Latin countries are indebted for almost all they know of the inner life of the Slavic races of our day.

No earlier Russian author has been read in Europe like Iván Sergeyevitch Turgenief; he is to be regarded rather as a cosmopolitan than as a Russian author.

He opened up to the European public a new world of subjects, but he did not need the collateral interest which his work gained for him thereby; for it is the artist and not the describer of culture which Europe has admired in him. Although he has hardly been read out of his own country in his own language, he has everywhere, even in those countries which possess the most taste, been placed on a level with the best authors of the land. He has been read everywhere in translations, which necessarily distort or diminish the impression of his superiority; but the perfection of his originality asserted itself so strongly in the various more or less happy forms in which his books were cast that any want of delicacy and clearness was overlooked. Great authors, as a rule, work most effectively through their style, because by this they come into personal contact with the reader. Turgenief made a very deep impression, although the reader who was not a Russian could appreciate only the coarser qualities of his style, and could scarcely imagine with what elegance he was wont to express himself, and would be just as far from understanding his allusions as from being able to compare his interpretation and description of persons and ways of thinking in Russia with the reality from which they were taken. Turgenief conquered in the artistic race, although he was heavily handicapped; he was triumphant in the great arena, although he wielded a sword without a point.

For the cultured people of Western Europe, he has peopled the great empire of the East with human beings of the present time. Thanks to him, we know the spiritual characteristics of its men and women. Although in the vigor of his age he left Russia, never again to dwell in his native land, he has never described anything else than the inhabitants of this country, and Germans and Frenchmen only as half Russianized or even only in contact with Russians. He only presents to us beings with whose peculiarities he was familiar from his youth. That gradually, during his long exile and the estrangement which existed between the Slavophile and European Russians, it came to be regarded as proper, in certain Russian circles, to depreciate his knowledge of his fatherland, and treat him as a kind of Western European, was natural. But, if he had been a degree less cosmopolitan, he certainly would never have made his way into the whole civilized world as he has done.

He has given pictures from the forest and the steppes, from spring and autumn, from all ranks and classes of society, and all grades of culture, in Russia. He has drawn the serf and the princess, the peasant and the proprietor, and the student; the young girl who is pure soul, endowed with the finest Slavic charms, and the cold, beautiful, egotistical coquette, who in his hands seems to be more irresponsible in her heartlessness than anywhere else. He has given a rich psychology of a whole human race, and has given it with a mind greatly excited, but yet so that his mental agitations do not in any way disturb the transparent clearness of the descriptions.

Of all the prose writers of Russia, Turgenief is the greatest artist. Possibly, it depends upon the fact that he is the one of those who has lived most in foreign lands; for if his long residence in France has not increased the stock of poetry which he brought with him from his home, yet he has plainly learned there the art of setting his pictures in frame and glass.

A broad, deep wave of melancholy flows through Turgenief's thoughts, and therefore also through his books. However sober and impersonal his style is, and although he hardly ever inserts poems in his novels and romances, still his general narrative makes a lyrical impression. There is so much feeling condensed in them, and this feeling is invariably sadness,—a peculiar, wonderful sadness without a touch of sentimentality. Turgenief never expresses himself wholly emotionally; he works with restrained emotion; but no Western European is sad as he is. The great melancholy authors of the Latin races, like Leopardi or Flaubert, have harsh, firm outlines in their style; the German sadness is glaringly humorous or pathetic or sentimental. The melancholy of Turgenief is, in its general form, that of the Slavic races in their weakness and sorrow, which comes in a direct line from the melancholy in the Slavic popular ballads.

All the later Russian poets of rank are melancholy. But with Turgenief it is the melancholy of the thinker who has understood that all the ideals of the human race—justice, reason, supreme goodness, happiness—are a matter of indifference to nature, and never assert themselves by their own spiritual power. In "Senilia," he has represented Nature as a woman, sitting clad in wide green kirtle, in the middle of a hall in the depths of the earth, lost in meditation.

" 'Oh, our common mother!' he asks, 'what art thou thinking of? Is it on the future fate of the human race? Is it on the necessary conditions for its reaching the highest possible perfection, the greatest possible happiness?'

"The woman slowly turns her dark, piercing, dreadful eyes towards me; her lips half opened and I heard a voice which rang as when iron comes in contact with iron.

" 'I am thinking how I can give the muscles of the flea greater power so that it can more easily escape from the persecutions of its enemies. There is no equilibrium between the attack and defence: it must be restored.'

" 'What!' stammered I, 'is it that you are thinking of? But we, the human race, are we not your children?'

"She wrinkled her eyebrows imperceptibly.

" 'All animals are my children,' said she; 'I care equally for them all, and I exterminate them all in the same manner.' "

Here you have his character of melancholy. When Gogol

is melancholy, it is because he is indignant; when Dostoyevski is so, it depends upon the fact that he is dissolved in sympathy with the ignorant and the obscure, with the saint-like, noble, and pure of heart, and almost even more with sinners both male and female; Tolstoï's melancholy has its root in his religious fatalism. Turgenief alone is a philosopher.

It will also be found that the other great poets have had a turning-point in their lives when they have been seized by a religious excitement which has given a new stamp to their career, according to their own interpretation a new consecration and a new earnestness, but which also operates greatly to hamper and diminish their poetic descriptive powers, nay, generally a little sooner or later it entirely destroys their poetic gifts. This turning-point comes in some cases from an independent conversion, and in others when they are filled with a national or a national religious mysticism. The disposition to such mysticism makes its appearance in this century as a common Slavic trait. It attacked in the Polish literature, in the forties, Mickiewicz, Slowacki, Krasinski, Zaleski, and others when Towianski and other dreamers made their influence felt. It has prevailed in Russian literature, in different forms, with men of so great ability as Gogol and Dostoyevski, and manifests itself, last of all, with Tolstoï—as it would seem, under the influence of Zhutayef.

Only for Turgenief, with his quiet contemplation, even religious enthusiasm is a theme like any other, although he, too, in "Clara Militch" and "The Love Song of the Conquering Lovers," pays his tribute to the mystical. He treats religious enthusiasm without losing his equilibrium. We recall, for instance, his Sophie Vladimirovna from "A Strange Story," the young girl of good family, who accompanies a wandering saint out into the world.

His melancholy, therefore, is less religious than philosophical; but it is that of the patriot who has become a pessimist. In spite of all his seeming cosmopolitanism, he was a patriot, but a patriot who mourned over his fatherland and despaired of it. He was attacked for this. Dostoyevski tried to make him ridiculous in the figure of Karmásinof in "The Possessed." He did not, indeed, lack confidence in the future of his fatherland; he admired its language and certain parts of its literature so much that he inferred therefrom what abilities the people must possess who had produced such results. But he did not share in the enthusiasm of his more simple and ignorant countrymen for the Russian people as such. He did not find their past history great.

Turgenief somewhere describes his dejection when at one of the great world's exhibitions he got an exact perception of how insignificant Russia's contribution was to industrial inventions, and he added bitterly, "We have invented nothing but the knout." His career as an author shows that the history of the more recent developments of his country was far from inspiring him with confidence.

Iván Turgenief lost his father early (1834), Col. Sergeï Nikolayevitch (of that Turgenief family which had already given two distinguished men to Russia), and suffered from the imperious and cold-hearted rule of his mother. But he was brought up in country quiet, on the family estate Spasskoye, and at an early age felt the most vital love for nature as well as the most passionate hatred to serfdom, whose unhappy results were constantly before him.

He studied first at the University of Moscow and then at that of St. Petersburg, travelled in 1838 to Germany and like Katkóf and Bakunin listened to lectures on philosophy and history at the University of Berlin (by Michelet, Werder, Ranke, and others). After several years' residence in foreign lands he returned home as a supporter of Western European liberal thought, was given a position in the department of the Minister of the Interior, but retired from the office at the end of a year, to live the free life of a Russian landed proprietor and huntsman.

He published his first hunting stories in 1847; then followed from 1847 to 1851 the others, which in 1852 appeared collected as "Recollections of a Huntsman," and created an epoch-making sensation. He at first began with things in verse like Byronisms and romanticisms, unsuccessful and without originality. It was in this first period that Alexander Herzen, as has been told me by an eye-witness, called him so affected that he could not eat without affectation. Byelinski tore him loose from Byron, Heine, and the romanticists, and brought him into the right path.

He expressed what he knew thoroughly: Russian nature and the life of the Russian people, and gave his hatred of serfdom expression in the forms which the censor would allow. This certainly had a beneficial effect on his talent,—developed, necessarily, everything that was pre-eminent, aristocratic, and discreet in it. If he sometimes, in his early youth, had an inclination to the pathetic, to declamation, to glaring effects,—pronounced it could have been under no circumstances,—then the relation to the censor must have suppressed it. To awaken a sympathy for the serfs, to show the lawlessness in which they passed their lives, and give pictures of the roughness which abused them even to death,—and that without making use of the whip or knout,—he relates incidents in his life as a sportsman, visits to the landed proprietors or to the physicians, and among these, now and then, little stories: of the miller's wife who, as a girl, had been guilty of a black ingratitude in wishing to marry, although her angelic mistress could not endure married servants, and who, when she would not give up her lover, was punished by a forced marriage, to another, after having seen her Petruchka put into the army. Or there is the story of the deaf and dumb but muscular man-servant Gerassim, whose sweetheart his gracious mistress married to a drunkard for her own amusement, and who was compelled to drown his dog, a little, emaciated puppy, Mumu,—his last consolation and sole company in the world,—because sometimes his barking irritated his mistress when, after too great indulgence at her meals, she was lying sleepless.

Both stories are told without comment, with no criticism of the events; the hatred of brutality which was manifested is expressed only in irony, and this irony, again, disappears in the pervading sadness.

What makes Turgenief's vein so rich and peculiar is that he is at once a pessimist and a philanthropist; that he loved the race of which he thought so poorly and esteemed so lightly.

But he had seen altogether too much go wrong and miscarry in Russia to be able to narrate any other incidents than those with unhappy or sad results. To him, a love story is not genuine Russian if it does not have an unhappy issue in consequence of the inconstancy of the man or the coldness of the woman. An undertaking does not seem to him to be genuine Russian unless it is beyond the capacity of him who attempts it, and falls through in consequence of the insusceptibility of those for whose sake it was to be carried through. But still he cannot refrain from dwelling again and again on vacillating love and fruitless struggles in Russia. For him, the land of Russia, where everything comes to grief, is a land of general shipwreck. And his chief emotion is one which awakens and is mingled with pain in the spectator of a shipwreck, in which the latter must give the sufferers themselves the greatest part of the blame. There is a strong and quiet emotion which is always softened in its expression. It is seldom that a great and productive author has made so little noise as he.

There is something aristocratic in this noble and simple attitude. It is not that, like Lord Byron or Prince Pückler, he has impressed the marks of superiority upon his works by any external stamp. But the impression forces itself upon us that the author has inherited his intellectual refinement, and has always lived in the best society. He was a man of the world, and we feel behind his works the experience in life of a man of the world, which the German authors generally lack. But this experience has neither made him cynical, like so many French authors, nor given to moralizing, like so many English. Although he has never shown any lack of good breeding in his style, still his tone is not the tone of the world. Even his contempt is not a cold contempt. There is always a soul in his voice.

It is difficult to say briefly and precisely what it is which makes Turgenief an artist of the first rank. We might almost say that it is because his style is so genuine. But even this word needs an explanation. The fact that he possesses in the highest degree the quality of a true poet, of being able to create men who live, is not all. What makes his artistic superiority so perceptible is the harmony which the reader traces between the author's conception of the person who is described, his opinion of him, and also the impression which is made upon him as well as upon the reader by that person.

The point is here. The relation of the author to his own creations is such that every weakness which he has as an artist or as a man must be exposed to the light. The author may have many and rare gifts, but if he calls upon us to admire that which is not worthy of admiration, or if he would extort from us admiration for a man, or sympathy with a woman, or enthusiasm for an act, without our feeling that there is any occasion for those sentiments, then he has injured and weakened himself. When the author of a novel, whose company we have kept for a long time with pleasure, suddenly shows himself less critical or more emotional or morally more lax than we are, then his descriptions lose their point for us. If he allows a person to appear as irresistibly winning, without our finding him fascinating; if he draws a man as more gifted or even more witty than he seems to us to be; if he explains his conduct by a magnanimity we have never met with, and in this case do not believe in; if he defies us by arbitrary, immature judgments, or disturbs us by coldness, or irritates us by moralizing: then there steals in upon the reader more and more a feeling of disappointing art. It is as if you heard a false note; and even if the music is afterwards correct, the disagreeable impression lingers in the mind. What reader of Balzac, or Dickens, or Auerbach—to speak only of the great dead—has not experienced this disagreeable impression! When Balzac becomes enthusiastic over vulgarity, or Dickens childishly pathetic, or Auerbach affectedly simple, the reader feels that he is in the presence of the untrue, the abortive, and is taken aback. Nothing abortive is ever met with in Turgenief.

The subjects he has selected are all the most difficult. He refuses to be interested in romantic characters and marvellous adventures, and he no less refuses the attractions of impurity. There seldom or never happens anything unusual in his books— a catastrophe like the falling-down of a house at the close of the "King Lear of the Steppe" is purely exceptional—and although he does not go out of his way on account of low and vile characters, or of incidents which no English novelist would relate, yet he does not dwell upon the obscene, as those authors who once for all have disregarded conventionality are so often tempted to do. As an artist he was a decided realist, but a modest realist.

His chief domain as a narrator is the poor, the weak, the

inconstant and untrustworthy, the superfluous and the abandoned.

He does not, like Dostoyevski, describe the misfortune which is externally palpable, nor the poverty, the roughness, the corruption, the crime, nor, above all, the misfortune, which can be seen at a distance. He describes the misfortune which avoids publicity, and he is especially the author for those who have submitted to their fate. He has pictured the inner life of reticent sorrow,—the still-life of the unfortunate, so to speak.

For instance read "A Correspondence." It is a young girl with whom we gradually become acquainted, who has lived isolated, misunderstood, despised by stupid associates in a little country village, and who is on the point of becoming an old maid. She has already resigned herself to it, deserted as she has been by her lover. She has given up her demands on life, and is trying only for peace and is on the way to success. Then begins—from an impulse of communicativeness, of idleness, of longing, of sympathy—a friend of her younger days to write to her. At first she answers declining the correspondence; after the receipt of other epistles she allows permission for him to continue the correspondence. He writes, and she replies, no longer briefly, but in a long, eloquent letter. In this manner the feeling of friendship grows up in her heart, and in no very long time occupies it and passes over into love. They are both in love for one short moment. He longs for and worships her, the day of his starting and arrival is already fixed;—then the correspondence is broken off, he allows himself to be carried away by a ballet girl, over whose vulgar graces he forgets everything, and she sinks anew, but this time more deeply wounded, back to her dreadful solitary life.

The highly elaborated novel "An Unfortunate Woman" treats of the life of another young girl, whose misfortune is equally quiet and uneventful. Her earliest remembrance is that her mother, a Jewess, the daughter of a foreign painter, and she herself sat daily at the table of the landed proprietor Kaltovskoi. Kaltovskoi is a grand old bugbear, who smelt horribly of ambergris, continually took snuff out of a gold snuff-box, and inspires the child with no other feeling than fear, even when he holds out his hard, dry hand, with lace cuffs, for her to kiss. At

the same time that the mother is made to marry the disgusting
steward Ratch, the child learns that the landed proprietor is her
father. The father never speaks a loving word to her, and not
even once a kindly one; he accepts her with stiff grandeur, as
his little reader. The mother dies. The old, heartless landed
proprietor dies some years later. His brother and heir, Semyón
Matveitch, gives Susannah some money, which her stepfather
immediately appropriates. Having grown up, her heart speaks for
the first time; she falls deeply in love with Semyón's son, her
cousin Mikhaïl, an excellent young officer, who loves her as she
deserves to be loved. But no sooner is the intimacy of the two
discovered than they are ruthlessly separated. Mikhaïl is sent
away and dies immediately after. The father, Semyón, pursues
his young niece with dishonorable advances and proposals. At
last he dies also and leaves her an annuity, which her stepfather
receives. Three years—six, seven years pass . . . time moves
on. She sees it gliding away indifferently and with it life. Then
a new ray of light falls into her existence; a fine young man,
whom she has won, also wins her interest; then he hears from
her associates, from her own depraved step-brother even, the
most scurvy calumnies in regard to her past history, and draws
back. She takes poison.

Or read "The Diary of a Superfluous Man." The title explains the contents. It is a man who is mortally ill, and who
occupies his last days in recording the chain of common events
which has made up his useless life. He has from first to last been
in the way in the world. Once he fell in love, but only to suffer
all the pangs of jealousy, and experience all its humiliations.
Elizabeth did not love him, but a dazzling young prince from
St. Petersburg, who is stopping for a short time in the provincial
town in which she dwells. He challenges the prince, who spares
him in the duel, succeeds only in passing for a bad man, and
appearing to the object of his affections as a murderer. Even
when the prince seduces and abandons Elizabeth, and when,
nevertheless, he is ready again to ask for her hand, her aversion
to him is unchanged. She gives her hand to another not less
magnanimous friend, who has got the start of the unhappy lover,
and who thus even on this occasion makes him a superfluity.

Here as always the poor fellow has been the fifth wheel to the coach. And yet we feel, through every line, how full of feeling, how nobly endowed and good he is. The last pages of the diary contain the farewell to life of the consumptive, who has been given up by his physician.

"Jacob Passinkof" is another story of the same kind. Passinkof belongs to the type of Russian personalities which Turgenief describes with partiality. He is not specially noble in his exterior, tall, thin, round-shouldered, and his nose even a little red. But his forehead is magnificent, his voice mild and subdued, and, as it is significantly enough said of him, "In his mouth the words goodness, truth, life, knowledge, love sound always like phrases, however enthusiastically he utters them." In his story Turgenief's fundamental theme comes out in a double form. He is in love with a beautiful young girl, who does not give him a thought. When he dies, forgotten and alone in an obscure corner of Siberia, he still has some mementos of her on his breast. He needed some faults, some selfishness, some levity, to win her favor. In the mean time, as a requital, without his knowing it, he was silently loved by her plain, rather ugly and awkward sister, who has always kept him faithfully in mind, and who for his sake had never been willing to marry.

Turgenief's story, written somewhat late in life, "The Living Relic," is certainly the best specimen of these monographs of misfortune, which are just as fine and perfect as they are simple. It is almost an unadorned soliloquy; it is only the account of her life which a young, formerly beautiful Russian peasant girl, now worn to a skeleton, gives to the author. He finds her lying on her back, after a fateful fall, and she has been lying thus for nearly seven years. Her head is emaciated, sallow as bronze; her nose sharp and pointed as a knife-blade; her lips sunken in, only the teeth and the white of her eyes have any lustre; some tufts of thin, flaxen yellow hair fall down over her forehead. Outside of the bed-clothing were lying a pair of very small hands whose fingers, like little dark brown pins, move slowly to and fro. And once she was the most plump, most graceful, gayest, and most beautiful girl in the country, always ready for laughter, song, and dance. She tells her fate, how after her accident she had become shrunken, dark-colored, had lost the power of standing and walking, appetite for eating and drinking; how they burnt her on the back with red-hot iron, and put her into solid ice, all to no effect. And she tells all this in an almost cheerful manner, without any attempt to excite pity. Her lover has left her, and married another. He is, she says, happy in his marriage, thank God. She finds his act natural and right. She is thankful to the people who take care of her, especially to a little girl who brings her flowers; she is not dull, does not complain: there are others who are more unhappy than she is,—the blind or the deaf and dumb; she sees wonderfully well, and hears everything,—hears when a mole is digging under ground, and smells every fragrance, even the weakest,—the flowers of the buckwheat, far out in the fields, and the linden trees far down in the garden. The great events in her existence are when a hen or a sparrow or a butterfly come in to her through a door or window. She has great pleasure in the recollection of a visit a hare made to her one day. And Lukeria reminds Turgenief of the time when she sang ballads. She still sings them sometimes, she tells him. The thought that this scarcely living being is preparing to sing inspires him with involuntary horror; and, trembling like a thread of light smoke, her poor little voice comes out in almost inaudible but clear and pure tones. She tells him the wonderful dreams she has had (unfortunately she sleeps but little),—one about Jesus, who came to meet her, and held out his hand to her; one about a woman whom she met, and who was her death, but who went past her, and, pitying her, did not complain that she could not take her with her. She contradicts the author when he expresses his ad-miration of her patience. What is there to admire! What has she done! No, the maiden who, in a distant country, with a great sword drove the enemy out into the sea, and then said, "Burn me now, for it was my promise that I would die at the stake for my people!"—that maiden performed a wonderful act. As he went away, Lukeria begs him to say a word for the peasants there in the village at her mother's, so that they might obtain a little bit of an abatement in the rent. She needs nothing herself, and has nothing to wish for in her own behalf.

Still it is not these minor works which have made Turgenief's name renowned throughout the world. It is his greater novels, his few romances, masterpieces, like "On the Eve" (Helen), "Rudin," "Spring Floods," "Smoke," "Fathers and Sons," and "Virgin Soil." No more subtle psychology is to be found in European literature, no more perfect delineation of character, and, what is almost unseen in the history of modern authorship, the figures of the men and women are here equally perfect.

In order fully to understand these best works of Turgenief, it is necessary to have some knowledge of his life and character.

Two decisive events occurred in his life. The first is his imprisonment and subsequent banishment to his estate in 1842. The second is his acquaintance with Mme. Pauline Viardot, née Garcia.

In the government circles a suspicious watch was kept on Turgenief, on account of his attacks on serfdom. Then, when Gogol died, and Turgenief, in a newspaper article (in which the censor in Moscow found nothing to strike out), eulogized the deceased with warm words, they at once seized upon the opportunity to give him a blow. They found—Heaven knows how—disobedience towards the Tsar in the said article, and on "the command of the highest of all" he was thrown into prison in St. Petersburg. Among his letters is to be found a communication which he wrote to the heir-apparent (Alexander) to prove his innocence. After having passed a month in prison, which the delicate condition of his health made doubly painful to him, he was exiled to his estate Spasskoye, where he was obliged to remain for several years. It is plainly enough the event which after his pardon led him to take up his permanent residence outside of his native land.

The acquaintance with Mme. Viardot imprisoned the author near to her for all the rest of his life—far more than half. She was born in Paris in 1821 and had made extensive artistic tours in America and Europe with her parents, first as a pianist and then as a vocalist. Her first appearance in Paris, which happened at the same time as Rachel's, is commemorated in verse by Alfred de Musset. From 1840 she was the wife of the author Louis Viardot. As early as 1847, Turgenief accompanied the married couple to Berlin and then to Paris. From 1856 he is to be re-

garded as a member of the Viardot family, and the influence
which the mistress of the house exerted upon the author was
great, and, so far as can be perceived, only for good. In 1847,
when his despotic mother refused to send him any money for
his support, Mme. Viardot assisted him out of her own purse,
and it was therefore only just that Turgenief in his will should
have made her his residuary legatee,—which, however, has given
rise to many fiendish comments on the part of Russians.

Turgenief's relation to Mme. Viardot was that of passionate
devotion and admiration. He could not do without her, and took
counsel with her about his affairs of every description. Genuine
Slav as he was, susceptible to impressions, intellectually productive and almost destitute of will-power, he was fortunate in
having a fair ruler over his life. When any friend complained to
him of his own irregular and unfortunate career, he usually answered: "Do as I do, my dear fellow; I allow myself to be ruled."
He did what Mme. Viardot told him he ought to do, and was
contented therewith.

She seems to have been the only woman of importance in his
life. Naturally, he had known women in his youth. At the age
of nineteen, in Berlin, he was the friend of a little sewing-girl
and was chagrined that Bakunin, with whom he was living, could
tell by his looks when he had been to see her.[1] At first in the
beginning of the fifties he lived in Russia, and then, 1851–53,
with a Russian serf, Avdotya Yermolayevna Ivánova, who must
have been very beautiful, but to whom it appeared to be impossible to impart the mysteries of the art of reading. She bore
to him, in 1842, the daughter whom he married to a Frenchman
in 1864. His letters show that he did not at that time even know
where the mother, who had married a Russian official, was living.
(Letter to Maslof, December 26, 1864.) But he was a good father
as well as a faithful friend and a magnanimous protector.

His character was noble; refined and pure even to the point
of tenderness; but gentle and undecided. Probably he was not
obliged to go far, as a young man, to find the model of single
traits of character in Rúdin. He was never guilty of any low act;
but, on the other hand, he hardly ever acted with any bold and

[1] Issac Pavlovsky: *Souvenirs de Tourguéneff*, p. 112 and following.

forcible energy. In reading his letters we are surprised to see with what rascals he corresponded,—apparently not to make enemies of them,—and with how little respect he speaks in confidential letters of persons to whom in other letters he shows great regard. When we find that Turgenief, with a character in which will-power was so weakly developed, during the whole of his life remained inviolably faithful to the old liberal convictions of his youth, we can scarcely err in attributing to Mme. Viardot no small degree of honor for this result. If she had influenced him in the opposite direction, he would probably have become conservative, and if her house and circle had not been decidedly liberal, perhaps an influence from some other direction would have succeeded in swaying him. On the contrary, he seems to have been entirely independent in his obstinate position as the exponent and pupil of Western Europe.

In perfect accord with the weak appearance of his will-power in Turgenief's character is the circumstance that as an author he comes forward with a confidence like that of a somnambulist. He said to Mikhaïlof, Professor of Physiology in St. Petersburg (from whom I have it): "I see a man who strikes me from some characteristic or other, perhaps of little importance. I forget him. And then, long after, the man suddenly starts up from the grave of forgetfulness. About the characteristic which I observed, others group themselves, and it is of no use now if I want to forget him: I cannot do it; he has taken possession of me; I think with him, live in him; I can only restore myself to ease by finding an existence for him."

Turgenief, as a writer, is more elegant than forcible. It is for that reason that female characters are so well adapted to his talents.

With tranquil tenderness he draws the young girls who have his full sympathy, Helen and Gemma, and with an indulgent love which, nevertheless, excludes all praise and admiration on the part of the author. Every word which is said of them is determinative, limiting. One, in play of features, gestures, laughter, train of ideas and love is wholly Italian; the other is impressed on the mind of the reader as the most beautiful type of Russian womanhood. Only the best authors of the world have produced anything so natural, so well sustained. And the worship of beauty that is to be found there has done no harm to the study of nature. They are not women whom the author has arbitrarily created, and who dwell in the fancy-land of poetry, like the forms of women in the works of so many other authors. They are not products of Turgenief's personal enthusiasm for the womanly, not merely an expression of his ideal alone, but studies built up on a foundation of a delicate sense of reality, and by the force of a thorough knowledge of the real.

In the more important male characters, from the nature of the material, Turgenief found his task expecially difficult. While the chief aim of an author usually is to sustain his characters and let them escape self-contradiction, the finest characters of Turgenief are made up of contradictions. He understood how to treat inconsistency as a fundamental trait of character without having the character disorganized thereby. With the regular Russian, as he describes him, there is nothing certain to be depended upon except instability. As Alexis, in "A Correspondence," leaves Maria in the lurch, so Rúdin abandons Natalia, Sanin, in "Spring Floods," Gemma, Litvinof, in "Smoke," Tatyana, etc.; they abandon youth, freshness, goodness of heart, beauty, happiness, to run after intoxication of the senses and degradation, or they deceive from pure weakness and instability in themselves. And to these men, whom no one can trust, and whose sudden outbursts of passion and sudden cessation thereof surprise themselves not less than others, correspond women on whom it is just as impossible to depend, women who are on the point of being able to love, but cannot, like Marie Odinzof, in "Fathers and Sons;" women who unintentionally insnare, abandon themselves, draw back, like Iriona in "Smoke;" and, finally, cold Bacchantes, like that Maria Nikolayevna who carries away Sanin from Gemma.

Sometimes, the inconsistency and treachery remain rather unsatisfactorily explained, as in "Spring Floods;" in that case, it depends upon the fact that Turgenief assumes, so to speak, that this trait of character of his young men is known. In his earliest great novel, "Rúdin" (1855), the study of inconsistency is so thorough and exhaustive that, through the weakness of this one character, we understand the weakness of the Russian character everywhere. That which most excites our admiration for the skill of the artist in this, is that he has been able to awaken a no small degree of sympathy for Rúdin; that in the milksop and phrase-monger he has shown us the sincere enthusiast. Rúdin, who speaks so warmly, tells a story so fascinatingly, and possesses all "the music of eloquence," is lazy, despotic, everlastingly playing a part, forever living at the expense of others, cold when he seems to be warmest, intellectually weak when he seems to be about to accomplish something. And yet Turgenief shows that he deserves our pity far more than our ill will, and that he rightfully exerts a great influence on young souls.

Men with constant hearts and strong wills do not appear among Turgenief's leading figures in his younger days. They are Hamlets who descend from Pushkin's Onyegin and Herzen's Beltov. When he describes a man who is wholly a man, and to whom a woman can look up, then, as in "Helen," in order to shame his countrymen, he chooses a foreigner, the Bulgarian Insarof, who has exactly those qualities which the Russians, from the best to the poorest, lack. The model of the figure was a real Bulgarian, Katianof, who has figured in his native land, and with whom Turgenief (1855) became acquainted through the papers of a neighboring landed proprietor, Karateyef. Otherwise, men whom Turgenief himself admires are named only incidentally, and they are placed as figures in the background, or used as contrasts to bring out the falsity and weakness of the leading character. Such, for instance, is Pokorski in "Rúdin," of whom Lekhnef speaks with so fascinating an enthusiasm, and in whom we really may see a portrait of the critic Byelinski, the friend and teacher of Turgenief's youth, to whose memory he has dedicated "Fathers and Sons," and by whose side he, on his deathbed, expressed his desire to be buried. It is said of him:—

"Pokorski made the impression of a very quiet and gentle, almost weak nature; he loved women to madness, enjoyed a little dissipation, and would not have suffered an insult of any kind whatever. Rúdin appeared to be all fire and flame, life, boldness, but at the bottom of his soul he was cold and almost a coward, so long as his vanity was not wounded, for then his self-control would be entirely destroyed by his frenzy. He continually sought to be the master of others . . . but acquiesced in bearing his yoke, but Pokorski submitted to all voluntarily . . . oh, it was a beautiful time and I cannot believe that it was wasted. How often have I not met people from that time, my former comrades, men who seemed to have sunken into a purely animal existence,—and yet it was only necessary to mention Pokorski's name; immediately all the good that had survived in them rose to the surface, as when one in a dirty, dark room opens a bottle of perfume which has been forgotten there."

Yet it was not until the publication of "Fathers and Sons" in 1861 that Turgenief gave a typical representation of the strong character and intellectual superiority of the Russian, this time in its modern form. The character of Bazárof introduced "nigilism" into light literature. Even if Turgenief has apparently specially desired to strike a blow against the idolization of simple utility, with its poverty of ideas, in the younger generation, still he has succeeded in drawing a man who by his firmness, his courage, and his steadfastness, towers up in the whole of European literature, which is not rich in types of true men. It cannot have escaped the observation of any one tolerably familiar with modern books that it is as if true manhood had disappeared. A man who has a will and mind and uses his will to aid his mind, sticks to his aim, is a support to his friends, is an everlasting thorn in the flesh to his enemies, and to whom the women, the defenceless, the beginners in life, naturally gravitate, such a man comes no more to the front, save in the dilute romances of boys and ladies.

In 1860, on a journey in Germany in a railway carriage, Turgenief met a young Russian physician, who, in the brief conversation that took place between them, astonished him by his original and startling views. He gave the poet the idea of Bazárof. In order to familiarize himself with the character, Turgenief began to keep "Bazárof's Diary," that is, as soon as he read a new book or met a person who interested him or exhibited some characteristic of a political or social nature, he criticised him in this diary according to Bazárof's manner of thought.

As is well known, it was not so much by the genius which

was displayed in the delineation of the principal character as it was from the effect the work created, the ill will, the misunderstandings, the passionate attacks, it provoked on the part of the radical leaders, that "Fathers and Sons" was an event in the history of Russian literature and in the author's own life. The book is a masterpiece without a blemish, besides being the original prototype of all the modern novels in different countries which treat of an older and younger generation in their reciprocal relations and conflicts; but in the beginning nothing else was seen in the depreciation of the younger generation to the advantage of the culture of the older.

In the face of this stupidity, Turgenief's own utterances about the hero have an increased interest. A certain Slutchevski had upbraided him that Bazárof had made so unfavorable an impression. He answers (1862): "Nevertheless, Bazárof drives all the other persons of the novel into the background. . . . He is honest, upright, and a democrat of the purest water. And you find in him no good quality! He commends 'Force and Matter' by name as a popular, that is a worthless book. The duel with Pavel Petróvitch is introduced to represent the intellectual vacuity of the elegant, noble knighthood; it is even then almost overdrawn, ridiculously represented. . . . According to my view, Bazárof is constantly Pavel Petróvitch wholly superior and unconverted. When he calls himself a 'nihilist,' we must read revolutionist. . . . On the one side a venal official, on the other an ideal youth. Such pictures I leave for others to draw; I strove for something greater. . . . I close with the remark: If the reader does not find Bazárof dear to him in spite of all his coarseness, heartlessness, merciless dryness and sharpness,—then the fault is mine and I have missed my mark. But sweet with syrup—to speak after the manner of Bazárof—that I would not have, although I had immediately won the youth over to my side thereby."

And twelve years later, after a fresh attack, he turns back again to his tenderness for Bazárof. He writes: "What! you also contend that I caricatured youth in Bazárof. You repeat this— pardon the freedom of the expression—insane complaint. Bazárof, my favorite child, for whose sake I broke with Katkóf, and on whom I lavished all the colors I could command! Bazárof, this intelligent man, this hero, a caricature!" . . .[1]

By the novel "Smoke," Turgenief fell out with another not less influential group in Russia than that which had been so much offended by "Fathers and Sons." It was almost a blow aimed at the Slavophiles, and imbittered them in every case against him. Katkóf and Dostoyevski were from this time his bitter enemies and persecutors. In this book certain twaddling and conceited Russian quasi-reformers are thrown aside with a cutting scorn, which recalls to a denizen of the North Henrick Ibsen's manner of treating certain reformers among his countrymen.

But in "Virgin Soil" (1877), Turgenief's last great work and the most versatile he wrote, he has brought his criticism of society to an end with a thorough unpartisan justice, by exposing to sun and air ranks, families, tendencies, and races in his great native land. "Virgin Soil" is inferior to the older, larger novels to the extent that here for the first time we feel clearly that the author has lived for a long time out of Russia, making up for the lack of personal observation by reading newspapers and legal reports; and still this book is the richest and most complete expression of Turgenief's humanity and worldly wisdom, and of his love of freedom and truth.

Here, perhaps in the most positive manner, his filial affection for Russia, his appreciation of the Russian youth, is brought to light; here appears unveiled his vision of its high idealism. It is quite true that everything miscarries here. With Turgenief all exertions miscarry; upon the whole, everything meets with misfortune. For the moment only hopelessness rules. The older generation, with the liberalism of Sipjaegin, is once for all given up; in the younger generation, there is much that is well meant, much is disinterestedly carried into effect, but all is fruitless. Nezhdanof wants to go out among the people, wants to distribute pamphlets among the peasants. It has the force of a symbol that the peasants misunderstand him. They will only drink with him; and the apostle of the common people is carried home deaddrunk. It was not without cause that Nezhdanof had previously

---

[1] Briefe von J. S. Turgenjev, Uebersetzt von H. Ruhe, 1886, i. 96 and following, 214 and following.

finished his poem, "The Sleep," with this picture never to be forgotten:—

"With a glass of spirit in thy hand, with head leaning against the North Pole, with feet pressed against Caucasus, oh, fatherland! Thus thou sleepest, holy Russia, deeply and soundly and steadily."

And yet in this last work a future is to be seen in vague, distant outlines. Young women like Marianne and Maschurin, young men like Markelof, like Solomin, like Nezhdanof even, prepared the way for it.

The last twenty years of his life Turgenief passed alternately in the two countries, Germany and France, to which he was most indebted for his culture. He lived in Baden-Baden and Paris. His relations to Germany and France were, however, quite different. Probably on account of ancient Russian tradition, and besides in consequence of the nationality of Mme. Viardot, he was far more closely bound to France than to Germany. He had studied in Berlin, and the criticism of young Hegelianism had refined and stimulated his mind. But, although he worshipped Goethe as the master above all others, and for a while in his youth was wholly absorbed in Heine, although he continued to have friendly relations with German authors and writers like Paul Heyse, Ernst Dohn, and Ludwig Pietsch, spoke the language fluently, and knew how to value the scientific greatness of Germany,—in spite of all these bonds binding him to that country, the Germans in his books, as in almost all Russian romances and novels, are continually represented in a highly satirical, and now and then even in a hateful light. It is a weakness of German criticism that it has not been able to see this evident fact. It is true enough, as a general rule, that all nations describe others without enthusiasm. A Russian woman, as drawn by Victor Cherbuliez or Paul Heyse (*Ladislaus Bolski*, "In Paradise," *Das Glück zu Rothenburg*), never has the good part. But there seems to have been a remnant of national hate at the bottom of Turgenief's soul.

Although, on the other hand, he did not fail to have an eye to the deficiencies in the French culture, he conducted himself in an entirely different manner in regard to it. He felt that his art was wholly understood and appreciated in that Paris which is otherwise so full of prejudice towards foreigners. He had equally warm admirers among those of the same age as himself (Mérimée), those of a little younger generation (Augier, Taine, Flaubert, Goncourt), and among the youngest authors (Zola, Daudet, Maupassant). With that circle of authors of which Flaubert was the centre, he associated on a friendly and brotherly footing as with the writers of no other land.

His relations to his own country were fluctuating. In his younger days he was popular and then a subject of hatred. It was first seen on his last visit to Russia that the misunderstanding—that he should have abandoned the ideals of his youth—had given way to a better understanding, and his journey became a kind of triumphal tour through the ovations which he received from the youth. It is true that these ovations created such uneasiness on the part of the government, that it shortened his stay in St. Petersburg. In Moscow, where Katkóf had attacked him as hostile to his fatherland and seditious, a festival had been arranged for him, to which Dostoyevski also was invited, his more recent, spiteful appearance against Turgenief having been overlooked on account of the convictions of his youth and his martyrdom.

In the mean time, the more the younger generation was reconciled to the author of "Fathers and Sons," and the more warmly he was greeted, the more the dissatisfaction of the Russian government with him increased. This was also very clearly shown at his death. A solemn funeral, with his house decorated, a long procession and addresses at the grave were forbidden. In perfect quiet, as if he were a convict, the man was buried who, in these later days, had given the widest reputation to the name of Russia.

For in the last ten years of his life, at least, he could have rejoiced in an admiration which was equally reverential over the whole of the civilized world.

Did he rejoice at it? I believe not. It affected him agreeably, but he did not delight in it, and it did not disperse his melancholy. Edmund de Goncourt relates of Turgenief, that at a dinner given by Flaubert, in March, 1872, during a moment of despondency, which sometimes seizes upon a circle of friends who are getting on towards old age, he allowed himself to be carried away so far as to say: "You know that there is sometimes found in a room an odor of musk which cannot be driven out; so it seems to me that about my person, and that continually, there is a perfume of dissolution, annihilation, death." His last works, the charming and original novel "Clara Militch," which is a variation of the theme of his youth, disappointed love, and his admirable collection of prose poems, "Senilia," likewise contain a deeper melancholy than the works of his youth, save that a lyrical, fantastic element most poetically flashes through them. Here, for the last time, he stands face to face with the secret of life, and explains it in unceasing sadness in symbols and visions. Nature is hard and cold; then let man not neglect to love. There is a scene here where Turgenief, on a solitary journey from Hamburg to London, sits by the hour with a poor, cowed, fettered little monkey's hand in his—the genius, whose spirit had ransacked the universe, hand in hand with the little anthropoid animal, like two kindred mortals, two children of the same mother,—there is here more true devotion than in any book of devotion.

At the last, Turgenief seems to have had a strong impression of man's ingratitude. No one who has read "Senilia" will ever forget "The Feast in Heaven." All the virtues were invited, and the virtues only; no men were invited, only ladies. Many virtues came, small and great. The small virtues were more agreeable and more modest than the great; but all seemed to be well contented and talked kindly to each other, as is becoming for those who are akin. Then the good God observed two beautiful ladies who did not seem to be acquainted with each other. The master of the house took one of the ladies by the hand and led her to the other, and he introduced: Charity—Gratitude.

It was the first time since the creation of the world that the two had met.

What sadness in the wit and what bitterness!

It also occurs to me that my gratitude towards this great benefactor has its first expression when he can no longer be sensible of any thanks.

VI

᳿§ In contrast to the national pessimism in Turgenief stands the national optimism in Dostoyevski. The great sceptic Turgenief, who believed in so little, believed in the culture of Western Europe. Dostoyevski despised the Occident, and believed in Russia. If the works of Turgenief are, to some extent, to be regarded as emigrant literature, then we stand with Dostoyevski wholly on Russian soil; he is the autochthonic author, "the true Scythian," the legitimate barbarian without a drop of classic blood in his veins.

Look at this countenance! half the face of a Russian peasant, half the physiognomy of a criminal, with flattened nose, small, piercing eyes, under eyelashes which tremble with nervousness, long, thick, untidy beard, and light hair; add to this the forehead of a thinker and a poet, large and shapely, and the expressive mouth, which, even when closed, speaks of tortures without number, of ingulfing sadness, of unhealthy desires, enduring pity, sympathy, passionate envy, anxiety, torture! Look at this body, which is nothing but nerves, small and slender, round-shouldered, and tenacious of life, from his youth up subject to epileptic fits and hallucinations! This exterior, at first sight plain and vulgar, on closer examination stamped with weird genius, thoroughly morbid and wholly extraordinary, speaks of Dostoyevski's epileptic genius, of the depths of mildness which filled his soul, of the billows of almost insane acuteness which frequently mounted into his head; finally of that ambition which creates greatness in its efforts, and the envy which creates smallness in the soul.

It is a character which reminds one of Rousseau's, irritable and suspicious, with fits of depression and the most exalted flights. Although his family belonged to the lower ranks of nobility of

Russia, from which the subordinate officials are generally taken, he has, like Rousseau, a thoroughly democratic stamp. Moreover, even if he is fanatical in his ideas, like Rousseau, he differs from him in his profound spiritual characteristics. Rousseau is a deist, but, in spite of his sentimentality, not a Christian, an enemy of the Christian humility, and of all submission to fate. Dostoyevski, on the contrary,—entirely regardless of the fact whether his dogmatic faith was orthodox or not,—is in his whole emotional nature the typical Christian. His works constitute a true repertory of characters and conditions of thought conceived from a Christian standpoint. All his persons are invalids, sinners or saints, of both sexes, and the transition from sinner to a convert, from fair sinner to fair saint, and from the bodily sick to the spiritually sound, happens, now after a slow purification, and now at a flash, as in the New Testament; nay, often the fair sinner is at the same time a fair saint, and the greatest criminal just as near being worthy of admiration as he is near being a scoundrel.

Physiologically and psychologically, all these types of paupers and poor fellows, of the ignorant good-hearted, of the simple emotional, of noble Magdalens, of the nervously distracted, of those seized with frequent hallucinations, of gifted epileptics, of enthusiastic seekers after martyrdom, are just the same types as prevailed centuries ago.

Feodor Mikhaïlovitch Dostoyevski was born in October, 1821, in a hospital for the poor, in Moscow, where his father was physician. There was a large family of children, and small means. Feodor and his brother Aleksei, to whom he was bound through life by an intimate friendship and common literary interests, were sent to the military school for engineers in St. Petersburg, and left it as sub-lieutenants. But, after the lapse of a year (1844), Feodor asked for his discharge from the military service, to devote himself to literature. He was even then suffering from the disease which was aggravated when he was subsequently whipped in Siberia; he had epileptic fits, and moreover he was visionary. With regard to the subjects which he treated later, and his ability to express the psychology of crime, this saying of his to a friend is characteristic: "The dejection which succeeds my epileptic attacks has this characteristic,—I feel like a great criminal; it comes over me like an unknown fault; a criminally guilty deed weighs upon my conscience."

At the age of twenty-four he wrote his novel "Poor Folk." Towards the close of his life, in the "Diary of an Author" he related the circumstances of his first appearance as an author. When he had written his novel, and did not know how he should get his manuscript disposed of, he got one of his friends, the subsequently well-known author Grigoróvitch, to take it to the poet Niekrásof. About three o'clock in the morning, Dostoyevski heard some one knock at his door. It was Grigoróvitch, who had come back with Niekrásof, who had already read the novel, and was so struck by it that he felt an impulse immediately to press the author to his heart. When early the next morning he left Dostoyevski, he went with the manuscript straight to Byelinski, "the oracle of Russian thought, the critic whose bare name frightened debutants."—"A new Gogol has arisen," shouted Niekrásof, as he broke in through the door. "Certainly, they shoot up nowadays like toadstools," answered Byelinski, fretfully, and reluctantly looked into the manuscript. But the effect on him was the same as on Niekrásof. When the author visited him, he said to him enthusiastically: "Young as you are, do you yourself understand how true it is what you have written? I don't think so. But true artistic inspiration is there. Respect the gifts you possess, and you will become a great author."

In order to understand this astonishment and this enthusiasm, we must remember that Russian literature even now does not possess a single attempt of this kind except Gogol's "Cloak," and that Turgenief's "Recollections of a Huntsman" did not appear till five years later. When a month or two after Byelinski's conversation with Dostoyevski "Poor Folk" (1846) issued from the press, the author's literary reputation was at once established.

The uneasiness and versatility of his nature is displayed in the circumstance that though he had made his *début* in a direction which is like that into which Dickens struck a little earlier, he continued his career with worthless and comic novels in Paul de Kock's manner.

He was an inordinate reader at an early day. At the age of twelve he had already ploughed through Karamzin and Walter

Scott, histories and historical novels by the quantity. Reading exhausted him, nervous, irritable, timid, emotional, precocious as he was, and with an unusual gift of placing himself in the imagined situation. In the School for Engineers, he read Balzac with special zeal, being carried away by "Père Goriot," which in its whole intellectual character furnishes one of the theories of his own novels, and translated "Eugénie Grandet," occupied himself in addition very much with George Sand and Eugène Sue, Dickens and Hoffman, the influence of all of whom is perceptible in his works. In this first period of his youth Dostoyevski was still a prey to varied influences.

He has himself told in his later years how Byelinski at the close of the forties drew him on to socialism, and, as he called it, tried to convert him to atheism. The same hatred and the same ingratitude towards the men who influenced his youth, Herzen, Byelinski, and others, which found its expression in the novel "The Demons" is shown in this bitter and poisonous attempt to cast the blame of his youthful conviction upon a man who is dead. We must remember that it is an old re-actionist who speaks, and in his defence consider that Dostoyevski was a man abused by life.

On the 23d of April, 1849, at five o'clock in the morning, he, together with thirty-three other young men, was arrested.

He had then for some time continuously belonged to the circle which had established itself around a certain Petrashevski, an adherent of the system of Fourier; in the meetings of this circle the talk had been loud and imprudent. The leader was a genuine Fourierist, an enemy of gods and kings, an opponent of marriage and property in the predominant forms. The indictment of Dostoyevski himself was to this effect: Participation in the meetings of the circle, observations about the strictness of the censorship, reading or listening to the reading of prohibited pamphlets, and finally promises of possible aid in the establishment of a printing office.

The accused were taken to the castle and isolated in the casemates. They were there eight months without any other amusements than their examinations by the magistrate. It was not until towards the end of their time of imprisonment that they were furnished with some books of devotion. The poor poet, who was reduced to the necessity of communing with his own thoughts alone, felt as if he had been under an air pump.

December 22, twenty-one of the accused who had been found guilty were taken out to Semenovski Place, where a scaffold had been erected. With the thermometer at —15° Fahr. they were compelled to strip to their shirts to listen to the reading of the sentence. This reading occupied a half-hour. When it began the perpetually optimistic Dostoyevski turned to his neighbor and said: "Can it be possible that they are going to execute us?" Instead of answering, the person to whom the inquiry was addressed pointed to some objects, which were concealed under the coverings of the wagons and which looked like coffins. The sentence ended with the words, " . . . are condemned to be shot." A priest with a crucifix in his hand now came forward and urged the prisoners to confess. They refused with a single exception. They then fastened Petrashevski and two others of the leaders to the stake. An officer directed his company to load their guns and wait for the word of command. At this moment a white flag was waved and it was announced to the condemned that the Tsar had commuted their punishment. At the foot of the scaffold sledges were waiting which were to carry them to Siberia. Dostoyevski was sentenced to ten years' hard labor. But his punishment was changed later to four years in the house of correction, and four years service as a soldier in the ranks with loss of his rank as a noble and his rights as a citizen. In Tobolsk the ways of the prisoners separated; they said farewell to each other. Their feet were fettered, their heads shaved, and they were sent to their several places of destination.[1]

What Dostoyevski saw, felt, lived through, and suffered in the Siberian House of Correction among the dregs of the world, the poor creatures, the ignorant and the barbarous, the criminals and the desperate, that he has indirectly told the world in his "Recollections of a Dead House," one of the greatest masterpieces descriptively and psychologically, which any literature has to show. If he had written it in his own name, and spoken of his crime as political, the book would never have passed the censor. Therefore

[1] De Vogüé: *Le Roman Russe*, p. 218 and following.

an imaginary narrator is found, who in a moment of passion has committed a common crime, and to whose account the observations are placed. What Dostoyevski does not tell is that he himself was the subject of the horrible corporal punishments which he describes.

From 1849 to 1859 Dostoyevski was wholly dead to literature.

At the age of thirty-seven he returned home from Siberia with his nervous system wholly destroyed. A great change had taken place in him. In the four years he had passed in the workhouse, he had only one single book with him, the New Testament, and he had read it again and again. All revolt was quenched in his soul. It was not simply that he saw with how little knowledge of men he had wished to reform the world, and how little this abstract idealism availed; but for once and all he had become meek and humble, obedient and submissive. He found his punishment just; nay, even more, he was grateful to the Tsar Nicholas for it. He imagined that without it he would have become insane; thought that the secret horror he always felt at the approach of darkness, under normal conditions would have deprived him of his reason; now it deprived real sufferings of their power.

In the next place he had obtained a thorough knowledge of the inner life of the Russian people. His fate had opened to him an insight into that which is generally regarded as the sewer of humanity; and there he found in every one, even in those who had sunken the deepest, something of value in spite of all their depravity. At the same time that he had lost all faith in the use or possiblity of a political revolution, he had found the faith in a moral revolution, starting from the bottom, in the spirit of the gospel. Thus he returned as the philanthropist among the Russian authors, as the author of the helpless pariahs. It has somewhere been justly said that what Wilberforce was in the English Parliament for the negro, he became in the Russian literature for the proletariats,—that is, their spokesman. As an artist he is true enough not to embellish the pariah; as a poet he is visionary enough to proclaim the presence of "a divine spark," even among the wretched. Nay more, the morality he preaches is, perhaps, the purest expression of the morality of the pariah, of the morality of the slave.

We are indebted to the philosopher Frederick Nietzsche for the establishment of the real and wide contrast between the morality of gentlemen and the morality of slaves. The expressions originate with him. By the morality of gentlemen is meant all that morality which emanates from self-esteem, positive animal spirits: the morality of Rome, of Iceland, of the renaissance; by the morality of the slave, all that morality which proceeds from contact with wretchedness as the highest virtue, from the denial of life, from the hatred for the happy and the strong.

This continual praising of the unselfish, self-sacrificing person, as contrasted to that person who lays all his strength on self-preservation, self-development, and development of power, does not by any means spring from a spirit of unselfishness. The *neighbor* commends unselfishness because he has the profit of it. If he thought himself unselfish, he would reject all that which would be to his advantage. Herein lies the fundamental contradiction of this morality, that the motive for it is in conflict with its principles. It is proclaimed for the advantage of the unsuccessful men, and generally has no more zealous or ardent advocates than that kind of unsuccessful men who do not have enough independent spiritual life to be able to live in the world of their own ideas, but do have so-called culture enough to suffer under it, and whose existence is at heart envy. Whatever qualities and culture such men have are strengthened by anguish; they live in a constant longing for vengeance on those whom they think are happy.

Dostoyevski developed into a colossal example of this type. With the worst ill-treatment of his life behind him, and now poor, soon in debt, and in continual endless debt, dependent on publishers, whose advances furnish him his means of subsistence, he is to begin anew to make his way into literature.

The first book which he wrote after his return from Siberia, "The Injured and Oppressed," does not belong to his best works, but it contains characters of which his first book had already given a hint, and which re-appear later. He had brought back with him from Siberia a young wife with whom he had fallen in love, the widow of one of the adherents of Petrashevski, who had died in prison. But she for her part was in love with another man; and Dostoyevski's letters show how for a whole year he labored to unite her to his rival, and set his friends to work to remove the obstacles out of the way of their union. Nevertheless, it ended in the marriage of her to Dostoyevski.

This is the reality which underlies the occurrences in "The Injured and Oppressed," in which the characters who remind one of Dickens do not, however, make any very deep impression.

He plunged into journalism, which during his whole life had a fascination for him, and on which he wasted much time and force. He became a contributor to the Slavophile newspapers published by his brother Mikhaïl, first "The Times," then "The Epoch," and preached the love and admiration for Russia "which cannot be understood by reason, but which is a matter of faith."

In 1865 he loses his first wife and his brother Alekseï. Mikhaïl's second newspaper is a failure, and he flies from the country to escape from his creditors. He does not enjoy the journey which he makes through Germany, France, and Italy. He continually has epileptic fits, and is obliged to return home to obtain new advances from his publishers, which they, it is true, concede to him, but only on the most unfavorable conditions. He brings back only one solitary strong impression from his travels, that of an execution to which he had been a witness in Lyons. This recalled to him the moment in his life in which he felt the greatest horror, and of which the recollection is continually coming back in his novels: that morning hour on the scaffold, December 22, 1849.

In 1862 he made a strong impression on the reading world by his "Recollections of a Dead House." In 1866 he made the greatest impression of his life in "Crime and Punishment" (*Prestuplenie i Nakazanie*). Hardly any other work has contributed so much to the psychology of the Russia of that time. What the book describes is only apparently something special; in reality, it unveils a great picture of society.

The problem of the book in a more limited sense is one which the most thoughtful minds have struggled with; the two apparently contradictory estimates which society places upon the value of human life. Bismarck has cleverly discussed this subject in his speeches.[1] It occupied the author of this book, when several years ago in Berlin a woman who was more than eighty-two years old was murdered by one of the many lovers whom she had won by her presents.[2] The problem was this: Has human life absolute value? Why does modern society answer this question in the most contradictory manner? It punishes with the severest penalty the murder by the mother of the new-born child without regard to the fact that she for fear of shame or of want inflicts upon herself a far greater loss and a far greater pain than she inflicts upon society; nay, it punishes her even if the motive of her act was to free the child from all the misery in store for it. Society demands that the full cup of earthly misfortune shall be poured out upon the little being's head. But society does not oppose the establishment of manufactories, the operation of which entails sickness and often death among the workmen, nay, even regards the founder of such a manufactory in a quarter destitute of industrial pursuits as a benefactor.

The one who in Dostoyevski's work struggles with this problem is Raskolnikof, a young Russian student, unusually good-looking, with fine features, and expressive black eyes, eminently gifted, but poor, as only a Russian student is poor, plunged in the deepest poverty, clad in rags, with a hat which cannot be seen without awakening laughter. He has given up his studies on account of his poverty, has tried in vain to support himself, has let himself go to ruin. He is reserved, gruff, suspicious, and hypochondriacal; he is proud, but also high-minded and good; he very reluctantly betrays his feelings. He is ambitious, with a tendency to boldness, but often so despondent that he seems to be cold and without sensibility to the degree of inhumanity. He is melancholy by nature, sombre and passionate, arrogant and magnanimous, sorrowful over the unhappy condition of the human race, with a constantly burning desire to be a benefactor on a grand scale. At bottom he is without ability. According to the opinion of the author, that is generally the case in Russia, where all wish to become suddenly rich without toil or trouble, and where every

[1] *Gesammelte Reden des Fürsten Bismarck* (by Hahn), i. 895.
[2] See G. Brandes: Berlin, p. 303 and following.

one is accustomed to have that which is generally attained brought to him all ready, accustomed to be led about in leading-strings, accustomed to get all the intellectual nutriment after it has been masticated by others. Capacity does not fall down from heaven, and for almost two centuries the people have been weaned from every public activity.

Even if Raskolnikof was melancholy from the first, poverty creates new melancholy in him. His wretched room is enough to cast an uninterrupted gloom over him. The low, small room contracts his whole soul. He cannot pay his rent and is frequently hungry. In the long winter evenings he has no light and lies in the dark, and at last does not even try to get a light; on his table his college text-books are covered with thick dust. He dreams, dreams continually. . . .

He dreams of a horrible old pawnbroker-woman, very rich and miserly, from whom he has had a loan now and then, and of a conversation about her to which he had once listened in a restaurant. A student sitting there said: "I should like to kill the old crone and sack her, and I assure you that I could do it without the least sting of conscience." He said it indeed as a joke, but continued seriously: "On the one hand, a stupid, wretched, malicious old crone, who not only never gives anything away, but does harm to everybody she comes in contact with; on the other hand, fresh, young powers, who fail for want of means of support, and that by the thousands; hundreds, perhaps thousands of existences, which might be brought on the right path, dozens of families which could be saved from wretchedness, from debauchery, from loathsome disease,—all for the money of this old crone. . . . And, after all, what weight on the universal scales of life has the life of this swindling, stupid, malicious crone? Not more than a louse's life or a cockroach's, and not even so much,—for the old woman does much more harm, for she undermines the life of others."

The words take root in Raskolnikof's mind, just because the same thought is ready to be developed in his head, peeps forth from his brain like a chicken from the shell, and especially because to his own wretchedness is added that of others who are dearest to him. His old mother, who is living in her country vil-

lage on an annuity of one hundred and twenty rubles a year, and
who by knitting and embroidery, which is spoiling her poor eyes,
earns twenty rubles a year more, sends him a letter, from whose
kind, considerate expressions he learns that his only dearly loved
sister, proud and beautiful as she is, is about to offer up herself
on the altar of a detested marriage in order to be able to keep
him at the university and support her mother in her old age. He
starts up against it, he kicks against the pricks, he will forbid his
pure sister from entering into this horrible marriage. But what
right has he to forbid it? How can he prevent it? What can he
offer her instead? To devote to her and their mother his whole
future, when he has first completed his studies and obtained a
position! In ten years perhaps! But by that time his mother will
be blind or dead from fasting or consumption, and by that time
his sister will be . . . what cannot happen in ten years!

He had early formed a theory of his own about crime, that
the extraordinary man has the right, not the official right, but one
which his conscience gives him, to overstep certain obstacles and
barriers which circumscribe other men; only, however, in the
case that his idea, an idea which looks towards the happiness of
mankind, demands such a step. If men like Kepler and Newton
could in no way have made their discoveries available to the
world without the taking of human life, which put obstacles in
the way of these discoveries, then they would have had the right,
nay, it would have been their duty, to take that human life. Experience teaches him that almost all the lawgivers and reformers
of humanity, from the oldest down to Lycurgus, Solon, Ma-
homet, Napoleon, have been criminals, from the very fact that
they have created a new law and set aside the old, which was
regarded by society as holy and had been handed down from
their ancestors, and that they had not shrunk from the shedding
of blood, and that even very often entirely innocent blood, which
was offered up with heroic courage for the defence of the old
law. The masses do not recognize the right of such men, they
execute or hang them when they can compass it, but the coming
generations place these executed men on pedestals and show them
honor. And is not he himself such an exceptional man?

But his whole being is roused against the act. It is altogether too shameful, far too disgusting. To kill a little old woman with an axe! All his pride, all the nobility in his nature, shrinks and groans.

Still the days roll on—and there is no other way out; slowly, slowly he becomes familiar with the idea; by the strangest accident he learns a time when the old woman on a certain evening will be alone . . . it is as if a corner of his coat had been caught on the wheel of a machine, which winds him in with it, and with a commingling of determined resolution and child-like recklessness, in a moment of crime, he accomplishes the murder—and still another murder; for her sister, a simple and good old being, comes in just as Raskolnikof has begun to investigate the drawers and chests of his victim, and he strikes her down with another blow.

But he was not equal to the task, or too nobly constituted for the misdeed,—just as you may regard it. He can commit murder in a somnambulistic insanity, but he does not know how to steal. He only appropriates one or two worthless things; with the greatest difficulty he escapes the fate of being arrested on the spot, and now begins that period of his life when he is in no condition to do anything else than brood over his misdeed. He obliterates all material traces of it; but he is absorbed in the thought of concealing it, and betrays himself inadvertently more every day which passes, to those who are seeking for the perpetrator of the crime. That, however, is not the chief thing; no discovery from without annihilates him, but an inner one, that he is not one of those chosen, exceptional natures to whom everything is allowed. After having committed his crime, he is no longer able to raise himself to the height from which he regarded it before it was accomplished. He is consumed by inches. "No," he says to himself, "these men whom we admire are not constituted as I am. The true ruler, to whom everything is allowed, lays Toulon waste, establishes his power in Paris by the bayonet, *forgets* an army in Egypt, sacrifices a half a million of men on a campaign to Moscow, then makes a pun in Vilno about it,—and after his death he is idolized. Such men must be of iron, not of flesh and blood." And a collateral idea almost makes him smile: "Napoleon, the Pyramids, Waterloo—and a disgusting, little usury practising old crone, with a red-strapped trunk under her bed. Would a Napoleon ever creep in under the bed of such an old crone? . . . Insanity."

He is not sorry for the murder of the old woman; he continues to regard her life as a useless one, her death as an indifferent, almost a beneficial act. The old woman is, and continues to be, a secondary matter; he would only by killing her bring a principle to life, kills not a human being, but a prejudice, and strides over the chasm which separates the every-day souls who possess the vulgar faiths from the host of the elect. He has killed the prejudice, but he remains just the same standing on this side of the chasm. He is excessively wretched, more wretched than ever before.

He has not done anything bad. He only wished not to be obliged to pass by his starving mother and keep her rubles in his pocket. And how conscientiously has he not acted! He assured himself first by a careful self-examination, that he would not overstep the barriers to satisfy sensuous impulses, but for the sake of a great object; so he himself selected, among all "the useless lice," the most useless of all, and finally determined, although he killed the woman, to take only so much as was absolutely necessary for the object nearest to him.

But it is not the old woman he has killed; it was himself, his own *ego*. His deed has grown up far above his head; it has isolated him completely, thrown him wholly back into himself. The secret gnaws him to insanity, and the agony of being himself "a louse," like all the others, paralyzes him.

Scarcely had he committed the murder before he began to feel lonesome, strange to himself, and doomed to everlasting dumbness. He it is who will nevermore be able to talk with others. Soon after, he is tormented by an insane impulse to disclose himself, to tell all himself. He prefers immediately to throw all that he has taken into the canal; he has no idea of using it, conceals it under a stone in a building-lot. He does not himself understand what has happened to him; but he has been separated from his past, as if by the clip of a pair of scissors. There comes a moment when he almost jumps into the water, to make an end of all. On his associates he makes the impression of a madman.

But he falls in with human wretchedness in its worst form—a drunkard who dies; a consumptive widow with a nest full of children, without bread; a noble young girl who has been compelled to sell herself to get food for her little brothers and sisters; and the need of showing generosity, of helping, restores to him, for a short time, faith in life. Still, this short rise is followed by new pangs. The thought whether the others did not know everything tortures him, so that he plays an entirely useless comedy when, towards certain people, he acts as if nothing was the matter. And really there are some who are on the track; one who has suspected everything and completely sees through him, and he is a genius of a jurist, an examining magistrate. Still Raskolnikof is neither arrested nor examined; no, what at last opens his lips and compels him to surrender himself is a purely inward, spiritual movement. Long before it gains the mastery, it presents itself to him, as the moment approaches when he must disclose himself, and he even draws a parallel of the feelings of the advent of this moment with his earlier perception of the necessity that the hour was come for murdering the old woman. Yet this feeling is continually crossed by the feeling of growing hate towards the whole world about him; he feels a murderous hatred towards those in regard to whom he suspects or feels that they know his secret. When, in his solitary ponderings, he puts to himself the questions what, under these or those given circumstances, he shall do in order not to be trapped, the outburst, "Then I shall kill him," is the constant answer to all such questions that arise. Nay, at last, he discovers, with horror, that even of his mother and sisters, who have always been so dear to him, he thinks now and then with a feeling of hate.

And this hatred and all this anguish have their root in love. If only he had not loved so much, all this would not have happened.

If his soul had been barren, if he had not been bold, magnanimous and earnest, he would never have become a murderer. During this horrible time he feels more and more drawn towards the young girl who has been named before, and who has fallen on account of her love for her little brothers and sisters. By her most strenuous exertions she could not earn what was necessary by her daily wages, and her own mother had driven her out into the street. Pity had brought him into relations with her, admiration for the nobility and purity of her being brings him to seek her out, for not a drop of real unchastity has as yet entered into her heart. He honors the one despised by the world. She also has "overstepped the barriers," she also has laid her hand upon a human life, her own, has sacrificed herself and sacrificed herself uselessly; but she stands spiritually high above him. Little by little she becomes his conscience. One day, when he has looked for a long time silently into her tearful face, he throws himself down before her and kisses her feet.

"What are you doing? What are you doing? That to me?"

He answers: "Not to you did I bow down—I bowed down to the total suffering of the human race."

It is Sonya's prayer that he shall himself confess his guilt, "take his martyrdom upon himself;" she will never leave him, will accompany him in his exile to Siberia as an inmate of the House of Correction. He hesitates a long time. His sister also urges him to surrender himself: she sees in this step his only salvation from the self-consumption into which he has fallen. But when she uses the word crime, he becomes excited. "That I have killed a disgusting, mischievous louse, an usurious old crone, for whose death one ought to be forgiven forty sins, a creature that sucked the blood out of poor folk,—that a crime!"—"Thou hast shed blood!" breaks in the sister amazed.—"Blood!" answers Raskolnikof. "All shed it—it flows and has always flowed on the earth in streams, it is poured out like champagne, and people are crowned for it on the Capitol and then called the benefactors of mankind—I myself only wished for the good and would have done a hundred thousand good deeds for this one blunder, and it was not even a blunder, only a clumsy act. By this blunder all I wanted was to put myself in an independent position, make the first step, and then all this would have been compensated by a proportionally large usefulness. But I have not been able to take the first step, because I am a milksop! That is the whole of it."

Still, in the long run, Sonya is stronger than he. He cannot withstand the prayer of the strong woman in all its humility and unworthiness, to make his deed known, and the novel ends with

Raskolnikof's self-accusation at the police-office: "It was I who murdered the old register's widow and her sister with an axe and then plundered their property!"

In this story Dostoyevski has plainly intended to give a picture of the times. "What is before us here," says the examining magistrate Porfyrius to the hero, in the third part of the book, "is, evidently enough, a fantastic, tragical product of the new tendency of the times; it is a deed which only the present time could bring forth, the time in which it is a custom to repress one's feelings and to give utterance to phrases like this: that blood operates refreshing; that is a fantasy which comes from books; it is a heart which is spasmodically overstrained by theories; it is a determination which leads to crimes as if strange feet carried him thither." The author evidently has political ferments in view, although he takes care not to say a single word directly about politics. There is undoubtedly contained in it an allusion to the murder of the Tsar. "Still it is well," Porfyrius says to Raskolnikof, "that it was only such a wretched old woman whom you killed; if, on the other hand, your theory had taken another direction, then your misdeed might have been a hundred million times more frightful." And indirectly, through a dream which Raskolnikof has, while he is brooding over thoughts of murder and is frightened at it, there is a description, which, it is true, is not anywhere pointed directly at the Russian people, but which undoubtedly is a symbol of the most sombre representation of the situation. The hero sees in his dream a miserable, emaciated, light brown peasant-horse, harnessed to a very large, heavy wagon, which it cannot possibly draw; but the horse is whipped again and again by the rough owner of the wagon, without mercy, over the muzzle, over the eyes, first with one whip and then with three at a time; the horse groans and puffs, can scarcely breathe, pulls, stops, tries to pull again, cannot escape from the storm of blows, and at last begins, to the general laughter of the men, to kick back. The horse is whipped again—while some beat on a drum in addition, one sings a shameless song, and a woman contentedly cracks nuts —is whipped over the muzzle and over the eyes. When even several heavy blows with a wagon pole over the back are not able to drive the horse forward, the owner seizes a great iron bar and

gives the horse a blow with that. The horse tries for the last time
to pull, then falls down on the ground and breathes his last. When
the social condition is of the kind described here symbolically, it
is no wonder that sanguinary thoughts spring up in the minds of
the youth.

Even if it is not a political crime which Dostoyevski has represented, it is a crime which has this in common with the political, that it is not mean, was not committed for the vulgar, low
object of procuring for the perpetrator greater personal profit,
but was in a certain degree unselfish, and, what is most important
above all, it was committed by a person who at the moment of
the crime does not harbor a doubt as to his right. In the mean
time, if we compare the men and women whom in recent years
we have seen sentenced in Russia for intent to commit murder,
and not less those who have been executed as accessories to the
assassination of the Tsar with this homicide, then the contrast is
striking. Those persons were not in any way ruined by the spiritual consequences of their deed; they had as conspirators in and
after the moment of the murder been in full accord with their
inmost being; their conviction continued to be unshaken and un-
moved to the last. If they had escaped detection, in all probability they would have lived to the end of their lives without any
other than peaceful and proud thoughts about their attempts at
the murder of a being whose extermination they regarded as a
good deed, nay, as a duty. Raskolnikof, on the other hand, is
destroyed by the consequences of the murder.

Like the political criminals, he started from a certain fixed
principle, which, it is true, is not mentioned in the book, but
which, nevertheless, lies at the foundation of his way of proceeding, that the end justifies the means.

This principle, which simplicity has misunderstood and Jes-
uitism has misused, is exactly and literally sound. The word "justifies" indicates that a good, valuable end is meant. He has a good,
valuable end who would maintain or produce results of real value.

Suppose that one could obtain his good end only by inflicting suffering, and suppose that this suffering is less than that
which will be produced if he avoids making use of the means.
Suppose, for example, that a man wishes the good of his fellow-

citizens, and can arrive at his end only by removing a single man (it may be one who is infected with a contagious disease, or a tyrant), then his act is deserving of honor, if of two evils—one or the other of which must necessarily be incurred—he chooses the lesser. The objection which lies near to this, that he cannot foresee the results of his act, signifies nothing, because the morality depends upon the intent and not upon the result. In our daily life no one entertains any doubt as to the soundness of the principle; we are quite familiar with the idea that there are no absolute duties. Society teaches: Thou must not kill, but adds: Except where your fatherland (the good end) demands it, for then it becomes not only allowable, but a duty, to kill the largest possible number of enemies. Society teaches: It is a bad act to cut off the arms or legs of another, but adds: when the physician amputates an arm or a leg to save the life of the sick or wounded, then the good end justifies the means.

In order that the principle shall be applicable, the following conditions must be fulfilled: The end must be good. The end must be such that it cannot be attained by any other means than those which inflict the pain, nor even by means which inflict less pain than those which are employed.—The suffering which is used as a means must be less than that which would exist without the use of the means.—With regard to all these points, the typical Russian terrorist, before as well as after his onslaught upon the course of events, would be without any concern whatever. Why, then, was Raskolnikof not so also?

Although Dostoyevski undoubtedly was not in the least degree partial to political terrorists, since even political progressionists were hateful to him, he has manifested on this point an extraordinary discrimination. He does not particularly deny the justice of Raskolnikof's reasoning, but shows that he is confused as to his end, uncertain if it is really good or not. In desperation he says to Sonya, a month after the deed, that he has continually been uncertain. When he examines himself he finds that in fact he has not committed murder to support his mother nor to become a benefactor of mankind, but in order to find out if he like the others was a "louse," not a man, that is, if he was in a position to overstep the barriers or not. He is uncertain about his end and uncertain about his inward authority to pursue this indefinite end, which, according to his own theory, only the elect are at liberty to use all means to attain. When he for a whole day has tortured himself with the question whether Napoleon would have done such an act, he already felt dimly that he was not a Napoleon.

Therefore he was wholly overwhelmed by the consequences of the deed. He wished only to kill an old monster; but that was hardly done before necessity compelled him, to escape detection, to kill a poor, kindly being who had never done harm to any mortal, nay, had continually been a sacrifice for others. Since then he has even been obliged to recognize Lisavieta's spiritual kinship to Sonya, whom he respects so greatly. He says somewhere, "Oh, how I hate this wretched old woman! I believe I could strike her down once more if she awakened to life. But the poor Lisavieta! Why must she come in! Strange that I almost not at all think of her, just as if I had not killed her! Lisavieta! Sonya! . . . Ye poor things, ye mild women with timid eyes, . . . ye dear women, . . . why do ye not weep? why do ye not groan? . . . They sacrifice everything with their mild and quiet looks."

Yet far more than the murder of Lisavieta, which had not been wished for, the fear of being arrested tortured him, and the system of dissimulation and denial and lying, in which he involves himself. His reason is not solid enough to endure it, and, until he confesses, he is continually on the verge of insanity. In an epilogue which takes place in Siberia, Dostoyevski then suffers Raskolnikof's defiant and yet troubled nature to be at once dissolved in tenderness and strengthened in spirit by the faithful, enduring love of Sonya. Raskolnikof is an "infidel," but Sonya a believer. Even before Raskolnikof has recognized his guilt, there is an affecting scene where Sonya reads aloud to him from the New Testament,—a scene where a tallow candle in the battered candlestick in the poor room at once shines upon a murderer, a fallen woman, and the gospel between them,—a truly Christian scene, stamped with genius. In the epilogue, for which Dostoyevski has plainly wished to make use of his experiences in Siberia, his religious convictions, direct and doctrinal, make their appearance. As I have heard a young Russian lady express it, we very often in reading Dostoyevski have a feeling that the characters which he has created are more profound than the author himself. He was not capable of understanding the scope of his own work.

If we should now study the subordinate characters only approximately with the same care with which the character of the chief person has been examined, we shall find that they, almost without exception, ten in number as they are, stand on a level with the hero by the force and truth with which they are drawn, and that all stand in some relation to him. There is no superfluous person in the book. Among the most admirably conceived characters are the examining magistrate Porfyrius, a legal genius, and the landed proprietor Svidrigaïlof, a very complex nature, a voluptuary, who is in love with Raskolnikof's sister, and who pursues her. He is a man of intellect, has an excellent head, and, although he has one or more unrepented murders on his conscience, he possesses both courage and sense of honor in his way. As the murderer from selfishness, by numerous details in regard to his way of acting and thinking, he forms a contrast to the hero of the book, who writhes under Svidrigaïlof's contention that they have one certain characteristic in common.

Dostoyevski's delineation of character here is of the first rank; it is profound, and bold. Nevertheless, after the manner of Dickens, it leaves almost the whole of the relations between the sexes, if not untouched, yet undescribed. In this domain, however, the poet does not escape the paradoxical; thus the morally irreproachable fallen woman reminds us more of an antithesis in human form by Victor Hugo than of a real person.

His aversion to describing the natural sensual life is all the more impressive since here, as in most of the author's other books, he dwells on unnatural, turbid appetites. We notice Svidrigaïlof's hideous passion for young girls. And we compare the amazing inquisition in "The Possessed," where Shatof questions Stavrogin if it is true that in St. Petersburg he belonged to a secret society which had for its object the satisfaction of unnatural lust, if he has really said that the Marquis de Sade could go to school to him, and if he has debauched and misused children.[1]

It is evident that Dostoyevski's fancy frequently turned on

[1] *Nihilister* (Danish translation), i. 319.

such unnatural inclinations, just because, according to his train of reasoning, there is no room left for a sound sensuousness. His inclination to describe bodily sufferings, the dwelling greatly on cruelties, are suggestive of unnatural desires. It is peculiar that Turgenief again and again returns to the comparison between Dostoyevski and De Sade. Quite evidently it is very much in consequence of his dislike to see his hateful rival installed as a hero, but also it is plain that it was Turgenief's conviction that there is to be found here physiologically and psychologically a real kinship.[1]

Thus much is clear at all events, that with Dostoyevski's gifts there was a perverse nervousness.

However high the delineation of character stands in "Crime and Punishment," the book suffers from the imperfections of the narrative style. The portions in dialogue are immeasurably the best. As soon as the author himself begins to talk, art ceases. Dostoyevski was not able, like Turgenief, to acquire the French art of narration; what he appropriated to himself from them was their ideal of humanity, a national, fundamental view, which is akin to that of Louis Blanc and of Victor Hugo in his later years.

Though an author of such a high rank, he was an artist of a low rank. He allowed all his writings to be printed as they ran off from his pen, without revision of any kind whatever, to say nothing of recasting them. He did not trouble himself to give them the highest possible degree of perfection by condensation or pruning, but only worked as a journalist works, and is therefore universally too prolix.

Thus so far as this, his best work, is concerned, it is clear that he in the first part had not known anything at all about the treatise which in the second part he states that Raskolnikof had written about his theory. Certain expressions in the first part are even at variance with what the hero must have written in such a treatise. Moreover, it is very little in harmony with the modern art of narration when in numerous places in the novel the author uses such turns as: "*Later* we learn that Svidrigaïlof that evening also had made a visit," or "When he *afterwards*, long afterwards, remembered this time, it was clear to him that his consciousness must have been confused," or "*Afterwards* it was wonderful to

[1] See especially Turgenief's letter to Saltykof of September 24, 1882.

Sonya that she thus at once had seen," etc. By such turns the author strives to fill up the gaps and omissions in the descriptions. Somewhere Dostoyevski even writes with the genuine olden-time naïveté: "We will temporarily leave the whole line of thought by which Raskolnikof reaches this result; besides we have already *anticipated* it too much. *Yet we add only*, that the actual material difficulties of the undertaking played only a weak part in his mind." Anticipations and excuses for anticipations have just as little place in a novel as gaps and gap-stoppers.

It is already seen from "Crime and Punishment" in what sense Dostoyevski can be said to be the author of the proletariats. As no one else he has known and understood the proletariat both of intelligence and of ignorance.

His chief characteristic, when he presents it, is a kind of psychological clairvoyance, which deserts him when he describes the upper classes. (See, e.g., the Prince in "The Injured and Oppressed.") The force and extent of his clairvoyance is especially traced where the healthy spiritual condition borders upon the domain of insanity. Towards the human spiritual condition he has the sure insight of a physician for the insane, but it acts with him, as sometimes with such physicians, that the habit of constantly having spiritual abnormities before him leads him to see the abnormal everywhere, and by degrees disturbs the equilibrium of his own mind.

He likes to take his stand on the dividing line which separates rational trains of thought from the exalted, and proper modes of action from the criminal. From the narrow and low embankment he looks on both sides and never forgets to call the reader's attention to how narrow and low the difference in reality is between health and disease, right and wrong. With a peculiar mastership he depicts the intellectual dizziness which makes men rush headlong into a gulf of crime or sacrifice. He knows, as no other person knows, the irresistible attraction of gulfs.

As a judge of spiritual life he is wholly pathological. The perpetual sensitiveness, which is the result of his epileptic nature, is also his strength. His own bad health, his nervous tremors, his hallucinations, his fits, pass through into the persons whom he describes. The horror which oppressed him when he first received the sentence of death, and afterwards when he faced the punishment of the lash, meets one in the attitude of his principal characters in the face of punishment (Raskolnikof, a number of persons in "The Dead House," Dmitri in "The Brothers Karamazof"), most distinctly perhaps in "The Idiot" (Prince Myshkin), where the hero, in the very beginning of the book, exhibits to his valet all the horrors of the man condemned to death. It is developed here that the putting to death in pursuance of a sentence of a court is disproportionately more odious than the most dreadful murder, and it is added, in conclusion: "Perhaps there is a man to whom a sentence of death has been read only to torment him." There is always this background of agony and terror.

The greater number of Dostoyevski's characters are visionary. Thus there are in "The Brothers Karamazof" alone, the youngest of the brothers, Aliosha, who reads in the souls of others and sees what is hidden, and the noble monk Zossima, the saint of the book, who foresees the temptation of Dmitri to parricide, and in the Christian mysticism casts himself on his knees before him, as before the most sinful, and therefore the nearest to salvation.[1] The hero in "The Idiot," Prince Myshkin, is epileptic, and so is the murderer Smerdiakof, in "The Brothers Karamazof."

Since Dostoyevski's strength is in pathology, it is quite natural that his three principal books should describe criminal natures. We find them in "The Brothers Karamazof," as well as in "The Dead House;" but "Crime and Punishment," nevertheless, contains the typical example of his masterpiece of psychological analysis; it unfolds the crime in its whole growth, from the first cell until it bears its last fruit. As a judge of the diseased condition of the mind, as an author of the "moral fever," Dostoyevski has not his equal.

It is natural that in an author who is so exclusively psychological, the natural environments play almost no part. What he needs of a landscape is the strip of the horizon, the glimpse of the blue sky, which is visible from a garret in the suburbs of a great city, or through the panes placed high up in a prison cell. With him it is all repartee, conversation; to that extent everything is dramatic.

[1] Dostoyevski: *Les Frères Karamazof*, by Halpérine-Kaminsky, ii. p. 223 and i. p. 38.

Dostoyevski is the greatest dialectician among the Russian authors. His great strength is his amazing skill of question and answer in dialogue. The soliloquy—and he is never tired of employing it—analyzes a matter from its different aspects in the most delicate details. Dialogue, with him, is a kind of inquisition, a continued contest between men, who seek to wrest their secrets from each other. De Vogüé's expression is very apt, when he says that he combines the disposition of a compassionate sister with the abilities of a chief inquisitor. The same author has also very truly said of him that his characters are never shown to us in a tranquil state, obeying the rule of reason. One of them never sits quietly at a table, occupied with one thing or another. It is said: "He was lying upon the sofa, with closed eyes, but not sleeping. . . . He went out on the street without knowing where he was. . . . He stood immovable, with his look persistently fixed on a point out into vacancy." They never eat, but they drink tea at night. They almost never sleep, and when they do they dream.[1]

Nothing is more foreign to them and their author than the code of honor of Western Europe, as it is most clearly stated in the dramas of Calderón, and still exists as a legacy from the age of chivalry in the Latin and German society. In the world which Dostoyevski opens up to us, the most insulting charges, nay, a blow in the face, are no disgrace to a man. They speak about a flogging as the most natural thing in the world. In a Christian spirit, and in perfect accord with the national mysticsm, suffering is regarded almost as a blessing. One of Dostoyevski's characters says, "I am afraid that I am not worthy of my torture." The torture is considered as a kind of distinction. It always ransoms somebody or something. When the torture is endured, the guilt which caused it is expiated.

Still more: suffering in this world turned upside down is a temptation. Shatof says to Stavrogin (*Nihilister*, i. 320): "Do you know why you made this low and shameful marriage? . . . You married from a desire to feel pain, pangs of conscience, from moral luxury. It was a nervous irritation." And this conception is not exceptional.

Therefore it is that the extremely significative desire to live

[1] De Vogüé: *Le Roman Russe*, p. 257.

which is purely characteristic of the Byzantine Christianity becomes the principle of evil with Dostoyevski. This is what he has
mystically embodied in the three brothers Karamazof. The atheistical Iván says to his younger brother, "Do you know that if I
had lost my faith in life, . . . still I would not have killed myself,
I would live in spite of everything! I have lifted the enchanted
cup to my lips, I shall not let it go till I have drained it to the
dregs. . . . More than once I have asked myself if there is a pain
in the world which is able to conquer this unquenchable thirst,
this thirst for life, which, perhaps, is unseemly; but I do not think
that before my thirtieth year any such pain has been given to me.
I know very well that this thirst for life is what the moralists,
especially those who write verse, the consumptive people, who
always have a cold in the head, call low and contemptible. It is
also true that this thirst for life is a trait which is characteristic in
the Karamazof family: to live! cost what it will! It is also in you.
But what is there low in it!" [1]

Although the thirst for life is an evil, yet suffering, without
something more, is not a good. Dostoyevski, with all his (unconsciously cruel) dwelling on torture, and the enjoyment of torture,
is too gentle and nervously weak and shattered not to melt
in pity thereat. Nay, pity is a kind of religion with him, and it
sometimes conflicts with his system, his faith in God, his Christianity. He is dialectician enough to evolve a fearful attack upon
faith in God from suffering upon earth. We read, for instance,
Iván's enumeration of all the cruelties of men towards defenceless
animals, little children; his busying himself with all the refinements of cruelties: a little horse, whipped over the eyes; a girl
seven years old, who is whipped with thorns; a girl of five, who,
on a cold night in winter, is locked up in a closet, and whose face
is smeared with filth, which she is made to eat; a serf boy eight
years old, whom a general suffers to be torn to pieces by his dogs,
—all this without the intervention of God,—and we ponder over
his conclusion: It is possible that all this fits into the heavenly
harmony of the Almighty; but I do not recognize it; it counter-
balances for me not a single tear of a child.

The young hero Aliosha, on Dostoyevski's behalf, disposes

[1] *Les Frères Karamazof,* i. 205.

of this doubt with the answer, "There is a Being who can for-
give all, for he himself has poured out his innocent blood for all
men and things."

The argument is not much better than that which, in another
place in the book (ii. 209), the devil in a hallucination uses with
Iván: "What pleasure can one have without suffering? It would
all be like an unending ceremonial,—holy, but unendingly tedious."

With a very extraordinary sublimity and greatness, Dostoyevski has developed the religious problem, as it appeared to him, in
the ingenious poem, "The Chief Inquisitor," which he puts into
the mouth of Iván, and for whose sake alone "The Brothers
Karamazof" ought to be translated.

Christ has come back upon the earth. He shows himself at a
great *auto-da-fé* in Seville, where hundreds of heretics are burned
in his honor, gently walking about in the ashes of the fire. All
know him, the common people throng around him, he blesses
them. Then the chief inquisitor, an old man of ninety, causes
him to be arrested, imprisoned, and placed in a cell used for those
who are condemned to the stake, and there visits him in the night.
A conversation then follows between the inquisitor and Christ,
or rather a long monologue of the former, which is not interrupted by any answer,—a monologue in which the cardinal shows
the Saviour how wrong he has been in coming again and disturb-
ing the work of his believers, and proclaims to him his fixed intention of letting him be burned alive as a heretic in order to bring
peace to his work. The inquisitor unfolds to Christ the faults, the
political faults, he committed in his lifetime. The most important
of all was that he did not accept the offer of the tempter to
change stones to bread, but showed himself to men with empty
hands. He thereby made it possible for them who rise up against
him to rally about the watchword: "Give them first meat, if thou
wilt that they shall be good." "We," says the cardinal, "give them
bread. We understand how to lie, and we speak in thy name. And
they end by bringing us their freedom, laying it down at our feet,
and asking us for chains and bread. There are only three forces on
earth which can keep that humanity in check, which is really so
weak and yet so rebellious, and these are: the miracle, the mys-

tery, and the authority. And thou hast rejected these forces to proclaim a freedom which it was particularly necessary to confiscate, and a love with which mankind cannot be governed; therefore it has been necessary to correct thy work, to correct it by the power of Rome and with the sword of Cæsar, and make some hundreds of thousands of progressive spirits unhappy, exterminate them when it was possible, in order to secure the weal of untold millions. To-morrow I shall have you burned. *Dixi*."

Christ does not answer a word, but looks into the eyes of the inquisitor with a mild but firm gaze, then he quietly moves his face close to the inquisitor's, and kisses the old man on his bloodless mouth.

Then the old man trembles, opens the cell door, and says, "Go your way, and come again never more . . . never, never more!"

This poem is condemned in the novel as the offspring of an atheistical train of thought, but even the composition shows with what seriousness and versatility Dostoyevski has asked the question and tested the different answers.

The period from 1871 to 1881 was the most peaceful in Dostoyevski's life. His second marriage was instrumental in introducing order in his household affairs. He eclipsed in popularity all the writers who were at first regarded as his equals, especially causing Písemski's reputation to grow pale in comparison. But he also eclipsed Turgenief, who had so long been regarded as his superior. All the ill will which this great author had stirred up among the Slavophiles and radicals enured for a long time to the advantage of Dostoyevski. When, in 1880, the unveiling of Pushkin's statue in Moscow was the occasion of a great national literary festivity, at which the greatest authors made speeches, Turgenief's was applauded, but Dostoyevski's excited raptures and sobs; and when he had finished, he was carried about in triumph.[1]

In his monthly periodical, "The Diary of an Author," he now

[1] The most of Dostoyevski's novels have been translated into Danish, as well as Písemski's excellent novel, "Thousand Souls." "Crime and Punishment" has been translated into English, and published by T. Y. Crowell & Co., New York.

preached faith in Russia as a duty and attacked with equal bitterness the Russian "intelligence" and the culture of Western Europe, which had become to him the culture of Babel and of Sodom. He was thus regarded as the greatest popular author of Russia at the time of his death. The sorrow at his loss was a national sorrow; forty thousand men followed him to his grave. The Russian students sent an open letter to his widow, in which appears, among other things:—

"Dostoyevski's ideals will never be forgotten; from generation to generation we shall hand them down as a precious inheritance from our great, beloved teacher. . . . His memory will never be extinguished in the hearts of the Russian youth, and, as we love him, we will also teach our children to honor and love the man for whom we now so bitterly and disconsolately mourn. . . . Dostoyevski will always stand bright before us in our battle of life; we shall always remember that it was he who taught us the possibility of preserving the purity of the soul undefiled in every position of life and in all circumstances."

It was, as we see, the Slavophile direction of thought which spoke the last word at his death.

VII

☙ Russia's last great realist and dreamer, Count Leo Niko-layevitch Tolstoï, is more powerful than Turgenief and more healthy than Dostoyevski. He approaches Turgenief in pessimism; in Slavic piety and faith in the Russian common people he approaches Dostoyevski. In common with the latter, he has a distrust of the culture of Western Europe, only he extends it so as to embrace all civilization.

His fancy is far-reaching, epic. So far as he is concerned, the proposition is true that the novel is the modern epic. He has not only like other authors given a phase of culture and the life of so-called good society in and out of the capitals of Russia, but in his greatest work he has depicted an age, an army, a people, and a historic catastrophe of the first rank, Napoleon's campaign and defeat on Russian soil.

He was born August 28, 1828, on the estate Yásnaya Polyána, in the department of Tula, lost his father in 1837, went to the University of Kazán in 1843, where he studied jurisprudence and the Oriental languages, but returned to his estate at the end of three years. In 1851 he served in the army of the Caucasus, where he made his first essay as an author, took part in the Crimean War, was in the battle at Tchernaya and the siege of Sevastopol, and, on the conclusion of peace, obtained his discharge. In 1857 he made his first journey abroad, visiting Germany and Italy. On his estate, where he came in close contact with the common people and studied their natures, he established a free school and busied himself in all directions with meditating on what could and ought to be done for the common people. He married in 1862. He first contemplated writing a great novel about the "Decembrists" (the heroes of the revolts of 1825), but abandoned this idea for another, of which "War and Peace" was the result (1865–1868). "Anna Karénina" followed in 1878, and later, novels, plays, sketches of the people, confessions.

It is indicative of the kind of Tolstoï's faith in reality that he began as an observer of himself, and an autobiographer. Turgenief keeps himself wholly in the background in his writings. When we catch a glimpse of the author himself in Dostoyevski's works it is in those characters which wholly sacrifice themselves for others, and generally in turn are despised, because they lack all the fascinating qualities with which the more ordinary persons are adorned. Thus it is with the narrator of the story, Iván Petróvitch, in "The Injured and Oppressed." There is a gleam of the same thing even in old Makar Alekseyevitch, in "Poor Folk." His description of himself in "The Dead House" is pathetically modest, even humble, although the author lets it be understood that the narrator is regarded by the others as an uncommon person. But when he uses himself as a model, Dostoyevski always draws a person of the most extraordinary goodness. In his novel, "The Idiot," he has presented himself in the guise of the hero, Prince Myshkin. Myshkin is a genius of the greatest ability, a child in simplicity and purity of heart. For four and twenty years he has been afflicted with that incurable disease, epilepsy, so that he acquiesces with mildness when, even although he is in possession of all his faculties, he is treated as one who is sick or insane, one who is on the point of "having a convulsive fit." He has no fine manners, is not able to husband his ideas, and therefore, as he himself says, uses words which are not suitable for the lofty thoughts he would express, and, as it were, disgrace them. But, notwithstanding this, there is no one in his circle of acquaintances, not one, who is worthy of such words. Dostoyevski proclaims that through the mouth of a young girl: "There is no one here who is worthy of your soul, your heart, nay, not even of your little finger. You are more honest than all of us, nobler and wiser than any one of us."

If Tolstoï begins by describing himself, it is because he wants to describe what he knows. He relates the life of his childhood and youth ("Childhood," "Youth"); then, indirectly, but in a transparent manner, his experiences, as an officer in the Caucasus

("The Cossacks"), his memories of war ("Pictures of War," "Sevastópol"). In every place where he gives a picture of himself the criticisms of himself and the use of irony towards himself are palpable. He unveils his own weaknesses, shows us his own follies. He never makes the impression of an ideal figure. On the contrary, it is he who less often than others succeeds in winning hearts, and who does not deserve any other happiness than that which falls to his lot. In "The Cossacks," his Olyenin, like Petschórin with Lermontof, is a Russian officer of the elegant world, living in the Caucasus. But while Petschórin, in spite of all his coldness, everywhere meets with a warm reception from the women, Olyenin, from his passionate love cherished for a long time for a child of nature, a Cossack girl, reaps only such ill will and contempt that she would not even turn her head towards him when he went away. In Lermontof's book the highly cultured man is attractive even when he is tired of the world; for Tolstoï the object here, as ever, is to extol the superiority of nature to the results of artistic culture. And to this love and admiration for nature we may attribute the fact that the Caucasian landscape, which in "The Hero of Our Time" was only a frame, in "The Cossacks" presents itself identified with the freshness and force of the nature of man: "the everlasting snow, untouched by man, and the exalted woman in her primitive beauty." . . . "I rejoiced over her as over the glory of the mountains and of the heavens, and could not help rejoicing, for she is as beautiful as they." . . . "Perhaps I love in her the nature, the embodiment of everything that is beautiful in nature," etc. We feel that something besides self-glorification is dear to the author, namely fidelity to reality.

It is this fidelity to reality which moves us everywhere in Tolstoï:—First, where the author's own character is traced in his created characters, as in certain heavy natures, strong and awkward men, who, without any special stimulus, for a long time allow themselves to float with the stream, until an awakening of their religious natures calls all their best qualities into action: Bezukhoï in "War and Peace," Levin in "Anna Karénina," are examples. In the next place, where Tolstoï describes the every-day life of strange natures, as in the finished, bitterly veracious story "Family Happiness," which is strongly effective, simply and only in the development of the way in which the illusions of life spring up, are nourished and lost. It describes the growth and blossoming of love, then the slow transformation which degrades the love of the two consorts to friendship, and at last allows tenderness for the children to displace every other sentiment. It is every-day life, without even a single romantic event.

Next to fidelity to reality the quality of divination, the gift of being able to anticipate, is noteworthy in Tolstoï. He possesses the extremely rare historical imagination.

It is quite true that he has a spirit sufficiently modern not to make any attempts to conjure distant persons, who have long since died. He does not go farther back than to an epoch where he is assisted by a tradition still vigorous. Nevertheless, his description of a past historic period, like that of Alexander the First, is admirable. His historical portraits make an impression as if the picture were painted on a foundation of personal experiences. His Napoleon, his Kutúzof, are instances.

There are perhaps in all only two artistic descriptions in which the appearance of Napoleon makes the impression of entire truthfulness, and which are drawn with genuine art. One is Alfred de Vigny's admirable description of Napoleon's conversation with the Pope, in *Servitude et Grandeur Militaires;* the second is the scene in "War and Peace," where Napoleon gives an audience to the Russian envoy Balashóf. It is written as if the author were present unseen.

How expressive is such a little trait as this of Napoleon: "His white and fat neck was set off sharply against the black collar of his uniform, from which there came a strong smell of eau-de-cologne." We feel the parvenu in this paltry detail.

Tolstoï's Kutúzof is a characteristic picture of the same rank. Nevertheless, however eminent it is as a work of art, it certainly has great defects as a portrait. It can hardly be doubted that, for national and religious reasons, the author has placed too high an estimate on Kutúzof, and too low an estimate on Napoleon. What is emphasized in Napoleon is the violence and the foolish arrogance which unconsciously stand before a fall; what we lack the impression of is of the force of his genius. In Kutúzof, even inaction, nay, imbecility, is extolled as the expression of a profound knowledge to what extent matters go as they will or rather as they must, without the interference of any single man having any special effect one way or the other.

This partiality, however, depends entirely on Tolstoï's peculiar views of life. Without the nervousness or exaltation of Dostoyevski, he is just as far as the latter from having a reverence for human intelligence and for political or scientific greatness.

In Germany authors believe in reason and culture, in England in the independent power of the individual, in France in abilities, in the North in morality; Tolstoï, as Russians so frequently are, is impressed with the insignificance of the single man in the presence of the universe. He cherishes a reverence for the universe and for fate, but has none for science, art, or culture.

In his view nothing depends on science or art. No, life and death are two great, earnest, inscrutable things. The great sermon which life and death daily preach into the ear of the author stifles the noise of the whole earth for him. The understanding of man seems to him so weak in the face of the enigma of life that the simplest intelligence here is no better than the highest.

And the will of man is to be counted as nothing in regard to the irresistible stream of historic events. It is not the leader of the army who in reality leads the army; fate drives it on; the battle is won or lost without his intervention, by the play of the secret impelling power.

A scene typical of Tolstoï is that where the wounded Prince Andreï, lying stretched out on the battle-field, looks up to the heavens. Napoleon, with his suite, stops by the side of the wounded man. The now feeble man, whose admiration for Napoleon had hitherto been so boundless, finds him small and unimportant in comparison with what is going on between his own soul and the immeasurable heavens.

It is significant that hardly any other author has described so frequently and with such confidence and versatility as Tolstoï, how people die. He is equally conversant with the feelings which precede suicide,—man's as well as woman's—with the emotions with which the wise and the foolish in sickness await the coming of death, and with the terror and the final release which death brings in battle.

From Tolstoï's lack of scientific culture and his weak faith in the intelligence of man results the ideal he has created for himself of a return to nature. It does not correspond to Rousseau's, for it has a religious character; but it reminds one of it. The peasant Karatáyef, in "War and Peace," makes so deep an impression on Bezukhoï, not only because he is a primitive creation but because he has the resignation and the Christian brotherly love which the civilized man lacks.

Tolstoï is a pure romanticist to the extent that he does not seek his ideal before us, but behind us, in the lowest classes. He is not a pure pessimist, in so far as, however black the situation appears to him, he continually tries to embody his ideal, and preaches its realization to others. In this the pessimism which appears in his writings differs sharply from that in which in our day French literature has culminated, the most characteristic expression of which is found in the writings of Huysmans, a conscientious artist and a man without hope. The pessimism of the latter consists in his being tired of life and disgusted with it. All that he has seen and experienced was to an intolerable degree vulgar and low. He suffers and is wounded by everything which there presents itself to his view, and it is very significant that he has created a character in a novel, who retires to a solitary life, to whom the reality is so hateful that he replaces the natural by the artificial, even natural by artificial light, and who from the simple classics, which are not spicy enough and which he despises, resorts to the very unnatural writers.

With this radical pessimism the pessimism of Tolstoï has one point of contact: the dislike of what is plain and rational. But for the typical French pessimist life is a worthless thing, whose enigma is not worth pondering over. The only thing which the pessimists of this literature honor and love is art. And the same thing which they loathe in real life, they honor when they find it in art. For only where the work of art almost exclusively represents that which in itself is purely commonplace and ungraceful are they sure that what they love in the work is the art itself. The lover of art indeed often prefers the low and the sordid as the subject in order to be able to the full extent to enjoy the art in the manner of its treatment.

For Tolstoï, on the other hand, life is so serious and inexhaustible a thing that his interest in art was from the first infinitesimal, in comparison with the interest which he bestows upon the questions of life and happiness. Upon the whole, art has never had an independent value for him, and in his last period he looks down upon his earlier works as far too artistic. He is wholly absorbed in a kind of Christian socialism of a wholly personal and eccentric nature, and it is evident that, so far as he gives art any importance, it is only as the organ of the sound views of life, as the power which elevates the people on the largest scale.

It is impossible to enter into the spirit of a view of art which despises the form, the style, even the element which makes the art an art.

There can, however, be no doubt as to which of the two constructions is best adapted to advance a literature which is not in its decadence, but in full prosperity; that which regards literature as an organ for ideas, or that which cultivates the form of art simply as form.

The teaching that art is its own end is sound enough, but must not be understood as sanctioning speaking or writing only for the sake of speaking and writing. Only where there are broad views and great thoughts is there to be found in literature that principle of life which saves it from being lost in its barrenness.

Therefore the intellectual life of Russia is in no danger from Tolstoï's more recent disdain of art.

Why speak of what all know who have in any way kept up with the times: of the great man's remorse for the thoughtless life of his youth, which—as his books of that epoch show—now appears to him far more thoughtless than it really was,—of his public confession, dignified and naïve, the confession of a contemplative man who was not created for a thinker,—of his self-made religious system, which adopts the instruction of Christianity about the unlawfulness of war, nay, of all armed defence, and in which the principle, that after the blow on one cheek we ought to turn the other also, becomes its chief corner-stone. That there are very great objections to this is more than evident: but what interests us is not that, but the genuine Russian character of this fundamental idea and of this predominant emotion. It is as if even this peace-loving, utterly unwarlike spirit of the people, which is peculiarly Russian, had become instrumental in the development of Tolstoï's religious teaching.

The philologian Carl Abel somewhere says, after having given the linguistic characteristics of the Great and Little Russian people: "There is still a nationality in Russia more important than either of the two already mentioned. This most remarkable kind of men consists of the higher classes of the empire. As a fusion of all the different races which are collected under the sceptre of the Tsar, these higher classes constitute one of the most gifted, courageous, and enterprising types of mankind produced anywhere on the face of the earth. In them sound Finnish reason is combined with Polish boldness, Armenian sagacity with the German reflective and methodical manner of thought, and to the patient endurance of the Tatar is added the suppleness of the Slav." And he declares that if Russia has accomplished much in diplomacy and war, it is due to this group of leaders.[1]

That interests Tolstoï least because war and diplomacy are just the things which do not interest him at all. And it is to those who have hitherto been under the necessity of blind obedience to this group of leaders that his whole sympathy is secured. It is with them that he in his employments, nay, in dress and externals, has gradually sought to identify himself, partly in order to become thoroughly acquainted with their manner of feeling, and partly not to look down upon them in any respect.

One of my acquaintances, a very dispassionate jurist, who visited him at his estate last summer, could not speak of his visit without emotion. Concerning the reports of a decay in Tolstoï's intellectual power he said: "Tolstoï has a clear, penetrating mind, especially tolerant of such as think otherwise, and of an angelic goodness. He reads everything, is interested in everything, and

[1] Carl Abel: Slavic and Latin, p. 51.

in his conversation does not attempt any propaganda. Poorly clad, half in rags, he lives in his family, which does not share in his convictions, but which honors and idolizes him. His wife is an intelligent woman, an excellent mistress of her house, a house which is kept up in grand style. The sons, practical men, take care of the estate. The daughter is beautiful, worldly; in her very elegant costume she goes out to walk with her half-dressed father, and worships him."

The people who surround him at the present time consist of three classes: the half-mad, who see in him what they want to see, and who get out of his words what they wish. In the second place, the good-for-nothings, who come to profit by his benevolent disposition, and who are often discontented, since he cannot satisfy all their demands. Finally, the correspondents of the different newspapers, who write about him entirely according to the tendency of the paper to which they contribute.

Tolstoï teaches, above everything else, that people ought to be happy just as they ought to be pure. To be happy we must have as few necessities as possible. Hence the return to the primitive condition, which he finds in the life of the peasant, which is so simple.

The moralizing propensity has been strong in Tolstoï from the beginning. It is always to be found in his writings, except, perhaps, in some of his very earliest little stories, like "Lucerne." It is unmistakable in "War and Peace;" it is very strongly stamped on "Anna Karénina," where it even weakens the result. The moral lesson which we should deduce appears quite too distinctly in his sketches. In other words: the fixed idea of the generations of the past is traced here; the idea of punishment: thus it goes, when, etc. Cause and effect, without its being expressly so stated, become transformed to guilt and punishment.

Of late Tolstoï has devoted his efforts to writing for the people. He has determined to turn to the hundred million instead of to the upper ten thousand. He has written a series of short narrative legends, symbolical stories and tales, which from his disinterestedness are sold for about one cent (1½ kopeks) for each number, and which are intended to give to the Russian peasants and workmen, who are now, for the first time, awakening from a sleep of a thousand years, the food which is suited to their minds and the ideas which they need.

These brief writings are not reading for us who have a different culture. But the great peasant drama of last year, "The Power of Darkness," stands far above these didactic sheets. Perhaps it is the masterpiece of this great eccentric and independent thinker. By its poetic meaning it belongs to the literature of the world, nay, so far as the dramatic literature is concerned, marks the discovery of a new world of material.

Although this play has the wonderful quality that there is not a single repartee which cannot be understood by the ignorant and untaught, it is food for the most cultured.

It is a peculiarity of Tolstoï, with his lack of scientific endowments, that his thought is not able to penetrate the economical causes of unhappiness and misery. No one who has read his essay "On the Importance of Art and Science," that is, its unimportance, this attempt of a self-taught moralist to pass judgment on things which are out of the scope of his intellect, will be surprised that Tolstoï regards money as the root of all evil. With his own hand he does all sorts of service for the poor; but he never assists them with money. He wastes his time in helping an old woman set up her stove, but does not give her the ruble or two which she needs to get the stove set up better and more solidly.

He is himself rich and has a large income, but he makes use of the expression that money affairs belong to the domain of his wife. He never has any money about him, only now and then gets from his home fifteen kopeks to pay for a bath in one of the bath-houses for the common people.

In the play "The Power of Darkness" there is a trace of this eccentricity. We notice Akim's indignation when Mitritch explains to him how it is that money put in the bank draws interest. All matters of interest and of banks are in his view a delusion. The author is to be heard here through the old peasant.

Otherwise, with exemplary self-control he keeps himself concealed behind his characters, and the play is a great work in its exceptional sense of reality and the great, kind heart which beats in it.

Here we look into a world where no one has the bearings, where no one really knows anything about what lies beyond the confines of the country town, not even the soldier who has roamed about. And how the women are regarded can be seen from what is said about them in one of the conversations: "There are millions of them in the Russian land, and all as blind as moles; no knowledge but a little superstition; when they die, they are just as wise as when they were born."

It is against this "Power of Darkness" that Tolstoï has directed the beams of light from the blaze of his fantasy and his enthusiasm. It is with this that he, as the educator of the people, has begun the fight. Behind his Asgaard's wall he kindles the bright fire into which the Spirit of Darkness, the giant in the Eagle's home, is to fall in the future.[1]

In the Russian monograph "Count L. N. Tolstoï and a Criticism of his Works," we have collected all the portraits extant of the great author. There is a group of the year 1856, in which the young officer is painted with Grigoróvitch, Gontcharóf, Turgenief, and Druzhínin, and the keen author of comedies, Ostrovski, and another of the year 1857, in which the group consists of Turgenief, Sollogub, Tolstoï, Niekrásof, Grigoróvitch, and Panayef. There is an admirable portrait by Kramskoï, and a great many photographs from later years.

We can thus trace how this characteristic head has been moulded and developed from within. There is the officer, not yet thirty years old, with the military mustache and the regularly cut, smooth hair, and the already peculiar, discontented, penetrating look, the expressive mouth, querying and uncertain,—a face which shows uneasiness, betraying a shy and violent spirit. All the others seem so tame, so mild by the side of him, capricious as he seems, and naïf and defiant.

Years roll on, developments take place, and this head becomes changed. A quality appears in it which conquers all the others: commanding power. In the later pictures this expression becomes very strong. There is Kramskoï's portrait, when Tolstoï was between forty and fifty years of age, with the smooth, black

[1] Tolstoï's works have been translated into Danish, German, French, and English.

hair falling in waves over the temples, the heavy, dark, full beard, which covers his throat and collar, with an expression of concentrated depth of understanding and strength. There is no more uncertainty about this mouth, no uneasiness in the brow; the look is the look of the seer and of the thinker penetrating into the very marrow of things. Then there is the portrait of Tolstoï at his writing-desk, a wonderful picture from the greatness of his style and bearing. The greatest gravity and absorption shine out from it. Every one who sees the portrait feels that what that man writes is not vanity, is not idle words, but strong, mighty words, worth pondering over. And there is still one later portrait, where the expression of the eyes and about the mouth comes very near to being frightful, appalling, it is so strong and commanding. The heavy eyebrows almost seem to threaten; the thick beard, growing freely, and besprinkled with gray, reminds one of the old prophets.

In the series of illustrations in the book come also the latest portraits: the well-known photograph of the sixty-year-old Tolstoï as a muzhík, in the dark blouse of the peasant, with the leather belt around his waist, with his hair parted in the middle of his forehead in the fashion of the Russian peasant, with his forehead furrowed with deep wrinkles curving down in the middle, the dishevelled, snow-white beard, extending almost down to where the arms are crossed upon the breast, and the anxious look of the mystic, whose firmness reminds us of the gaze of the careworn.

Last of all is Riepin's masterly painting, which is also known in other lands from the chromo-lithographs: a broad field with a background of woods; peasants are ploughing in the middle distance; in the foreground Tolstoï as a peasant is ploughing in the Russian style, with a white horse harnessed to an antique wooden plough, leading by a halter another white horse behind him, which draws the harrow. For it is Leo Nikolayevitch himself, this strong, broad-shouldered frame, with the soft white hat, which protects the sunken eyes from the sun, with the blue peasant's-frock, open about the neck, exposing his naked breast, and the high boots, which sink in the rich mould. There is nothing here which reminds one of the count, of the born aristocrat.

The thick, broad nose, the heavy jaws, are those of the Russian peasant. But what a wonderful peasant! this bearing, this immense force in simplicity! It is the peasant in contemplation, as a hero, as a genius, as a civilizer. It is the Scythian prince of Herodotus, Kola-Xais, the Prince of the Ploughshare; it is Mikula, the child of the village, the hero of agriculture, with the wonderful plough, who draws his furrow rich in blessings in the boundless Russian plain. It is the national hero Ilia of Murom himself, risen from his death of a thousand years to cultivate again the Russian soil and earth,—he who, stronger than fate, went on the road to riches and "did not become rich," but was wholly engrossed in the fundamental Russian idea of community.

Thus with Tolstoï we turn back to our first impression of Russian intellectual life and literature. He, to whom Turgenief directed his last words written with a pencil, and whom, when dying, he addressed as "my friend, the great author of Russia!" he in our days is the last great one of the group of cultivators in this immense empire.

What is it that he cultivates? what is it that all these, young and old, the men with good will, prepare and cultivate?

Black land, fertile land, new land, grain land, . . . the broadly constituted, rich, warm nature, . . . the broad, unlimited expanse which fills the mind with melancholy and hope, . . . the incomprehensible, darkly mysterious, . . . the womb of new realities and new mysticism, . . . Russia and the future.